HEMINGWAY'S SECOND WAR

Hemingway's Second War

Bearing Witness to the Spanish Civil War

ALEX VERNON

UNIVERSITY OF IOWA PRESS, IOWA CITY

University of Iowa Press, Iowa City 52242

www.uiowapress.org
Printed in the United States of America

Design by Ashley Muehlbauer

The University of Iowa Press is a member of Green Press Initiative and is committed to preserving natural resources.

Printed on acid-free paper

Library of Congress Cataloging-in-Publication Data
Vernon, Alex, 1967–
Hemingway's second war: bearing witness to the Spanish Civil War / Alex Vernon.
p. cm.
Includes bibliographical references and index.
ISBN-13: 978-1-58729-981-0 (pbk.)
ISBN-10: 1-58729-981-X (pbk.)
1. Hemingway, Ernest, 1899–1961. 2. Americans—Spain—Biography. 3. War correspondents—United States—Biography. 4. Authors, American—20th century—Biography. 5. Spain—History—Civil War, 1936–1939—Journalists. 6. Spain—History—Civil War, 1936–1939—Press coverage. 7. Spain—History—Civil War, 1936–1939—Literature and the war. 8. Hemingway, Ernest, 1899–1961. For whom the bell tolls. I. Title.
PS3515.E37Z913 2010
813'.52—dc22 2010046249
[B]

for Pat C. Hoy II and Linda Wagner-Martin

master teachers

constant advisors

dear friends

"We know war is bad. Yet sometimes it is necessary to fight.
But still it is bad and any man who says it is not is a liar.
But it is very complicated and difficult to write about truly."

—Ernest Hemingway to Ivan Kashkin, 23 March 1939

CONTENTS

ACKNOWLEDGMENTS

Somewhere I read that it takes one hundred books to write one book. Sometimes it takes nearly that many people, too.

First and foremost I must thank those who have supported me professionally and personally over the years: Pat Hoy and Linda Wagner-Martin; Joanna Hildebrand Craig; Tim O'Brien; and James Meredith, Carl Eby, and the entire community of Hemingway scholars, past and present. Denis, Chris, and Peter Wood were amazingly kind, generous, and gracious sources of information and insight about their father Jasper and their family life. Richard Alderson, a close friend of Jasper's, was equally open and helpful to my research.

I am deeply grateful to the libraries and library staffs that made this project possible: the John F. Kennedy Presidential Library, the Harry Ransom Humanities Research Center at the University of Texas–Austin, the Library of Congress, the Firestone Library at Princeton University, the European Foundation Joris Ivens (André Stufkens and Bram Relouw), the Beinecke Rare Book and Manuscript Library at Yale University, and the Special Collections at the University of Delaware. At Hendrix College, special thanks to Amanda Moore, Peggy Morrison, and the rest of the Bailey Library staff; and to several students for their assistance: Russell Moore, Carolyn Harder, and Sally Cunningham. Students and colleagues have provided unceasing support, collaboration, and inspiration.

Financial assistance was provided by the Ransom Center, the Kennedy Library, Hendrix College, and the Hendrix-Murphy Foundation. Without this assistance, this project would never have gotten off the ground.

Finally, I must thank Holly Carver, Charlotte Wright, Joseph Parsons, and the rest of the University of Iowa Press, for letting this book become what it could be.

An adaptation of chapter 2 initially appeared as "Style, Politics, and Ernest Hemingway's Spanish Civil War Dispatches" in the *Mailer Review* 4.1 (Fall 2010). A small excerpt from chapter 4 was adapted and published as "*The Spanish Earth* Makes a Book" in *Ivens Magazine* 16 (October 2010).

INTRODUCTION

In one photograph, on a rise among scraggly trees and behind a pile of rocks—their fighting position—two soldiers crumple into the Spanish earth. In a second photograph, on a rise among scraggly trees and behind a pile of rocks—their fighting position—two soldiers crumple into the Spanish earth, and beside them, studying them, stands Ernest Hemingway.[1]

Was it outside Teruel? Were the soldiers government troops, loyalists for the Spanish Republic?

The Republic launched an offensive against Francisco Franco's insurgent Nationalist forces occupying Teruel in Aragon, northeast of Madrid, on 15 December 1937. The cold and snow created the most difficult conditions of the war. Hemingway arrived to report on the battle three days later for the North American Newspaper Alliance (NANA), along with Herbert Matthews of the *New York Times* and a British reporter, Sefton Delmer. On 21 December, the trio plus a Belgian, Mathieu Corman, maneuvered with the infantry through the close-range hill fighting, and at one time intensive firing leveled at them by rebel troops covering their own withdrawal killed two loyalist soldiers nearby. Matthews's dispatch wired to the *Times* by radiogram describes the scene: "IT MEANT FLATTENING OURSELVES ON GROUND AND THERE SEVERAL PERIODS WHEN VERITABLE SHEET BULLETS CRACKLED SO CLOSE THAT TO RAISE OUR HEADS OFF GROUND MIGHT WELL MEANT DEATH STOP TWO SOLDIERS KILLED CLOSEBY DASH HEADWOUNDS

WHICHS WHAT ONE GETS SUCH FIGHTING."[2] The following pause in the action mentioned by Matthews would have given the correspondents time to take the two pictures.

A little later that day, as they drew closer to the town, they came across a dead Republican officer. Hemingway's dispatch documented this one:

> In the pleasant autumn falling dusk, we walked the road down hill and into Teruel. It was a peaceful feeling night and all the noises seemed incongruous. Then in the road was a dead officer who had led a company in the final assault. The company had gone on and this was the phase where the dead did not rate stretchers, so we lifted him still limp and warm to the side of the road and left him with his serious waxen face where tanks could not bother him now or anything else and went on into town.[3]

In another photo, taken on the approach to Teruel and most likely by Matthews, a single stiffened corpse on a treeless slope foregrounds a mountainous landscape.[4] Is it the same man? And can any reader of Hemingway see this photo and not think of Robert Jordan dying on the mountain slope at the end of *For Whom the Bell Tolls*?

But the landscape in the photo is too remote and too elevated to match the scene of the dead loyalist lieutenant which, according to Matthews, they "ALMOST STUMBLED OVER" as they "DESCENDED" through "SAN JULIAN QUARTER POOR WORKING CLASS DISTRICT."[5] Earlier in the action the correspondents had seen another corpse, and Matthews's description of it very much fits the one on the treeless slope in the photo he probably took: "SO WE WENT DOWN SAGUNTO ROAD STOP HERE WAS BODY REBEL WHO DIED IN THEIR LAST COUNTERATTACK DURING PREVIOUS NIGHT HIS FACE GREY FOR HED BEEN WOUNDED HEAD ANDS LEFT ARM HANGING STIFFLY IN AIR AS IF EVEN IN DEATH HE TRIED MAKE FASCIST SALUTE."[6] In the photo one leg and the left arm are indeed off the ground, the body slightly canted but generally supine—most assuredly not Robert Jordan, who dies kissing the pine needle floor.

Jordan died kissing the pine needle floor as befitting a stalwart defender of the common, the laboring, the poor, the decent. In an unpublished musing, Hemingway contrasted the Italian aristocrats flying above, fighting for Franco's fascists, with the corpses of working-class and poor Italian infantry who died fighting for the wrong cause. He wished somebody would turn them over, to face and commune with mother earth, the source of their lives and of their true allegiance, allied in their heart of hearts with Hemingway's vision of the Spanish people.[7] He might have drafted this piece with the two soldiers in the two nearly identical photos in mind—they lay facing the sky, just like the rebel corpse with its fascist salute, and it turns out they were in fact Italians fighting against the Republic. They can be glimpsed in the pro-Republic documentary *The Spanish Earth* that Hemingway helped produce with the Dutch filmmaker Joris Ivens. Ivens's cameraman John Ferno took the pair of photos in late March 1937, just after the Battle of Guadalajara (or Brihuega, as the battle is also known) and just after Hemingway's arrival in Spain.[8] In the film, Hemingway's voice captions the image on the screen: "These dead came from another country. They signed to work in Ethiopia. We took no statements from the dead but all the letters that we read were very sad. The Italians lost more killed, wounded, and missing in this single battle of Brihuega than in all the Ethiopian war."[9] The correspondents didn't talk to the dead, but they did talk to some of the surrendered and captured, who numbered twelve hundred according to freelancer George Seldes, and read some of the letters: "These original troops, these 4 divisions, had been told they were going to Abyssinia on police duty. They didn't even know they were in Spain."[10]

Hemingway's presence in one of the two otherwise identical photographs calls attention to the paradoxically objective and subjective nature of the medium. With him the scene becomes posed, and by association the other photo does too. Bearing witness in whatever medium is always paradoxically objective and subjective. In photography the tension between the act of witness and the art of witness, between documentation and beauty, vitalizes the encounter. As Susan Sontag muses in her last major work, the book-length essay *Regarding the Pain of Others*, in looking at an arresting photograph the viewer feels partially if not wholly responsible for the transformation, for seeing beauty where one shouldn't, for feeling moved by an object mechanically produced. Sontag's essay specifically tackles the unsettling aesthetic pleasure produced by horrific war photographs. "To find beauty in war photographs seems heartless," she writes. The idea that "photographs that depict suffering shouldn't be beautiful" implies that "a beautiful photograph drains attention away for the sobering subject and turns it toward the medium itself, thereby compromising the picture's status as a document."[11]

Written reportage is particularly complicated in its reception, perhaps because if camerawork generally pushes toward art, daily journalism rarely does and arguably actively resists. Their commingling of subjectivity and objectivity also operates differently. Whereas the documentary photograph we insist to ourselves happens at the spur of the moment, with the objectivity of the raw unmediated encounter, even the hurried dispatch occurs afterward with the possibility of limited crafting and fact-checking to get the story objectively straight. Yet both are ipso facto acts of personal witness: in the cabled version of the dispatches from reporters like Hemingway and Matthews, "Eye" communicated the first-person pronoun. Matthews in particular underwent great grief over challenges by his editors to his authority as eyewitness. The sentiment from one message to his editors became something of a refrain: "IF YOU DONT TRUST YOUR CORRESPONDENTS EITHER RELIEVE OR DISCHARGE THEM BUT EYE WONT STAY MADRID UNLESS EYE HAVE YOUR FULL CONFIDENCE."[12]

Hemingway wrote his eye-witnessing into news reports and other nonfiction, which many readers have found self-centered; into *The Spanish Earth*, for which he is credited with writing the commentary and recording the narration, and which he then permitted to be turned into a small book of the same name by a seventeen-year-old Ohio kid, Jasper Wood, a self-declared anarchist from the upper-crust Cleveland Heights neighborhood; and finally into fiction, amounting to several stories, one play, and his 1940 non-autobiographical novel *For Whom the Bell Tolls*. It might even be the case that the novel's apparent detachment from Hemingway's experiences boosted its perceived artfulness among its readers and reviewers. In the context of his novels of the 1920s, and in the context of his very public participation in the war, this novel was a refreshing surprise. To those who believed in such things, it proved the transforming, universal power of art. To Hemingway it proved his own maxim, that the truest part of any story is what one invents. One of the most memorable chapters in the book details El Sordo's last stand, the one event with no surviving witnesses. This story for all intents and purposes is imagined by Robert Jordan and Pablo's gang as they listen to the battle from across the valley. It's this piece of invention, along with the portrayal of a real event he did not witness, the Caporetto retreat from *A Farewell to Arms*, that Hemingway chose for his 1942 anthology *Men at War: The Best War Stories of All Time* (along with one piece of his nonfiction from the Spanish Civil War, "The Chauffeurs of Madrid").

The novel's other great set piece, and the source of much envy for the aspiring writer Robert Jordan, is Pilar's story of Ronda. In nonfiction terms Pilar's story of the town's heartless executions of its establishment figures by driving them off a cliff resembles the "informant narrative" or "informant documentary" that became so popular in the 1930s. "All documentary tends to direct quotation, but documentary can be all quotation and nothing else," writes William Stott in defining this genre.[13] Inevitably confessional (as Pilar's is), such stories in the 1930s were chiefly a colloquial, proletariat form. In addition to the fully imagined story of El Sordo and the entirely quoted story from Pilar, *For Whom the Bell Tolls* gives us Robert Jordan's tale. Jordan pines to live and think in the moment, a kind of camera-eye narrative not unlike that of Jake Barnes in Hemingway's first novel of Spain, *The Sun Also Rises*. Still, Jordan can't stop himself from reflecting, and not simply reflecting but truly using narrative to shape his life. And his death.

Whatever else the novel addresses, it certainly attends to the relationship among personal experience, historical accountability, imagination, and art. Pilar's story, so arresting, so testimonial, so direct, challenges us as gruesome photographs do, our repulsion to the obscene violence clashing with our appreciation of its perfected expression. In *Writing War in the Twentieth Century*, Margot Norris argues that *A Farewell to Arms* challenges the reader compelled to turn a novel about disillusion, desertion, selfishness, murder, and tragic death into a tender romance. Following Norris, and departing from readers who valorize Robert Jordan's self-sacrificing heroism, I wonder if *For Whom the Bell Tolls* poses a similar challenge. The Spanish Civil War was a brutal, savage affair on both sides, while the United States and its European allies like Great Britain and France did nothing. In his history of the war, Anthony Beevor records that the May 1937 Republican offensive in the Guadarrama Range on which Hemingway based the novel—and another event he did not personally witness—became "the first example of unrest in the ranks of the International Brigades as a result of being sacrificed for little benefit."[14] Robert Jordan, a fictional international brigader, has sacrificed his life in vain: the bridge is blown but the battle is lost, the war will be lost and the dear 1940 reader has already been lost—the Second World War is well underway, the Allied refusal to take on Hitler and Mussolini in Spain having failed, as so desperately desired, to prevent it.

Are we supposed to believe that for Maria two overly poetic lovemaking scenes have transcended the gang rape? Does art have such power? The earth moves only figuratively during the lovemaking, but literally when the planes bomb El Sordo's gang to oblivion. And why on earth does Hemingway, in a letter to his wartime comrade and peacetime composer Gustavo Duran written right around the time of the novel's publication, call Robert Jordan a "chickenshit"?[15]

Michael Reynolds's *Hemingway's First War: The Making of* A Farewell to Arms is a landmark text, and I am acutely aware of the possible perception of presumption in naming this book as I have. I would never claim to have produced a work on par with that one. Nevertheless, the books share a similar spirit in their discussion of the author's experience, their attention to the creative process, and their analysis of a major Hemingway war novel independent of biographical consideration.

The full story of Hemingway and the Spanish Civil War has not been told. This book does not purport to fill that tall order either. I set out to learn as much as I could about the film and book versions of *The Spanish Earth,* though it did not take long to realize that to understand the documentary I needed to study Hemingway's experience of the war, his war correspondence, and his fiction. *Hemingway's Second War* began with the film, but it begins with the war.

Part I, "Spain in Flames," treats Hemingway the war correspondent. Chapter 1 charts his encounters with the Spanish Republic from 1931 through 1938. The basic story is similar to those told by previous biographers though the approach and details—the composite—differ. This chapter is also necessary to set the stage for the rest of the book. Chapter 2 analyzes the journalistic output and aims to restore some measure of appreciation for a corpus discountenanced by most commentators. (Herbert Matthews's dispatches prove a wonderful comparative tool.) In terms of the journalism, this book and Scott Donaldson's recent essay "The Last Great Cause: Hemingway's Spanish Civil War Writing," included in his *Fitzgerald & Hemingway*, nicely complement one another.

The two chapters of part II, "*The Spanish Earth*," explore the film and its book version and I daresay constitute the fullest published account and study of these texts to date. Chapter 3 discusses the film's inception, production, and initial appearances. (The biography is thus divided between chapters 1 and 3.) Chapter 4 studies the completed film and documents its post-release life, including young Jasper Wood's translation of the film into the book.

From the actual to the fictional: *Hemingway's Second War* proceeds as this introduction has. Thus part III turns to the final act and art of witness, *For Whom the Bell Tolls*. Chapter 5 advances the first parts of the book by thinking through the historical canvass on which the novel draws. It does not detail all of the connections, and some of what it discusses will be familiar to some readers, though again it makes a necessary contribution to the entire book and in certain cases contributes to or qualifies earlier scholarship. I hope teachers will find useful material here, such as the internet availability of motion footage of the actual Guadarrama offensive taken by Robert Capa and Gerda Taro. (Teachers and others interested in exploring the war's many dimensions should consult the Modern Language Association's marvelous *Teaching Representations of the Spanish Civil War*, edited by Noël Valis.)

The sixth chapter examines gender roles and rhetoric as they played out during the war and in the novel, moving from the wartime realities and discourses to their functioning within Robert Jordan. Finally, chapter 7 attempts to answer the question posed above about Robert

Jordan by reading him alongside Frederic Henry, of *A Farewell to Arms*, in terms of their profound similarities as opposed to their apparent differences: Are they both chickenshits?

Among its many shortcomings, *Hemingway's Second War* neglects sustained attention to the creative essays in *Ken* (including "The Old Man at the Bridge"), the play *The Fifth Column*, and the short stories—"The Denunciation," "The Butterfly and the Tank," "Night before Battle," "Under the Ridge," and "Nobody Ever Dies." All receive mention as part of the larger tale, but none receives scrutiny. Readers interested in the publication history of *For Whom the Bell Tolls* will also be disappointed but can and should turn to Robert Trogdon's *The Lousy Racket*.

The major shortcoming involves the nature of the beast. In literary biography there are always other facts, other leads, other contexts, other documents and material, other considerations. Writing literary biography engenders a deep appreciation for and a respectful skepticism toward previous biographers. I have done my best to rely on primary material in piecing together this narrative, yet one can't escape the fraught necessity of relying on others. I am incalculably indebted to Hemingway biographers like Carlos Baker, Jeffrey Meyers, Linda Wagner-Martin, Scott Donaldson, and Michael Reynolds for their research and narratives. The Baker papers at Princeton University contain a wealth of information whose use in no way fates one to a repetition of his foundational *Ernest Hemingway: A Life Story*. The works of Allen Josephs and William Braasch Watson on Hemingway and the Spanish Civil War have proven crucial. I am equally dependent upon biographers and historians of other subjects—Caroline Moorehead for her life of Martha Gellhorn, Hans Schoots for his life of Joris Ivens, and Hugh Thomas, Anthony Beevor, Paul Preston, and Helen Graham for their histories of the Spanish Civil War.

Literary biography is one part detective work, one part library science, one part journalism, one part literary criticism, one part history, one part pop psychology, and one part gossip column. Writing this book has been a pleasure and an education.

I
SPAIN IN FLAMES

ONE

Hemingway's War

The Spanish Civil War began in mid-July 1936 when a large portion of the Spanish army rebelled against the legitimately elected government of the Second Spanish Republic. The Republic of July 1936 consisted of a loose coalition of political entities, from revolutionary anarchists and regional separatists to unionists, socialists, communists, and middle-class republicans, all vying for support from the working class and the unrepresented poor and never overcoming their differences in ideologies and interests. Even individual political groups generally loyal to the Republic struggled to achieve a common agenda. To talk about anarchists or communists or socialists in Republican Spain, for example, fails to recognize the diversity of anarchists, communists, and socialists in Republican Spain. Unifying the war effort of the various militias, the remnant regular army and internal militant police forces (the Civil Guard), and the brigades of international volunteers, proved no small feat. The history of the war is very much a history of Republican internal dysfunction.

The government's distrust of some of its own factions caused it to withhold arms from its citizens and militias early in the war; some historians think that if it had decided otherwise, it could have stopped the rebellion in the opening days.[1] As it was, in this underdeveloped European country with "communications difficult or non-existent, each town [found] itself on its own, acting out its own drama, apparently in a vacuum. There were soon to be not two Spains, but two thousand."[2]

The insurgent military wore the Nationalist mantle with the support of the conservative elements of Spain—the monarchists, the Catholic Church, the landed classes, and generally all the beneficiaries of the quasi-feudal system the Republic had recently and incompletely replaced (including a share of the middle class). Within the first three months of fighting, General Francisco Franco emerged as the Nationalist leader as the rebel movement took a decidedly fascist turn. Those nations who might have aided the Republic—England, France, and the United States—abided by a nonintervention treaty that the Nationalist's fascist friends, Germany and Italy, did not. The Republic's potential allies believed intervention in Spain against fascism would spur a far more devastating war across all of Europe. The Soviet Union did provide essential war material and advisors to the Republic, though at heavy financial and political costs, in terms of further discouraging democratic nations from assisting what increasingly appeared to be becoming a "Red" state.

Madrid finally fell to the rebels in March 1939. Franco declared victory over the Republic on 1 April. Five months later Franco's ally Hitler invaded Poland, and the world war Ernest Hemingway had predicted in 1935 was underway.

In his preface to Gustav Regler's autobiographical novel *The Great Crusade,* Hemingway wrote that the war "was really lost, of course, when the Fascists took Irún in the late summer of 1936. But in a war you can never admit, even to yourself, that it is lost. Because when you will admit it is lost you are beaten."[3] Hemingway's historical pronouncement names as decisive and climactic a battle that occurred quite early and well before his arrival in country to report the war, and sounds the same forgone note that resounds in *For Whom the Bell Tolls.* Both books appeared in 1940. Hemingway's retrospective analysis answers for the ungrounded optimism of his wartime writings, and it excuses him and his comrades for their failure. Regler, a German exile who had worked with Joris Ivens in 1934 in Moscow on the anti-Nazi short film *Saar Plebiscite and Soviet Union,*[4] was the political commissar for the XII International Brigade and one of Hemingway's chief combatant associates.

Irún fell on 3 September. Nearby San Sebastian, a town dear to Hemingway, followed ten days later. As Hugh Thomas explains, not only did the Nationalist victory at Irún secure "about 1,000 square miles of rich farmland, densely populated, with many important factories," it was "of incomparable strategic importance" because it severed the Republic's loyalist Basque region from France, the overland source of aid and support.[5] With the battle still underway, six freight cars loaded with ammunition, sent from Republican Catalonia through southern France, were intercepted and held by the French in strict observance of the August nonintervention policy. Though it's unlikely the shipment would have saved Irún, France's interference at this hour of need symbolized the non-fascist international community's contribution to the eventual defeat of the Republic. The defense of Irún also revealed a schism in the ranks between the anarchists and the Basque Nationalists, as well as between the central government in Madrid and the Basque government, again potentially symbolic of the Republic's disarray. Finally, in naming Irún, Hemingway managed to spite Franco, as Irún had fallen to General Emilio Mola's northern command, and at the time Mola still contested for supreme authority over the Nationalist forces. Mola, in fact, had been the revolt's chief architect. The war had begun on his command.

On 17 July 1936, the rebels mutinied first in Morocco, then the next day throughout mainland Spain. But Spain had been aflame for years, with Hemingway watching. He arrived in May 1931, shortly after the inception of the Second Spanish Republic on 14 April, to spend the summer working on his bullfighting book *Death in the Afternoon*. In Madrid he passed many afternoons with his friend Luis Quintanilla, the artist he had met in Paris nearly ten years before. Quintanilla's talk of Spain in those days had helped inspire Hemingway's first visit, back in 1923, the same year he wrote about Spanish politics for the first time.[6] A century of antagonism between the powerful and the powerless arrayed the royalty, the landowners, the financiers, and the church against the rural and industrial workers, and the dissatisfied portion of the middle class.

Nationwide municipal elections on 12 April yielded significant victories for the latter groups, under both Socialist and Republican parties, sending a clear message to the traditionalist elite.

Within forty-eight hours King Alfonso left Madrid by car, headed for exile abroad, and Quintanilla found himself before the Royal Palace surrounded by an "agitated" crowd: "The moment appeared critical, and it occurred to me that the best thing to do at that moment would be to put a Republican flag on the Palace." A "wildman" with "a beautiful tricolor flag" of red, yellow, and violet refused to give it up. Others descended upon him, and a street urchin emerged with it. Quintanilla told the boy to mount the flag on the main balcony, and "Agile as a monkey, he climbed up along the wall's outer architectural adornments: there was a brief silence as the golfo attached the flag to the balcony. Then the overwhelming ovation of those seventy thousand people prolonged itself like a monstrous explosion which went on and on, and when calm finally returned they began to leave."[7] In Hemingway's version of the story, Quintanilla raised the flag by his own hand.[8]

A temporary government was established to manage state affairs and administer elections for the constitutional congress (the Constituent Cortes). On 10 May an incident between a monarchist group and hopeful citizens of the Republic led to an outbreak of mob arsons, first against the offices of a monarchist paper, but then to churches — perhaps one hundred churches — in Madrid and throughout Spain in a matter of days. The infant government declared marital law.[9] Hemingway arrived soon thereafter.

Quintanilla's son Paul, summarizing and quoting from his father's own memoir, describes Hemingway's attitude in Madrid:

> Hemingway was "euphoric" about the arrival of the Republic. Though totally nonpolitical, my father tells us he was "profoundly democratic and liberal in his ideals," and so great was his enthusiasm that he saw the Republic's creation as a "personal victory," for he hoped the new government would finally rectify the numerous abuses the Spanish people had endured for centuries.[10]

Luis Quintanilla's memoir, *Pasatiempo: La Vida d un Pintor*, was published almost thirty years later, in 1960. Yet even accounting for fallible memory, for Quintanilla's loyalist agenda (writing during Franco's dictatorship), and for the possibility that he heard what he wanted to hear, his account testifies to Hemingway's long engagement with Spanish politics. But Hemingway also tempered his optimism and aspiration with a realistic concern:

> But one day as Ernesto stood at a window in my father's studio he could hear a company of cadets training in a nearby open area. And, "like a sudden blow," listening to their machineguns, he experienced a presentiment of the future. Turning to my father he said: "The Republic should begin to prepare to defend itself. It is a democracy born in a bad moment—Europe is moving toward dictatorships."[11]

Two days before the elections for the Constituent Cortes, Hemingway wrote to John Dos Passos about the upcoming Republican landslide: "Madrid loves the Republic—which, as soon as anyone takes power—Lerroux etc., they shift from left to right faster than even France. The King is permanently out. . . . Chances for Marxian revolution nil—may yet have a terror though. If worst comes to worst history of 1st Republic will repeat."[12] The First Republic, declared in February 1873, lasted a few violent months, with the army restoring the old conservative order of monarchists, church, and landowners.[13]

The elections on 28 June were remarkably peaceful. But the new government, a liberal coalition mostly of socialists and republicans, had not won power from a coherent, organized position but rather found themselves thrown together in the wake of the old ruling class's collapse. It had to manage, for example, the agenda of northern Spain's industrial working class, generally respectful of Spanish Catholicism, and the agenda of central and southern Spain's exploited agricultural laborers who saw the church in cahoots with the system that abused them. Moreover, the progressive Republican government remained thoroughly centrist and traditional in its belief in the authority, processes, and tools of the state. Its leaders were middle-class professionals who sought to free Spain from the stranglehold of the traditional powers but who balked at the idea of revolution. Helen Graham's brilliant history *The Spanish Republic at War, 1936–1939*, characterizes the government as having a "statist, *top-down*," and self-interested old-school approach that "feared rather than sought political mobilization of the masses" despite its deep democratic beliefs.[14] It had not yet embraced the far left (nor even some elements of the near left) and had inherited the instruments of civil control that had a history of violent responses to public dissent. July and August saw several strikes organized by anarchists turn violent when the government authorized the Civil Guard and the army to end what it considered illegal actions. On 22 July, the new government declared a state of war.[15]

Hemingway had spent the summer following the bullfighting season and retreating to work, often but not always accompanied by his wife, Pauline. When the Hemingway's left Spain at the end of August, the Republic had made enemies on both the left and the right.

The government's violent suppression of the strikes had turned many workers against it and reignited the passion for social revolution. The right, meanwhile, blamed the far left and the progressive government for the social unrest and for the violent tactics used to put it down. And it began to rally its various groups and personalities against the Republican agenda: separation of church and state, agrarian reform, Catalonian autonomy, and military reform.

Hemingway followed the upheaval as best he could from abroad, referencing its troubles in occasional letters and in a January 1934 *Esquire* article.[16] For the next two years, strikes and civil unrest met with violent responses as the government struggled to preserve order and enact progressive legislation. For many on the left, the reforms did not go far enough or fast enough; agrarian measures to relieve the laborers oppressed by the old system, for example, often went unfunded or unenforced. For everyone on the right, any reform went too far. Secularization efforts did go too far, with an anticlerical frenzy that turned churches into ash-heaps and "infringed the democratic rights and sense of identity of ordinary Catholics."[17] The right began to organize itself more determinedly, and many of those with money removed significant capital from the economy just when it needed it the most—this was, after all, the height of the Great Depression in a country caught lagging far behind its modernized peers. Occasionally some members of the left even sided with the right, as for example when the government prematurely removed Jesuit control of education before it had a working replacement.[18]

The disorder led to elections in November 1933, this time won by the right. The left could not consolidate, and ironically, the government's passing of suffrage for women led to more votes for the right. Predictably, the new government of the Second Spanish Republic worked to reverse its predecessor's reforms and moved toward control by monarchist sympathizers. Several parts of Spain erupted in October 1934. Most of these local efforts, chiefly in Madrid and Barcelona, were immediately crushed. The revolution in the Asturias area met with the most success, though pillaging and atrocities against priests and businessmen eroded its legitimacy. Government suppression this time involved importing General Franco to command Foreign Legion and Moroccan troops to quell the Asturias region, and a brutal post-uprising pacification campaign of imprisonment, torture, and execution.

Among those thousands arrested as political prisoners that season was Luis Quintanilla:

> On the night of the fifth of October, nineteen thirty-four, my father was arrested in his studio for being a member of the Revolutionary Committee which had intended to overthrow the Madrid government. . . . And though once again more sympathetically than actively involved he had indeed hosted a large group of revolutionaries who were awaiting the moment when they would go out onto the streets to oust the central government: though when the police arrived he vigorously protested they had all gathered in his studio merely to look at art. . . . What had given their presence away was a lapse among some of the more youthful members of the committee who had gone out onto the studio's terrace to discuss the day's events, and a neighbor overheard them and reported them to the police.[19]

This was the very studio from which Hemingway, three years earlier, had predicted a violent future for Spain. Its centrality and its view made it an ideal staging and coordination position; Quintanilla had been helping distribute arms among the revolutionaries, though at the time of the arrest the police only found four pistols in the place. Quintanilla's own, hidden in a planter, escaped discovery.[20] Had they been caught after taking up arms, the consequences would have been less kind.

Hemingway learned of the arrest from an October cable from Madrid, reading "Luis hoosegowed."[21] His friend Lester Ziffren wrote from Madrid on 1 November, telling Hemingway that Quintanilla "happened" to be with the conspirators in his apartment and so "packed off with them to jail," where he sits while the government "drum[s] up some charges against him so that he may get a good long jail sentence."[22] Jay Allen, working in Madrid for the *Chicago Tribune*, wrote Hemingway two weeks later to report on Quintanilla's condition. His morale was high during Allen's one o'clock visits, and he was even putting on extra weight—according to Allen, Quintanilla's friends would bribe the guards with whiskey to get him food, utensils, and sketching supplies.[23] A *Newsweek* article presented his luxuries as aboveboard: "By paying 1 peseta a day he has the comparative luxury of an upstairs cell, which he shares with six others. Pen and pencil are allowed him; also the privilege of buying his food at the restaurant across the street." But he faced a sentence of either thirty years or death. The article described a one-man show of his work in New York City, at the Pierre Matisse Gallery, noting that when he was arrested "he was working on six large panels for the monument in Madrid's Montcloa Park to Pablo Iglesias, Socialist leader who died in 1925," the panels "among Quintanilla's best work."[24]

Hemingway put up money for the show, and he and John Dos Passos wrote bits for the brochure. According to Paul Quintanilla, proceeds went to Quintanilla from Hemingway through Allen in Madrid. Hemingway also helped organize a picket line in front of the Spanish consulate.[25] Pierre Matisse and Jean Lucrat, a radical French painter Matisse assumed to be a member of L'Association des Écrivaîns et Artistes Révolutionnaires, concocted a plan to petition President Zamora of Spain for Quintanilla's release,[26] and the petition was signed by, among others, Sinclair Lewis, Theodore Dreiser, Waldo Pierce, and Hemingway and Dos Passos.[27] A draft of the letter at the gallery bears Henri Matisse's signature.[28] But according to Paul Quintanilla's recounting of his father's tale, "The petitions, letters, and pressure the British government put on the Spanish government didn't obtain my father's release [in June 1935]. It was the nagging of his military judges' wives."[29]

The right's reversal of progressive legislation and its violence during and after the failed October revolution brought the various centrist and leftist groups together as the Popular Front for the purpose of ousting the right's National Front. Political scandals hitting the government at the end of 1935 brought about new elections, scheduled for February 1936. Voting sites opened 16 February, and the official word of the Popular Front's victory by a tenuous margin of "less than 2 percent"[30] came on 20 February. In her memoir, Dolores Ibárruri of the Spanish Communist Party (PCE), called La Pasionaria for her role as impassioned motivator for the Republic's war efforts, spins the Popular Front (as espoused by the communists) as "a weapon of unity wielded by the workers and the democratic forces in the electoral and postelectoral fight to restore and consolidate democracy in Spain" rather than as a "mere election-ticket coalition."[31] Perhaps the new government had that potential, but its major members' (including the communists') continued hostility toward its more radical coalition allies thwarted such hopes.

The unrest continued. The two-hundred-fifty–plus deaths from February to July were topped off with a series of political murders.[32] When the war began, Quintanilla became an impromptu soldier and fought to win the surrender of the rebels in Madrid's Montana barracks, which he then commanded for a brief time.[33] Hemingway was in Key West.

The military historian S.L.A. Marshall and his wife, staying in their Key West home for about ten days that summer, went fishing several times with Hemingway. The two of them, plus Harry Sylvester, "talked the whole thing over several times. Hemingway was quite disinterested. He said: 'It means nothing to me; I have good friends on both sides.' . . . Then he gave me the key to his apartment in Madrid, saying he had no intention of going to the war. However, I never used it."[34] But Prudencio de Pereda, a young writer who idolized Hemingway and had been corresponding with him since 1934, thought from letters and conversations that Hemingway "had made up his mind to go immediately after the war started, wanted to go, felt committed."[35] In a short letter of 23 July to de Pereda from Key West, Hemingway had in fact written that they should have been in Spain that week[36]—the week that the Nationalist forces in the north were advancing on Madrid through the Guadarrama Mountains, closing to within forty miles of the capital before being stopped. He also wrote of his desire to get to Spain in September to his editor Maxwell Perkins.[37]

Hemingway's different audiences explain his apparently different attitudes. De Pereda, of Spanish descent, considered volunteering for the loyalist side; Harry Sylvester, as Marshall noted, "was a very devout Catholic and hot for the Rebel cause." Indeed Hemingway's neutral response and simple acknowledgment of loyalist friends "shocked Harry."[38] (Hemingway would later write to Sylvester explaining his Republican sympathies.[39]) One wonders if Hemingway's very Catholic wife, Pauline, was around for any of these conversations as well. A few days after writing to Sylvester, he wrote to her family—who had turned a room of their Piggott, Arkansas, home into a Catholic chapel—to soften the news of his politics. Acknowledging that the so-called Reds of the Republican side might have earned their reputation for brutality, the country nevertheless belonged to them, not to "the absentee landlords, the moors, the italians [sic] and the Germans." These "Whites" were certainly "rotten," and he wanted to go to Spain to compare the two sides "on the basis of humanity," and to write antiwar dispatches to encourage the United States to stay out of the "inevitable" general war in Europe.[40]

The Hemingways left Key West in late July, on their way to the Nordquist ranch in Wyoming (east of Yellowstone and just south of Montana) after visiting Pauline's family in northeast Arkansas. John Dos Passos's letter to Hemingway that October—"gosh I hope you get to go"—suggests Hemingway had shared the possibility with him.[41] By late October, Hemingway was already talking publicly about getting to Spain, to the *Billings Gazette* the last days of his western vacation.[42] Sometime before Thanksgiving John N. Wheeler, the general manager for the North American Newspaper Alliance (NANA), learned of Hemingway's plans from the syndicated print and radio columnist Walter Winchell and wrote Hemingway to propose that he cover the war for NANA.[43] On 9 December, Hemingway wrote to de Pereda from Havana about his plan to travel to Spain after finishing *To Have or Have Not*. He offered to loan de Pereda the money to go over to fight: "If you didn't get killed you would get wonderful material and if you did get killed it would be in a good cause."[44] De Pereda never went, but Hemingway paid the passage for two other volunteers.[45]

Hemingway began wiring money to the Medical Bureau of the American Friends of Spanish Democracy in mid December.[46] Eleven days into the New Year, the American Friends named him "chairman of a committee formed to send an ambulance corps to Spain" and announced his plans to leave for Spain soon.[47] He arrived in New York City on 13 January.[48] On Friday the fifteenth, he inspected the surgical and ambulance unit's equipment before it shipped aboard the *Paris* the next day; the group consisted of "sixteen men and women with four ambulances and twelve tons of medical hospital supplies valued at $30,000."[49] (On 1 February the unit arrived in Barcelona and, after attending a banquet in its honor, proceeded to Valencia on its way to the front.[50]) Hemingway's NANA agreement letter to cover the war for two to three months is dated 22 January 1937.[51] To Roger Chase, chief of the Medical Bureau of the American Friends of Spanish Democracy, he would later write that he had borrowed the contribution for the ambulance fund and had signed with NANA to repay it.[52] By the end of January he had also already agreed, at least to Archibald MacLeish, to help with the pro-loyalist film that would become *The Spanish Earth*.[53]

After a few weeks back in Key West, Hemingway sailed for Europe from New York aboard the *Paris* on 27 February 1937. Though the January notices of his intentions cited his ambulance mission and his desire to observe the war, the *New York Times* and the *Washington Post* reports of his actual departure cite only his NANA assignment. With him were Sidney Franklin, an American bullfighter (from Brooklyn) who would serve as his assistant, and Evan Shipman, a friend from Paris in the 1920s, who would manage transporting the ambulances from France to Spain. His Scribners editor Maxwell Perkins saw them off.[54]

Hemingway went to Spain because he loved Spain. He had to see the war for himself. He also had to do what he could to save Spain from fascism, by providing the ambulances and by promulgating his perspective through his writing and the film — the proceeds of both he turned into material support. Spain had to be saved for her own sake, and for Europe's. Stopping fascism in Spain might have prevented the next world war; at the very least, it would have added Spain to the Allied nations. George Seldes would recall a late night with Hemingway in Paris during the war and Hemingway's remark that "I had to ('go to Spain' or 'do this' or something like this phrase, meaning commit himself to the loyalists) before you liberal bastards would believe I was on your side."[55] Hemingway's sensitivity in the 1930s to criticism by other writers, that his writing did not engage the pressing social issues of their times, offers another reason for going to Spain, though a secondary or even tertiary one. His December letter to de Pereda offers a reason he was perhaps less conscious of: new stories and people for his fiction. His writing needed it—none of his books since *A Farewell to Arms* in 1929 had met with satisfactory success. The war in Spain came along at just the right time. According to one acquaintance from Key West late that fall: "I thought then that he was getting himself into a situation with diminishing resources. He didn't find any pleasure in research or reading; only sex, violence and the agony of writing interested him. He drank and hung out with essentially dull people like Sidney Franklin who turned up there for a few days. But these people gave him nothing much."[56]

Josephine Herbst, a fellow correspondent in Madrid the spring of 1937, described Hemingway as

> undergoing some kind of transformation, and part of the reason he had come to Spain was doubtless because the forces of that process were already at work. It wasn't only that he was giving up his wife for Martha Gellhorn. He had answered a definite call when he came to Spain. He wanted to be *the* war writer of his age, and he knew it and went toward it. War gave answers that could not be found in that paradise valley of Wyoming where he had fished or even in the waters of Key West when the tarpon struck. What was the deepest reality *there* was in an extreme form *here*, and to get it he had to be in it, and he knew it.[57]

Hemingway met Gellhorn in December, and she was anything but dull company. A fellow writer, a beautiful young blonde who shared his passion for the antifascist Republican cause, she was, according to Regler, "the most devoted of all"[58] among the correspondents. They would pursue their affair in Madrid.

The night before the *Paris* made Plymouth harbor in the United Kingdom, Miss Great Britain of 1936, twenty-three-year-old Muriel

Oxford, threw an after-midnight champagne party in her cabin to celebrate the end of the journey. Hemingway and Franklin attended, as did a thirty-seven-year-old British theater actor, Frank Vosper. Vosper disappeared, presumed lost at sea. One friend suspected he had slipped when climbing down to his own cabin. Others spread the rumor that he leapt overboard from Oxford's cabin veranda after she refused his hand in marriage.[59]

It was not a propitious beginning.

The initial rebellion failed to win a quick victory, largely due to the miraculous improvised defenses of various political and union militias and of unaffiliated citizen-workers, including women. By the end of July, however, the Nationalists controlled one-third of the country: the Moroccan territory, a large northern stretch from the Atlantic to France surrounding the Basque region, a substantial salient emanating from the southwestern port of Cádiz (north of Gibraltar), and the Balearic Islands of Mallorca and Ibiza in the Mediterranean. The transportation of soldiers from Morocco to Spain by German aircraft "was the first major 'airlift' of troops in history."[60]

By August, Mola's Nationalist northern forces and Franco's southern forces closed the western gap. With each seized town, retribution followed. Bullrings proved convenient sites for mass executions. Jay Allen of the *Chicago Tribune* watched as the Nationalists marched their prisoners into the bullring at Badajoz: "There machine guns await them. After the first night the blood was supposed to be palm deep on the far side of the lane. . . . There is more blood than you would think in 1,800 bodies." Men and women. In twelve hours.[61] The idea occurred to some loyalists, too. In Oropesa, they had gathered the bourgeoisie "in the bull-ring to be killed by fighting bulls"—only the rebels intervened and "took a bloody revenge."[62]

Hemingway's delayed arrival caused him to miss some of the war's significant battles. Málaga fell to the Nationalists in February 1937, an event of great consternation and controversy within the Republic resulting in a blame-game among the various political interests. Back in September, in addition to the Republican losses of Irún and San Sebastian, he missed the relief of the besieged Alcázar, a fortress serving as a school for infantry officers to which the city of Toledo's rebels had retreated.[63] Franco's decision to save the defenders of the Alcázar may have given Madrid's defenders enough time to prepare and eventually repel the Nationalist's November offensive against the capital. But it also became a symbol of Nationalist heroism and of Franco's role as savior. *Spain in Flames*, a pro-rebel book published in the closing months of 1936 by the Paulist Press in New York, held up the Alcázar to its American audience as the war's symbol of Nationalist sacrifice, determination, and eventual victory.[64] Paul Preston historicizes the symbolism: "In the middle ages, Toledo had been the first major Muslim city to be reconquered by Christian forces. Now, Franco was symbolically associating himself with the great warriors of the *Reconquista* and the Republican defenders with the infidel."[65] The irony that Franco led Moorish troops escaped less attentive observers. Saving the Alcázar and winning Toledo assured Franco's installation as supreme commander on 1 October.

October also saw the initial shaping of the future Republican military. The government ordered the formation of the Popular Army with "mixed brigades" of militia and old regular army battalions (a process that took many months to complete and never fully worked). Volunteers from around the world entered Spain to join the first of the International Brigades, and the Soviet Union decided to answer German and Italian support for the rebels by sending its first shipment of weapons to the Republic, including dozens of aircraft and T-26 tanks. These developments saved Madrid and the Republic from the Nationalist's monthlong offensive in November, the month the government moved to Valencia.

The brutal street fighting converged at University City, the campus on the northern edge of Madrid whose administration building sported Quintanilla murals. As one international volunteer described it,

> we started a ruthless fight for every path, every house, every floor, and every threshold. Here, the front line sometimes goes through the most valuable laboratories and libraries. Sometimes breastworks are constructed from huge volumes of the Encyclopedia Britannica. Here the fascists have come the closest to Madrid; it is only between three and five hundred metres from the Casa Velázquez to the nearest café in town.[66]

The Nationalists won the School of Architecture and the clinic while the Republic won the Departments of Agriculture, Medicine, and Philosophy and Letters.[67] The front line would divide the campus for the rest of the war.

From December 1936 to March 1937, Franco tried several times to break the Republican lines surrounding Madrid, first down the Corunna road to the northwest, then into the Jarama River valley to seize the Valencia road to the south in a campaign that included the fight for the Arganda Bridge featured in *The Spanish Earth*, and finally from the northeast toward Guadalajara. All these offenses saw their immediate gains stalled and even slightly reversed. The Guadalajara campaign of 8 March through 18 March ended, for the time being, the costly Nationalist efforts to capture the capital. Italian forces fighting for the rebels suffered an embarrassing defeat at Guadalajara, alerting the world to the extent of Mussolini's support for Franco. Among the loyalist fighters who drove the Italian army back by recapturing Brihuega was a contingent of Italian volunteers. The day the campaign ended, Hemingway cabled from Valencia his first NANA dispatch from Spain, describing young recruits in Alicante

> celebrating their enlistment and the victory over Italian regular troops on the Guadalajara front, walking four abreast arm in arm, singing, playing accordions and guitars. The pleasure boats of Alicante harbor were packed with couples holding hands, taking last rides together, but ashore, where the recruiting stations' jammed lines formed far down the streets, the atmosphere was a wild celebration.[68]

Ten days later he would write that "the battle of Brihuega will take its place in military history with the other decisive battles of the world."[69] However hyperbolic and optimistic, this claim captured the mood in Republican Spain of both Spaniards and foreigners. Not long after the battle the U.S. ambassador to Spain, Claude Bowers, wrote to Secretary of State Cordell Hull gushing in his prediction of government victory and beating Hemingway to an American Civil War analogy: "This national army no more resembles that which made a mess of things, clinging to their trenches, in the early stages of the war, than did the Union Army of Bull Run resemble that which fought at Gettysburg."[70]

But Hemingway had missed it. By the time he arrived in Madrid, the war "was no longer [one] of rapid manoeuvre, but of head-on slogging."[71]

Hemingway's first NANA dispatch was hardly newsworthy—filed from Paris on 12 March, it complained about the U.S. State Department's reluctance to allow Sidney Franklin into Spain as Hemingway's assistant. Four days later he used Franklin's troubles to open his second dispatch, contrasting the refusal to permit Franklin's trip with the arrival of twelve thousand Italian troops for Franco purportedly on the same day. "French Border Airtight, Hemingway's Check Shows" wryly salutes the vigilance and effectiveness of the border guards given the porousness of the rest of Spain to Italian and German soldiers (which he numbered at just over a hundred thousand[72]). The wry salute was only mildly disingenuous, if and to the extent that Hemingway knew of European and American volunteers for the Republic who had slipped across that very border since its closing on 20 February—handfuls at most.[73] Hemingway's trip had another potential purpose, in assessing the feasibility of the planned overland route from France for his ambulances, and possibly for medical personnel as well. The dispatch mentions the refusal of a sixty-year-old Swiss woman, a former Red Cross nurse, to cross the border with supplies for refugee children in Madrid. The U.S. State Department had recently begun refusing passports to those medical volunteers assembled by the American Friends of Spanish Democracy on the grounds that the organization's partiality to the Republic constituted political rather than humanitarian aid and violated the United States's official neutrality (although two other units managed to make it to Spain through Barcelona by mid April, at least one of which the Spanish press reported as sent by "Medical Bureau—American Friends of Spanish Democracy").[74]

Quintanilla tells a different version of the "French Border" story: he and Hemingway had "met on the French side of the border" and "engaged, as they always did after a long separation, in *la Gran borrachera*, the great drunk, and touring the border inadvertently wandered into the rebel zone. Hemingway took notes on what he saw and that night, in his hotel room in Hendaye, wrote the first of his journalism pieces for NANA," which he admitted was "the dirtiest of dirty journalism," an easy "thousand dollars."[75]

Once in Madrid, having just missed the battle for Guadalajara (Brihuega), Hemingway went to the battlefield to see what he could see. He wrote a dispatch about the battle on 22 March, but he first visited the battle (and perhaps drafted the dispatch) a day or two before. The dispatch mentions leaving Valencia "at five o'clock in the morning."[76] Joris Ivens's trip notes indicate that he and Hemingway could have been traveling together to Spain, as Ivens arrived in Valencia on 17 March, the day before Hemingway's Valencia dispatch, and so possibly on the same date and the same flight, explaining Hemingway's use of the first-person plural pronoun.[77] They stayed at least through 19 March and arrived in Madrid on 20 or 21 March. They saw Guadalajara and Brihuega on 21 March, then visited Valdesaz five miles from Brihuega on 22 and 23 March to meet with the French and Italian units of the XII International Brigade involved in the fighting and returned to Guadalajara on 24 March.[78] On these trips to the battle site, Hemingway met Regler, Regler's commander General Lukács, and Werner Heilbrun, the German doctor to whose widow Hemingway would direct any proceeds from Jasper Wood's *The Spanish Earth* book.[79]

NANA's "precede" to Hemingway's dispatch of 22 March introduces Hemingway's description of the Italian defeat by reminding readers of the Italian retreat from Caporetto he so famously depicted in *A Farewell to Arms*.[80] Hemingway's dispatch actually distinguishes the two: "Italians defending the line of the Piave and Mount Grappa against invasion are one thing and Italians sent to fight in Spain when they expected to go on garrison duty in Ethiopia are another." In obeying the republican press standard rules forbidding the mention of internationals fighting for the Republic, however, Hemingway does not write about the Italians who had won the battle. Instead he draws a picture of the letters and papers strewing the battlefield and the Nationalists' Italian dead—"small and pitiful," they looked less "like men" than they did "curiously broken toys" and "doll[s]."[81] These are the papers and the dead we see in *The Spanish Earth*, including the two beside whom Hemingway posed. Though his next dispatch exaggerates the historic magnitude of the battle, in this one he demonstrates operational foresight: "There will still be bitter fighting for Guadalajara and the ground south of the main Valencia road, but studying the terrain I believe an encirclement of Madrid is now impossible unless General Franco gets huge reinforcements of a better class of troops than those who fought at Brihuega."[82] Franco did in fact abandon hopes of encirclement, and within a couple of weeks Hemingway would witness fighting south of Madrid for control of the Valencia road.

News dispatches were filed from the tall Telefónica building on Madrid's Gran Via, "telephoned to London and Paris and from there cabled to various parts of the world." According to Virginia Cowles, because most reporters had to submit for morning papers, "the greatest rush came at nine o'clock in the evening" as they competed to be the first to file on one of the two available lines. "It sometimes took four or five hours to establish connections," so some correspondents slept on cots in the room until it was their turn. Government censors approved each page, and an operator would cut the line if the journalist diverged from his approved copy.[83]

Ivens's notes for these intervening weeks are difficult to read, but several entries clearly track his days: 25 March with the 11th Brigade; 28 March to Fuentes; 29 March to Morata de Tajuña and the 15th Brigade; and 1 through 4 April in Madrid.[84] Hemingway accompanied Ivens for most or all of these events. Ivens's cameraman John Ferno and Hemingway's sidekick Sidney Franklin joined them most of the time, too. On 5 April, Hemingway and Ivens "operating behind infantry" filmed tanks climbing the steep, "grey olive studded broken hills of the Morata de Tajuña sector" to the southeast, headed into action. This dispatch is the first to record Hemingway's experiencing combat: "A high cold wind blew the dust the shells raised into your eyes and caked your nose and mouth and, as you flopped at a close one and heard the fragments sing over you on the rocky dusty hillside, your mouth was full of dust."[85]

Hemingway filed this dispatch four days later, on 9 April. That day he, Ivens, Ferno, and Henry "Hank" Gorrell from the United Press left their hotel just before six o'clock in the morning to watch a government attack designed to sever the insurgent salient into University City. Machine-gun fire had woken Hemingway and Ivens. "After eight minutes of unbreakfasted downhill walking, loaded with cameras and gastric remorse from an excellent pre-battle celebration, we arrived at Brigade headquarters in the Casa de Campo," the old royal hunting grounds and the site of fierce fighting during the rebel's advance on Madrid in November. The dispatch is notable for establishing the first-person participant style that would characterize most of Hemingway's combat correspondence. The group escaped artillery fire and headed to high ground, first to a ruined building Hemingway identified, but after several bullets struck uncomfortably close, the four men moved to the third floor of a safer one Ferno found, "where, in the shade of a balcony with the camera camouflaged with old clothes we found in the house, we worked all afternoon and watched the battle" unfolding below.[86]

The crew returned to watch the battle the next day, and the day after that, Sunday, 11 April, Ivens and Ferno drove to the village of Fuentedueña to prepare for filming, returning the next day.[87] Hemingway stayed behind. In the morning the Nationalists bombarded Madrid with twenty-two rounds by Hemingway's count:

> They killed an old woman returning home from market, dropping her in a huddled black heap of clothing, with one leg suddenly detached whirling against the wall of an adjoining house. They killed three people in another square who lay like so many torn bundles of old clothing in the dust and rubble when the fragments of the "155" had burst against the curbing. A motor car coming along the street stopped suddenly and swerved after the bright flash and roar, and the driver lurched out, his scalp hanging down over his eyes, to sit down on the sidewalk with his hand against his face, the blood making a smooth sheen down over his chin.[88]

This shelling, Hemingway declared, "seeking the Sunday promenaders was not military." Afterwards he headed back to the observation place to watch the continuing battle. The infantry advanced to "within fifty yards of the houses" occupied by rebel troops,[89] but as night fell Hemingway could no longer watch, so he closed his dispatch: "The outcome of the offensive designed to free Madrid from Fascist pressure depends on the result of tonight's and tomorrow's action."[90] The outcome favored the rebels, a fact Hemingway did not then relay.

The bombardment had struck about eleven o'clock, according to Virginia Cowles's diary. Despite Hemingway's graphic description, it did not phase anyone much. Shortly after it ended, Cowles and another correspondent, Sefton Delmer, bumped into Ernest and Martha at the hotel,

> and arranged to meet at twelve to go to a festival for the benefit of the FAI [Federación Anarchista Ibérica] and hear Pastoras sing. Pastoras never sang and the show was bad; a tap dancer in tails and top hat, a very old flamenco singer and a skit between a priest and a housewife, both of whom kept their backs turned squarely on the audience so that no one could hear what they said. Everyone cheered a lot, so it was evidently a success.[91]

That afternoon Cowles accompanied Hemingway and Herbert Matthews to the ruined house, dubbed the Old Homestead, for the battle. Professor J.B.S. Haldane joined them, sitting in what remained of a red plush chair watching the battle in full view, against Hemingway's caution. Hemingway also warned him that the sun's reflection in his binoculars would attract attention. Haldane dismissed the danger. "Ten minutes later there was a loud whistle as a shell plunged into a flat next door. Two more screamed overhead and we all went down on the floor—all except Haldane, who scrambled down the stairs and disappeared." At night in the hotel lobby Hemingway bought Haldane a drink, "and more than one." Cowles's memoir confirms that the loyalist offensive "was repulsed with heavy casualties." It quotes her diary's entire entry for the day to illustrate "what was perhaps a routine day."[92]

A routine day of a remarkable historical moment. The gathering of personalities in Madrid in April 1937 made for something like a condensed, wartime version of Paris in the 1920s, with foreign journalists instead of expatriate artists and Hotel Florida instead of the Left Bank. As Cowles describes the scene:

> I don't suppose any hotel in the world has ever attracted a more diverse assembly of foreigners. They came from all parts of the globe and their backgrounds read like a series of improbable adventure stories. There were idealists and mercenaries; scoundrels and mar-

> tyrs; adventurers and *embusqués*; fanatics, traitors, and plain down-and-outs. They were like an odd assortment of beads strung together on a common thread. Any evening you could find them in the Florida; Dutch photographers, American airmen, German refugees, English ambulance drivers, Spanish picadors and Communists of every breed and nationality.[93]

The Guadalajara victory had lifted the town's spirit and contributed to Madrid's "gay" mood—it was "like a strange carnival" to Cowles.[94]

The usual dining place, other than the hotel and the foodstuffs the guests brought with them and ate in their rooms, was the Gran Via. The Puerta del Sol was a popular café. In the evenings the reporters congregated at the Telefónica to send their dispatches out. A tall building with a commanding view and a communications center for the Republic, the Telefónica was a primary artillery target. In the few weeks Cowles stayed in Madrid, the building survived over eighty hits.[95] And because the Hotel Florida sat between the Nationalist artillery in the surrounding hills and the Telefónica, rounds that fell short of their target sometimes struck the hotel.[96] It did not take long to grow accustomed to the bombings. Hemingway's and Delmer's rooms were the main meeting places at the Florida. At night, in addition to the hotel lobby and each other's rooms, two favorite watering holes were Chicote's and Molinero's, which "every afternoon . . . were crowded with soldiers with guns dangling from their hips and platinum blondes whose hair was growing out very black due to the fact that all the peroxide had been confiscated by the hospitals." Employees now collectively managed most businesses, as the owners "had either been shot, were in gaol, or had fled from the city."[97] Hemingway also spent time at the Gaylord Hotel, the Soviet and Communist International (Comintern) watering hole, where he met, befriended, and to an extent came under the influence of Mikhail Koltsov, the *Pravda* correspondent and Soviet agent featured in *For Whom the Bell Tolls*.

At the theaters one could catch such films as Charlie Chaplin's *Modern Times*, Al Jolson's *Casino de Paris*, Greta Garbo's *Anna Karenina*, and the Marx Brothers' *A Night at the Opera*. Once a shell hit when Hemingway was in the theater, "watching Marlene Dietrich get herself shot as a spy, or almost shot, or something like that. Anyway, there she was, baring her bosom bravely to the bullets' chill blast when wham! the building shook." The audience laughed "so long," nonchalant about it all, that he didn't notice what happened to Dietrich's character.[98]

People formed long queues for what little food was to be had. Guarded barricades blocked many streets:

> At the end of the avenue the streets grew desolate and blocks of houses were gutted and empty. Some had only frames standing where bombs had plunged through the middle; others looked like stage sets with whole fronts ripped off. High up on one was a table all set for dinner, napkins in place, chairs pulled up, but for a wall it had only a piece of blue sky.
>
> It was ghostly and sad with the wind blowing through the window-frames, and doors high above banging back and forth on empty caverns.[99]

Nearing University City, the muddy trenches began.

That was the "most convenient front" to visit, and it stretched from University City to Casa de Campo, "only two miles from the main shopping district of Madrid. You took a tram halfway, walked the other half, and you were there." Otherwise, "when you wanted to go to the front, you just got in a car and went."[100]

Throughout April the correspondents and their companions visited the war in various configurations. One day Virginia Cowles and Sidney Franklin drove to a village forty miles away.[101] Another day Franklin and Ivens dropped Josephine Herbst off in Morata.[102] One visited jails and hospitals. Herbst spent a night in the caves above Alcalá de Henares, between Madrid and Guadalajara, where the people of the ruined town resettled.[103] Colonel Gustavo Duran recalled a visit to his unit stationed around Torrejon de Ardoz and Loeches east of Madrid by Hemingway, Dos Passos, Matthews, the poet Rafael Alberti and his wife, and Robert Capa, bringing cigarettes and bourbon from the U.S.[104]

Hemingway's dispatch dated 14 April uses the present tense to convey a general sense of daily life in Madrid. About a third of the way into it, he describes a visit to a hospital run by the American Friends of Spanish Democracy, behind the Morata front toward Valencia, where a wounded soldier asks to see him. "The voice came from a high mound covered by a shoddy gray blanket. There were two arms crossed at the top of the mound and at one end there was something that had been a face, but now was a yellow scabby area with a wide bandage cross where the eyes had been." He was a social worker from Pennsylvania, "where once we fought at Gettysburg."[105] Hemingway hadn't believed the man's story of his wounding—after all, Hemingway had "lied a little" about his own[106]—until running into the man's commanding officer, who told him it was true: "This was a strange new kind of war where you learn just as much as you are able to believe."[107] This is the first Hemingway dispatch to acknowledge American or indeed any international participation for the Republic.[108]

From the fourteenth to the twenty-first of April, Hemingway, Ivens, Ferno, and Dos Passos filmed in Fuentedueña, a town south of Madrid and Morata which Ivens and Ferno had discovered earlier.[109] It's unlikely, but possible, that photographer Gerda Taro and presumably her companion and colleague Robert Capa, joined them for at least one day.[110]

In Madrid on 21 April, Hemingway's cable describes eleven days of "indiscriminate bombardment." This dispatch interests for subtle reasons. First, he informs his audience of government censorship by casually mentioning the press censor in a post-bombardment scene—a scene otherwise innocent enough to escape censoring. He also, for the first time, discusses the Moors occupying University City. Finally, he considers the bombardment as a tool of mass, indirect execution of "the supposedly Red population of Madrid" in opposition to rumored direct individual executions in the city by the Republic or an allied group. In Madrid "not one friend of this correspondent from the old days when I lived here, regardless of politics or religion, has been executed or is missing in this war, except for those killed fighting at the front," including people he "met and passed the time of day [with] recently."[111] In fact all sorts of Reds and radicals did populate Madrid, although many of them hardly fit a standard definition of communism. According to Cowles, "Although the propaganda was concentrated on the German and Italian invasion of Spain, rather than on the class issue, the character of Madrid was distinctly revolutionary. Apart from a handful of Government officials, Madrid was proletarian with a vengeance."[112]

Revolutionary and *communist* were hardly synonymous during the war; following the Comintern, the Spanish Communist Party no longer actively sought revolution. Cowles acknowledges that many Madrid citizens of the Republic, such as the "*petits bourgeois*" and the "deeply religious, did not sympathize with the revolutionaries,"[113] and her memoir might overstate the case. Hemingway's attempt to undercut American paranoia of a communist Republic was honest if read as countering charges that all of Madrid was Red. It was also a little beside the point.

Then there's the matter of executions and disappearances in Republican Spain. Everyone knew that these events happened. During the Nationalist campaign against Madrid back in November, over one thousand prisoners were removed from Madrid's Model Prison for transit and then slaughtered. Herbert Matthews accused Comintern agents, citing Vittorio Vidali's history of "briefly interrogating prisoners brought before him and, when he decided, as he almost always did, that they were fifth columnists, he would shoot them in the back of the head with his revolver. Ernest Hemingway told me that he heard that Vidali (aka 'Carlos') fired so often that the skin between the thumb and index finger of his right hand was badly burned."[114] It has also been speculated that Mikhail Koltsov gave the order for the Model Prison executions.[115] But Helen Graham argues that it is just as likely "that what occurred was the result of the anger and outrage" of those transporting the prisoners rather than a direct order from the government or a Comintern or Soviet agent.[116] (The latter two possessed little power this early in the war.) George Seldes wrote to Hemingway's biographer Carlos Baker with the standard judgment that the Republican side committed far fewer atrocities relative to the Nationalists, and whereas Republican crimes were committed by individuals or mobs taking matters into their own hands, Nationalist crimes were officially sanctioned, encouraged, and frequently documented: "I do not doubt that the communist leaders in the International Brigade, notably Marty, did commit crimes. . . . Now Hemingway knew these facts much better than I did."[117] Hemingway would in fact vilify André Marty in *For Whom the Bell Tolls*. When Marty assigned Gustav Regler to the XII International Brigade as its political commissar, he gave him "*full* powers," which Regler understood to mean discretionary capital punishment.[118] On meeting Hemingway at

Arganda in late March, Regler told the newcomer about two anarchist soldiers he had ordered to a sanatorium for cracking up in battle but who wound up being executed presumably on Marty's order. "'Swine!' said Hemingway, and spat on the ground."[119] Marty eventually said he executed five hundred international volunteers.[120]

At the time, Hemingway and John Dos Passos were risking their great friendship over a dispute about Dos Passos's old friend José Robles. Dos Passos—who was also participating in *The Spanish Earth* production—suspected Robles had been secretly imprisoned or murdered under the guise of valid capital punishment. Hemingway refused to agree, and his reportage was technically accurate: he had never known anyone "disappeared." The day after the dispatch, 22 April, they both learned that Robles had indeed been executed, though they did not see eye-to-eye on its legitimacy.

Marion Merriman, who had joined her husband, Robert, in Spain after learning of his wounding at Jarama in late February, describes meeting Hemingway and Dos Passos with her husband on 24 April 1937:

> I was fascinated by Dos Passos, whom I had always thought was a better writer than Hemingway. John Dos Passos was, without question, a seasoned writer of the prose of war. But as a man, he didn't impress me. I thought he was wishy-washy. I couldn't make out everything he was saying, but his message was clear—for whatever reasons, he wanted out of there, out of Hemingway's room, out of bomb-shaken Madrid.
>
> I was scared too, with good reason. But somehow Dos Passos acted more than scared. I guessed it was his uncertainty, his facial expressions, his general attitude that this was a lost cause, given the superior strength of the Franco forces. Dos Passos criticized the Spanish Republic, for which Americans were fighting and dying.[121]

Marion Merriman did not know at the time, or apparently even when writing her and her husband's story in the early 1980s, of the Robles affair. In contrast to Dos Passos's resignation, she found Hemingway's certitude almost inspiring: "Hemingway, on the other hand, let you know by his presence and through his writing exactly where he stood. Hemingway had told the world of the murder in Madrid, including the murder of children by Fascist bombing. . . . Hemingway knew what the war was all about."[122] While his attitude certainly matched her own, his position in her eyes, and her glowing validation of him, may have been influenced by her later knowledge that Hemingway might have drawn on her husband to invent Robert Jordan.

The Merrimans had come to Madrid to help make a radio broadcast to appeal to the United States. According to Marion's memoir—based on memory, her and Bob's separate diaries, and some research—Hemingway knew of her husband before this first meeting. (And he would have: Bob Merriman had commanded the American battalion at Jarama; the Associated Press reported his wounding and leadership there. It was his wounded soldiers Hemingway had visited in the hospital.) About midnight or shortly thereafter, with Hemingway and Sidney Franklin as moderators, the broadcast aired. In Washington, D.C., guests at a banquet honoring the city's volunteer combatants in Spain tuned in.[123] Merriman spoke first, for about six minutes, followed by Dr. William Pike, the battalion doctor; Dos Passos; Josephine Herbst; and finally Martin Hourihan, who only a few weeks before had assumed command of the battalion. What a scene that must have been, with Hemingway and Dos Passos at the hour of their rupture, plus Franklin, a man generally described as not particularly bright but eager, who initially hadn't even understood the politics nor knew which side to be on (never fully committing[124]), joining the soldiers to inspire the homefront.

The broadcast became something of a coda. Ivens and Dos Passos left in the morning for Valencia,[125] Ivens on his way to Paris and eventually New York to edit the film, Dos Passos on his way to Barcelona, arriving perhaps on the very day, 26 April, that Franco's air force bombed Guernica. In meeting with the Partido Obrero Unificación Marxista (Workers' Party of Marxist Unification) or POUM leader Andres Nin in Barcelona, given the POUM's and the PCE's rivalry, Dos Passos once and for all proved himself untrustworthy to Ivens. Herbert Matthews had left Madrid for a respite a week earlier.[126] As he later reminisced, "Madrid, amidst many other happy memories, has that one for me, too—of great days with a man who exemplifies for me so much that is brave and good and fine in a somewhat murky world. Ernest

Hemingway is great-hearted and childish, and perhaps a little mad, and I wish there were more like him—but there could not be."[127] Both Herbst and Cowles recount a meal at the Gran Via on 28 April with Hemingway and Pepe Quintanilla, Luis's brother, whom Hemingway knew as "the chief executioner of Madrid," who admitted that morning to "mistakes,"[128] and who would become a character in Hemingway's play *The Fifth Column*. In Milton Wolff's fictionalized recreation *Another Hill*, the next fall after Wolff read a draft of the play and expressed doubts about torture and executions by Republicans, Hemingway retorted: "We're not playing games, *mi capitán*. They play dirty, we play dirty."[129] Herbst knew Pepe as "the man who had not told Dos Passos the truth about Robles."[130]

Hemingway would file but one more dispatch before his own departure. Wired on 30 April, it refers to "a hard ten days visiting four central fronts, including all high positions, hours on horseback, and climbing to important positions 4,800-feet-high in the Guadarrama Mountains, which, when the snows melted, can be studied intelligently."[131] Hemingway clearly did not spend ten consecutive days and nights away from Madrid. He and Ivens and their crew had been filming in Fuentedueña only eight days earlier. He had been in Madrid for the broadcast, the meal with Pepe, and other events. He might have spent a couple of more days with Ferno and Franklin, 27 and 28 April, completing filming at Fuentedueña. Thus those "ten hard days" may have been the hardest that spring, but they still consisted of daytrips with perhaps some overnight stays and presumably with various companions. Cowles accompanied Hemingway on at least one foray to the Guadarrama Mountains. She was with him when their armored car received fire, and she does not mention Martha Gellhorn's presence.[132]

Most of the 30 April dispatch concerns the insurgent drive toward Bilbao in the north. Hemingway's tone is resigned to the Basque capital's fall, which would "give the Fascists an important port, a rich mining region, and release aviation, artillery, and possibly twenty thousand troops for an attack on Madrid again." Hemingway also digs at Franco and his international supporters by reminding his readers of the Basque's Catholic Nationalist population killed by bombs. "But neither the destruction nor the capture of Bilbao can win this war for Franco," only delay the government's victory.[133] The dispatch also sends a message of explanation and apology to the Basques and to Republican supporters outside Spain. Given its isolation from the rest of the Republic, neither Madrid nor Catalonia could come to its rescue. At present, the government might attack Franco's forces outside Madrid to redirect rebel troops and resources away from Bilbao. The shelling of Madrid, Hemingway concludes, is a ruse to draw Republicans out to attack and thus suffer heavy casualties from the rebels' well-entrenched machine guns. Another "possible tactic, if worst comes to worst, is to allow Bilbao to fall and await a Fascist attack on the Castilian plateau where the war will eventually be decided."[134]

On 1 May, Hemingway, Cowles, Gorrell, and Herbst visited the Garibaldi Battalion (Italian) of the XII International Brigade. After another day of shelling, Hemingway, Herbst, Franklin, and probably others went to Werner Heilbrun's hospital and ended up having a party. Gustav Regler was there, as were Heilbrun's wife, Almuth—"blue eyes very happy laughing"—and Dr. Pike. A large hammer-and-sickle banner adorned the salon where they danced and sang to piano music; a small child did her best imitation of a Shirley Temple tap routine. Hemingway fell asleep on an operating table. According to Herbst's diary, "Regler [is] very low. Thinks he will be killed in next few months. Thinks he will or all be lost in next few months. Bilbao at this moment looks bleak—may fall any moment."[135]

On 2 May, a Republican civil war within the civil war erupted on the streets of Barcelona pitting the anarchists and other revolutionaries—in particular the radical Marxist POUM—against the Catalonian government and its sympathizers. After a week of fighting, one "contemporary press estimate of the casualties was 500 killed and 1,000 wounded."[136] This was followed by several weeks of excessively violent repression and the ceding of control of the region's military and police to the central Republican government. Hemingway and Gellhorn left Madrid on 3 May for Paris.[137] On 9 May (or 10 May) in Paris he wrote a dispatch that was never published, and probably never filed—nothing beyond the typescript exists. The piece begins with a paragraph about the U.S.'s civil war and, like Bowers's letter to Washington a month earlier, making an analogy with the First Battle of Bull Run. At the beginning of that war, Federal troops ran from the battle just as some Republican militiamen fled during the early battles of Spain's civil war. Four years later, the Federal side won; implicitly, in several years, the Republican side will win. He reports that when he arrived in Spain two months before, he anticipated witnessing Madrid's capture by the Nationalists, given the international community's apparent abandonment of the Republican government. He then praises the Republican successes repelling Italian forces at Guadalajara and Bilbao. He describes Madrid as "impregnable"; outlines some of Franco's next possible moves; finds the Republican air force of capable size; and attempts to tally the number of foreign troops fighting for the Republic—two hundred Americans, a far smaller number than he's read in other papers—once again drawing an American analogy by estimating the percentage (including French naval support) as possibly equivalent to the percentage of foreigners who fought for the colonies during the American war for independence; and finishes by discussing possible future Republican offensive operations: "That is what this correspondent looks forward to seeing this summer."[138]

A few days later he left Gellhorn in Paris on his way back home, to Pauline. He debarked the *Normandie* in New York on 18 May. On 30 May, the Republicans launched a surprise offensive in the Guadarrama Mountains to relieve pressure on Bilbao. The operation, the military setting of *For Whom the Bell Tolls*, failed within the week. Anthony Beevor concludes that "the nationalist assault on Bilbao was delayed by no more than two weeks at the most."[139] General Lukács was killed and Gustav Regler very nearly killed on 11 June when an artillery round hit their car; the next day Werner Heilburn drove from unit to unit to suppress the news, and when he had finished an "enemy plane spotted him and emptied its guns into his zigzagging car, and a bullet cut one of his arteries and he died."[140] Hemingway might have cried on learning of Lukács's death. "I don't remember. I know I cried once when somebody died. It must have been Lucasz because Lucasz was the first great loss. Everyone else who had been killed was replaceable. Werner was the most irreplaceable of all; but he was killed just afterward."[141]

Bilbao fell to Franco 18 June. On 25 July, at Brunete, the twenty-five-year-old Gerda Taro, already a minor legend, was crushed by a Republican tank.

The strange carnival had come to an end.

Brunete became the contested town during the Republic's greatest offensive thus far, a deep penetration west of Madrid at the base of the Nationalist salient that extended into University City both to provide elbow room for Madrid and to draw pressure off of the Nationalists' Basque campaign. The July operation mimicked Nationalist attacks toward Madrid earlier in the year: after an initial gain, the attacking forces were beaten back and suffered heavily, and the original lines were more-or-less reestablished. The government claimed a major victory for the Battle of Brunete. It was anything but. Fascist air superiority won the day, and the Republican forces experienced terrible morale problems. Four hundred soldiers from one division who fled the battle were shot. Another unit set up machine guns behind its own lines to prevent retreat. The extreme heat and lack of water—not to mention ammunition—did not help. Paranoia turned the blame against fifth columnists. Discontent, anger, and even insubordination infiltrated the International Brigades. One officer committed suicide.[142]

During the battle, a conglomeration of writers from around the world had descended on Spain for the Second International Congress of Writers, which really amounted to a great photo opportunity.[143] Hemingway spent the summer of 1937 finishing and promoting *The Spanish Earth*, and resting with his family in Key West, knowing he was going back to Spain in August.

On 14 August, the rebels resumed the Basque campaign, and Hemingway set sail on the *Champlain* (carrying money and messages for family members of the Stork Club's captain of waiters, Andre Boucher).[144] By the end of the month the Basque region had fallen, and the Republican army had regrouped from the loss at Brunete to strike along the long, relatively quiet and unfortified Aragon front west of Catalonia. In the first week of September the Nationalists began their advance on the last Republican territory along the northern coast (Asturias). The same day that Ernest and Martha left Paris for Spain, 6 September, the

Republicans won Belchite, but it was a pyrrhic victory—heavy losses, a destroyed town, and the Aragon offensive ground to a halt.

Hemingway, traveling with Matthews and Gellhorn, wrote one dispatch from the Aragon front after the major fighting had ended, but an interruption in the telephone line while he was dictating forced him to send the second half the next day, causing NANA to run them as separate articles.[145] The first article celebrates the Americans who participated in the siege against Belchite. Bob Merriman led the final assault against the cathedral in the central square: "Unshaven, his face smoke blackened, his men tell how he bombed his way forward, wounded six times slightly by hand-grenade splinters in the hands and face, but refusing to have his wounds dressed until the cathedral was taken." Hemingway visited the town on 10 September, and "two hours after it had been bombed by Fascist aviation" the town "had such a smell of death from bodies in the smashed houses that Government burial squads digging to reach them would be unable to remain there without gas masks."[146] Republican corpses, Nationalist corpses, and animal corpses.

The second article—the second half of the interrupted dispatch—heralds a loyalist victory in the Aragon campaign: "The offensive was only completely successful in the Belchite and Quinto salients, but this was much the most difficult and important operation."[147] In fact the modest territorial gains accomplished nothing, according to Anthony Beevor: the effort "a total failure in its main objectives of taking Saragossa and diverting the nationalists from their campaign in the north."[148] The dispatch also comments on Republican problems by blaming the war-long "stalemate on the Aragon front" on "inactivity of Anarchist and P.O.U.M. troops"—the groups blamed for Barcelona's May civil war within the civil war. The campaign had, in fact, the internal political objective of asserting governmental military control over the region by moving its Popular Army to conduct the campaign. Hemingway's criticism neglects to mention that the rough terrain made infantry operations all but impossible, and that the government had never directed offensive operations out of Catalonia and only minimally supported defensive troops with materiel. ("There is very little doubt," wrote George Orwell of the situation back in the early spring, "that arms were deliberately withheld lest too many of them should get into the hands of Anarchists."[149]) The internal political objective was partially achieved: the Catalonian units were placed under direct Popular Army operational command, but harsh government tactics against local organizations and leadership, and the communist-directed military campaign's failure, did little to unify the Republic.[150]

Hemingway's dispatch glossed over Franco's certain victory in Asturias, for good reason. The rebel's eventual conquest of the region gave them Asturias's coal and Bilbao's factories: "From now on, the nationalists could make their own ammunition" which "freed 65,000 men of the Army of the North, and its armaments, to fight in the south."[151] And a later dispatch would downgrade the government force's Aragon campaign to a "nibbling offensive," a part of a larger strategy of "a series of small offenses with limited objectives," but constantly "improving their positions" and "teaching an army to maneuver in preparation for operations on a grand plan."[152] It had been a training mission all along.

Accompanied by Herbert Matthews, Hemingway next spent three days inspecting the Nationalist defenses at Teruel, at the southern end of the Aragon front due east of Madrid, to study the possibility of a Nationalist attack from Teruel to the Mediterranean to split in half what was left of the Republic. They were, Hemingway reported, "the first U.S. correspondents permitted to make a thorough and complete survey." He concluded that the "mountain ranges and broken hills" would make for an extremely difficult operation in normal weather and all but impossible with winter's approach.[153]

The rest of the fall Hemingway spent in the relatively quiet Madrid. It was not quite the "strange carnival" of the last spring, though more International Brigaders joined the more somber Madrid expatriate revelry.[154] Hemingway filed two dispatches, one about city life in Madrid, with stores open and bars crowded and only occasional shelling, and another after visiting the Brunete battlefield.[155] He traveled to Alfambra on 20 September, and enjoyed a rare safe-conduct pass for all sectors for a month beginning 27 October, during which time he very well may have accompanied a guerilla demolition operation.[156] He mostly worked on his play, later titled *The Fifth Column*. The diary of a North American Committee to Aid Spanish Democracy delegate—Paul Patrick Rogers, a professor of Spanish from Oberlin—describes the fairly quiet Madrid front that fall, with barricades of various material, walls, and wire throughout the city making it seem impenetrable. Rogers was able to visit the trenches of University City:

> Sporadic and desultory firing by snipers, with only occasional rattle of machinegun fire. We were cautious always to keep head below top of parapet. Many underground trenches, for safety against mortar or heavy fire. Most peep-holes, or firing holes, partially stopped up, leaving only small cracks for observation. This avoids the perception of movement by enemy, who have their guns trained and are always watching for some motion. Many such holes bore bullet marks. Through some unstopped ones we were allowed to observe, sans movement and always from the side, the trenches of the enemy a few hundred feet away. . . . The ground, trees, buildings between are exactly the shell torn pictures of "no man's land" on which we were fed during the Great War.[157]

Rogers described the trenches as being a little less than five feet deep, with another foot or two of sandbags or dirt on top as parapet. At one point the two sides' trenches were a mere eighteen meters apart.

Eventually Franco would attack out of southern Aragon and achieve the Mediterranean coast, but not until the next spring. At the moment, the threat helped prod the Republican government to uproot to Barcelona by the end of October; at the moment, Franco was turning his army from Aragon toward Madrid to strike at the capital once again through Guadalajara. Instead the Republic struck first. At Teruel. In winter.

The Republican attack on Teruel initiated a two-and-a-half-month struggle that would be "the most horrific of all the battles of the civil war."[158] It began on 15 December in "zero degree weather, with wind that made living a torture and intermittent blizzards," as Hemingway later reported.[159] Hemingway, Herbert Matthews, and Sefton Delmer drove from Madrid to Valencia on 17 December and linked up with the operational headquarters the morning of 18 December.[160] The "next day the weather became so bad," wrote Matthews, "that men died of the cold, waiting for orders to charge, while casualties from frost-bite ran into the thousands."[161] Hemingway's first Teruel dispatch is characteristically optimistic. After all, Napoleon had taken Teruel in December:

> Making due allowance for Government optimism, any military observer must admit they have shown again in this very large offensive their attacking power demonstrated in the early stages of the Belchite offensive and Aragon. They have flown when Rebel planes could not fly and by their clearing of snow-blocked roads had shown an admirable material and military organization. Most of all they had attacked when outsiders expected them to wait passively for the long hailed Franco final offensive.[162]

The three had "rushed back to Valencia to get their stories off by courier to Madrid" and drove all night to rejoin the battle at dawn on 21 December. (Hemingway's dispatch beat Matthews's by ten hours, for which Matthews received much grief from his *Times* editors.) "It was to be the greatest day of the war for the Republican arms," Matthews would later reflect, "and—quite incidententally—one of the greatest days of my life."[163] Accompanying the infantry through the tough fighting, Hemingway, Matthews, Delmer, and the Belgian reporter Mathieu Corman reached the streets of Teruel that evening. After a brief celebration with a group of civilians, they found an abandoned car and drove back to Valencia, arriving at midnight. Matthews and Hemingway wrote their quite similar stories before sending them by courier to Madrid for cabling and, finally, sleeping.[164] Later that morning they returned to Teruel, and according to Matthews for "three days running" watched the loyalists taking the town.[165]

The three correspondents drove to Barcelona on Christmas Eve, where Matthews filed another dispatch on the street fighting. Hemingway had written one too, the "most godwonderful housetohouse fighting story," which NANA chose not to use.[166] That piece of writing has been lost, but probably resembles Matthews's in many details. Nationalist soldiers, with Italian soldiers and German officers, took refuge in the seminary with priests and perhaps two hundred novices; one hundred and twenty rebel soldiers were holding their own in the Civil Guard barracks. Rebel forces outside the city were not yet able to mount a counteroffensive. "EVEN IN TWENTIETH CENTURY ONE

MUST EXPECT SEE ALL HORROR TRAGEDY PATHOS WHICHS EVER ACCOMPANIED MOPPING UP OF CAPTURED CITY," radiogrammed Matthews. The street fighting in Teruel was awful. Street by street, house by house, room by room. The rebels moved among critical buildings in underground passages. Soldiers blasted holes in side walls between buildings to avoid exposing themselves in the street.

> CIVILIANS AND SOLDIERS WHOVE SURRENDERED BEEN TREATED UTOMOST CONSIDERATION STOP EYEVE SEEN SOLDIERS SHARE THEIR SCANTY FOOD THEREWITH COMMA CARRYING BUNDLES AND EVEN BABIES AND NONE US TANY TIME SAW OR EVEN HEARD OF EXECUTIONS OCCURRING DASH AND WE TOOK PAINS CHECK CAREFULLY.

The two of them watched a tank pull up an artillery piece to help bring down the seminary. "HERE IN TERUEL ON CHRISTMASEVE ONE FEELS THAT SENSE OF POWER MOREN ANYWHERE STOP SOMETHING GREAT HAS HAPPENED BUT GREATER THINGS ARE IN AIR."[167]

By Christmas Eve the government had declared victory in Teruel. The group of reporters drove to Barcelona that day, where on Christmas a show of one hundred and forty drawings by Luis Quintanilla opened at the Hotel Ritz. Hemingway performed as one of the show's hosts;[168] it was his last duty before beginning his journey out of Spain. Within a day or two after Christmas, Matthews, Delmer, Robert Capa, Jay Allen, and Luis Quintanilla all made their way back to Teruel. Matthews would visit Teruel about ten times total.[169] The weather continued to be hellish. Vehicles froze in place, and some broke. People froze in place, and some died. The first rebel counterattack came on 29 December, while the street fighting was still raging. The remaining Nationalist forces in Teruel surrendered on 7 January, but the counterattacks persisted until Teruel was back in Franco's control on 22 February. Once again, immense losses gained the Republic no ground.

Arriving in Miami on 27 January 1938, on his way home to Key West, with the Teruel fighting still unresolved, Hemingway predicted a government victory "if the Italians don't send any more troops."[170] Still convalescing from his wounds, Gustav Regler and his companion Marie Louise arrived in New York on 2 February on their way to spend time with the Hemingways, getting to Miami by train on Monday, 7 February.[171] Regler had been sent by the Republic's prime minister, Juan Negrin, "to raise funds for the needy hospital-service of the Spanish Republican Army."[172] On 17 March, Regler spoke as the guest of honor at a reception in Washington held by the Women's Committee of the Friends of Spanish Democracy. Hemingway had supplied a written introduction read by Marquis Child, a journalist: "Gustav Regler has no right to be here; he should be in a cemetery in the outskirts of Valencia, beside Gen. Lucasz and Werner Heilburn [sic], two heroes of the International Brigades, killed in the same offensive against Husca [sic]." Regler talked about the good work performed by political commissars, such as moving women and children to safety, saving Goya paintings, halting atrocities "on both sides," and teaching soldiers how to read and write. Josephine Herbst was there, along with Spanish Ambassador and Señora Fernando de los Rios and several "socialites and senators."[173] (Regler would also speak in New York, Buffalo, and Detroit, with Hemingway's introduction read at each stop.) The next day Hemingway sailed out of New York aboard the *Ile de France* on his way to Spain by way of France, presumably missing the exhibition of Quintanilla war drawings at the Museum of Modern Art for which he had written the brochure copy on 10 March in Key West—and which he had first seen in Barcelona on Christmas.[174] He thwarted his own plan "to sail secretly" with his name "kept from the list of passengers" by showing up "hatless and with no overcoat."[175] On the boat he found it impossible to draft a preface for Quintanilla's book of drawings from the show, originally announced as "Guns and Castanets" but published in 1939 as *All the Brave*.[176]

Meanwhile, after recapturing Teruel, the Nationalists had begun their methodical eastward push. If they could reach the sea, they would cut off Madrid from Catalonia's industry as well as supplies from abroad routed through Catalonia. They had regrouped far more quickly after Teruel than had the Republican military, and the Aragon front was long and spottily defended. The Nationalists took Belchite on 10 March and crossed the Ebro River on 23 March. On 28 March, the Minister of Government for Republican Spain reported to the U.S. Counselor of Embassy in Spain that "the military situation is in fact hopeless," a "matter of weeks," but the government "will continue the war as long as possible."[177]

In Paris, Hemingway received instructions to cover Franco's side of the war. He traveled to the border where, as he reported back to NANA, Nationalist Spain proved inaccessible.[178] (A year earlier Virginia Cowles had managed to secure permission to report from Nationalist territory.) The success of the Nationalist advance distressed Hemingway. In St. Jean de Luz, on the border with Spain, he visited the U.S. ambassador to Spain to begin making arrangements to evacuate by ship wounded Americans ("several hundred"[179]) as well as medical personnel in the event of the government's imminent fall: "Hemingway suggests that money necessary may be had from the Medical Bureau for Aid of Spanish Democracy, from Friends of the Lincoln Brigade, et cetera. Believe all this important in event collapse, since danger otherwise of massacre of wounded and of incidents involving personnel of hospitals, doctors and nurses, here properly with our consent."[180] Hemingway would have felt a humanitarian need to intervene as well as no small measure of responsibility, given his role with the Medical Bureau. Other correspondents, in particular John Whitaker and Edgar Mowrer of the *Chicago Daily News*, and Hemingway's old friend and soldier-of-fortune Charles Sweeny, joined him in these efforts. By 2 April they reported to the ambassador on having secured enough money for a French hospital to care for the wounded who "cannot at once be repatriated" to the U.S. because of their wounds, and they began seeking repatriation funds for all of them. The U.S. would not pay for either hospital care or repatriation because of the possible perception of a violation of its nonintervention policy. Bowers swore Hemingway to secrecy about their plans: "These correspondents and Hemingway will take on themselves the task of assembling these people at the port."[181] I've found no evidence that these plans were realized; the government in fact held on a few months longer.[182]

Hemingway flew into Barcelona on 2 April,[183] a day before Lérida fell. He later complained that NANA's request that he investigate working from Franco's side cost him coverage of the Lérida story.[184] The fascist Serrano Súñer announced that "the war approaches its close."[185] Meanwhile, Hemingway and Matthews left for the front. They ran into refugees outside coastal Reus. "Bedding, sewing machines, blankets, cooking utensils, mattresses wrapped in mats, and sacks of grain for the horses and mules were piled in the carts and goats and sheep were tethered to the tailboards. There was no panic. They were just plodding along." Soon enough they saw soldiers among them, initially "only a few troops, then finally there was a steady stream with whole units intact." The "migration" swelled over the road, filling "all the old paths for driving cattle" alongside it. They turned back to Barcelona.[186]

The next day they headed out again hoping to stumble across and link up with the American Lincoln-Washington Battalion of the International Brigades. Eventually they found eight survivors, three of whom had swum across the Ebro without clothes. There had been four hundred and fifty when the unit was last together on a hilltop near Gandesa, but the reporters "learned that probably 150 more" besides those eight had made it.[187]

Peter N. Carroll's *The Odyssey of the Abraham Lincoln Brigade* tells one version of their story. The battalion had been retreating and regrouping again and again for a month. They made their last stand, at one-fifth the strength of early March, on high ground around Gandesa: "But heavy fire forced them to retreat to higher ground. Surrounded and vastly outnumbered, they waited for nightfall to attempt an escape. After an anxious day's stay, the Americans quietly moved off the hill into a single file. . . . Around midnight, the leaders of the column marched directly into an enemy camp." Some ran; others, including their acting commander, Bob Merriman, attacked. He was never seen again.[188] The disbanded survivors worked their way east to cross the Ebro into Republican territory. A few made it across the bridge at Mora la Nueva only to look back and see the bridge swept away into the river after being bombed—Hemingway saw the shelling from Reus.[189] Of the rest, "Some managed to reach the river's edge only to attract enemy fire when they entered the cold, rushing waters; many drowned in the effort to cross."[190] A few made it; most did not.

> Those who were captured could expect no mercy. As in any war, there is no count of the men who may have been shot while attempting to surrender or of those wounded who received a coup de grace

> to hasten their deaths. But an exhaustive study made by a former American prisoner of war, Carl Geiser, found that of the 287 known American captives, the fascists killed 173. That statistic accounted for one-fifth of the total American dead in Spain.[191]

One of the eight men Hemingway found was with Merriman when they walked into the enemy. This officer "ran through the orchard to pass north of the town. But no one followed. I could hear them running towards the town." Toward the enemy. "Then I could hear commands of 'Hands up! Hands up!'"

Hemingway drove on to his original destination, Tortosa, only to find it "almost demolished," its civilians evacuated and the Republican soldiers fifteen miles away fighting to protect it.[192] Hemingway and his driver turned back, once again, to Barcelona. Passing through Tortosa the next day, the correspondents drove "carefully between the boxes of dynamite set to mine the small stone bridges on the narrow road" on their way up the Ebro toward the front, to Cherta and a little farther[193] until a motorcycle dispatch carrier warned them that the road ahead was under fire, and they turned back to Tortosa,[194] where he filed his next dispatch: "today, you see extent and seriousness of the Government resistance. It is not over yet by a long shot, and one thing that has been learned in this Spanish war is that anything can happen and the experts are always wrong."[195]

His next four dispatches from Tortosa continue in this remarkable vein as running optimistic commentary on a battle that will be lost—something of a synecdoche for Hemingway's entire wartime correspondence. In these dispatches, as Watson writes, "when nothing seems to be happening, that is just the point" because the rebels did not overwhelm the Republican Army "as many outside observers as well as many within the Government itself expected at any moment."[196] Hemingway's optimism follows suit. On 10 April, he reports that of the Nationalists' three axes of advance, the one through Tortosa has been halted. The one to the south, toward Vinaroz, "has been progressing spottily for several days, but the Government forces have still not fallen back on the best positions." The one through the north, paralleling the French border, "is the danger."[197] He argues that the government must get serious in the north, and once again deprecates Catalonia's anarchist and revolutionary militias: "In the far north, under the shadow of the Pyrenees, Franco's troops have advanced steadily north and eastward in a country where positions could be held by the determined graduates of any good girls' finishing school." That he does not name the militias he associates with girls' school graduates could indicate his understanding of the Republic's dependence on these soldiers as never before.[198]

Three days later, Hemingway slightly modifies his conclusion: Tortosa in the middle is holding and won't fall; the southern route is of more concern, with "Government troops . . . putting up the same fight they made to defend Tortosa but with slightly harder positions to defend"; and the northern route remains "a grave problem which can only be solved by a resolute defense of the magnificent positions the Government holds there and which has plenty of troops to defend." But the Italians above Tortosa still sit within sight of the sea, and to the south the rebels "were just thirty seven kilometers from the coast" as of the day before.[199] The optimism of the previous dispatch has lessened in this one's description of Franco's blitzkrieg-like tactics of punching through soft spots with mechanized forces and leaving the infantry to clean up, and in the rumor of Navarrese and Moors replacing the Italians on the southern axis.

The next day, 14 April, the southern advance succeeded. Nationalist soldiers celebrated in the Mediterranean Sea. The Republic was cut in half. Hemingway's dispatch of 15 April to NANA was misleadingly titled "Bombing of Tortosa." The first three paragraphs describe the bombing of the city and defensive positions outside it, but the rest of the article reports mournfully of the successful rebel advance and the beginning rush of refugees toward Barcelona. The enemy planes "swung round and round in a slow circle like vultures waiting for an animal to die," it opens. An infantry company makes "a last stand on the hillside"; another "lay behind rocks in hastily dug foxholes and in simple folds of the ground trying to hold up the advance of the army." The dispatch finishes with an understatement: "It is a bad night for the west bank of the Ebro."[200] Gellhorn, Matthews, and Delmer watched with him that day as sortie after sortie of German and Italian planes filled the sky, as that company protected its retreating comrades.[201] The final Tortosa dispatch, of 18 April, is aptly titled "Tortosa Calmly Awaits Assault by Insurgents":

> Sometimes in war there is a deadliness which makes all walking upright within a certain range either foolishness or bravado. But there are other times before things really start when it is like the old days when you walked around in the bull ring just before the fight. . . .
>
> Now, as you watched, you saw another man come slipping through the green trees on the other bank and then three more. Then suddenly as they were out of sight came the sharp sudden stabbing close clatter of machine guns. With that sound all the walking around, all the dress rehearsal quality of before the battle was done. The boys who had dug shelters for their heads behind the railway banks were right and from now on theirs was the business. From where you stood you could see them well protected, waiting stolidly. Tomorrow it would be their turn. You watched the slant of bayonets angling above the rails.[202]

It was not the next day but that very day, 18 April, that Tortosa fell.

That same day, "one of the very worst," Hemingway received a cable threatening to cancel the contract for Quintanilla's *All the Brave* if he did not submit a preface. He wrote one that night by candlelight, a disjointed and depressing piece, and one of his most powerful from the war:

> Compared to the necessity of holding the line of the Ebro everything, including drawings of war by a great artist and one of your best friends, seems like chicken crut, and that is what makes this an unpleasant and churlish piece of writing. . . .
>
> So now let's see. How many words are there to be? Put in a few more words for the publisher. The reader does not need them because the reader can look at the pictures. They are nice pictures, too. Are they not, reader? That is something of what war looks like; a very small part of it. And you must not be shocked at the dead Moors or think they are disgusting because there is one thing that you learn in war and that is that a dead enemy always smells good.[203]

Six days later Hemingway attended a morning showing of *The Spanish Earth* in Barcelona. Different music and sound effects weakened this Spanish-dubbed version. Bombs falling at the edge of the city and antiaircraft fire interrupted the film for forty minutes. Hemingway received five minutes of applause.[204] The moment must have felt like a rather paltry swan song.

The Republic, however, had some fight left. The Nationalists had claimed Lérida on 3 April, but by the end of the month government forces still held the eastern roughly one-third of the city. Hemingway visited the government defenses on 29 April. They reminded him of the positions around Madrid from the year before: "Trenches angled through kitchen gardens full of peas, beans, cauliflower and cabbage," with the enemy "less than a hundred yards away." Given his assured predictions of a Republican victory for the last eighteen months, and given the present state of the war, his new uncertainty still registers as optimism:

> After a week along the Ebro and Segre rivers and a month on the front your correspondent has been unable to see a conclusion to the Spanish war. Ordinarily, after the Aragon defeats and Franco's cutting Valencia [off] from Barcelona, one would expect a military collapse. There has been none. If it were war game manoeuvers and divisions were surrounded, they would be announced as destroyed by the umpires. In the last ten days I have visited four divisions, all of which would have been destroyed under this classification.

A twenty-three-year-old battalion commander explained that they had learned how to break out of an encirclement: Throw bombs, and "rush them bombing as you go. If you know you will be shot when captured it makes for new tactics." Hemingway's dispatch concludes by noting that the front has not moved in four weeks.[205]

Hemingway's last two dispatches of the war sent to NANA convey confidence in the Republic's new defensive posture. After flying down from Barcelona, he describes in the first one a brief driving tour from Alicante north through Valencia to coastal Castellón close to the front line with Franco's wedge between Valencia and Barcelona. "There is no richer stretch of country in the world, and the Government holds

Spain's granary in La Mancha and Spain's kitchen garden and fruit orchards and a big part of the olive orchards with the provinces of Murcia, Alicante, and Castellon." The Republican front lines he found quite strong, with "excellent third and fourth line entrenchments and great natural defensive positions in his rear." As one officer expressed, "the panic is over."[206] Two days later, on 10 May, he surveys Madrid, "unchanged and more solid than ever," with a unit nicknamed "the moles" hard at work extending the trenchline to attempt to outflank Franco's forward position on the hill of Garabitas. The unexpected finding in this dispatch is "the one unaccountable factor that foreigners never figure out when analyzing the Spanish campaign"—regionalism.[207] "It can have a bad effect when desiring to link up operations on a very big scale. But once one sector is isolated from another, instead of being panicked they seem relieved at not being bothered by the necessity of contact with another region."[208]

In other words, the regionalism that helped save the Republic in the opening days of the insurgency—and one factor of disunity that doomed it from the beginning as well—Hemingway believes will save it now. He sees "a year of war" to be fought, whereas "European diplomats are trying to say it will be over in a month."[209] What he also does not say is that salvation will most likely come from these regions simply holding on until the general European war breaks out, when Hitler and Mussolini can no longer afford to supply Franco and when the Republic will become by an ally of France and Great Britain by default. His first essay for *Ken* magazine appeared 7 April, before Franco had reached the sea, before Tortosa had fallen, and perhaps even written before he saw the refugees at Reus and encountered the eight survivors of the destroyed Lincoln battalion. That essay argued for arms and support to the Republic to beat the Italians in Spain, to prevent or at least delay the world war.[210] His next essay, published after Tortosa's fall,, is more angry and adamant: "The resistance of the republican government in Spain against the first combined fascist invasion is the great holding attack to save what we call civilization."[211] That spring Hemingway thought the world war all but inevitable, but to say as much would undermine his case. Many of his *Ken* essays should be read in the context of the imminent Nazi threat to the rest of Europe. In one of his last essays for *Ken* he quits his public hedging: "There is going to be war in Europe."[212]

If the Spanish Republic could last that long. Hemingway was not alone in holding this last hope for the Republic's survival, though others would not accept it until after the Republic's next and last offensive, the Battle of the Ebro.

Hemingway left France on 25 May on the *Normandie*,[213] landing at New York on 30 May along with four stowaways from the International Brigade whom a *New York Times* subtitle meanly characterized as "Loyalist Army Deserters."[214] Whether Hemingway knew they were aboard or even helped stow them away isn't known. (Back in Spain, some deserters from the International Brigades were executed.[215]) His casual remarks to the *Times* reporter, summarized as giving the government "a good chance of winning" and believing "the war would drag on for an indefinite time," followed the terms of his last dispatches from Spain and his *Ken* articles. This time he did not know if he would go back. On 2 July, eighteen wounded American volunteers to Spain landed in New York, "the first considerable number of wounded Americans who served with the International Brigade and the Abraham Lincoln Battalion to be returned through the efforts of an American committee in Paris headed by Ernest Hemingway and Louis Bromfield. Heretofore most of the wounded have returned as stowaways."[216]

At the end of July, the Spanish Republic launched its last great offensive of the war, aiming to reunite its two split halves. Late at night on 24 July the Popular Army out of Catalonia crossed the Ebro using boats, makeshift footbridges, and pontoons. The surprise attack gained them several miles of Nationalist territory in a few days before stalling. Three-and-a-half months later, those gains would be reversed, the Battle of the Ebro lost, and the Republican army effectively finished.

Hemingway had made one last trip, arriving in September and visiting the Ebro front but without journalistic duties. One of the few things we know about this trip is the story of a nearly fatal boat crossing of the Ebro. Hemingway, Capa, Vincent Sheean, and Henry Buckley, in heavy winter coats, had successfully crossed over to inspect the front. It was 5 November, just above Mora; the Republican army was in the process of retreating, ten days from the battle's end. Matthews related the story in an interview the next spring:

> Coming back, though, we ran into trouble. The current, aided by a strong wind, carried us more and more toward the bridgehead. The soldiers, each using an oar, couldn't cope with the situation. Hemingway, a powerful man, saw the danger we were in. He grabbed a spare oar, manipulating it on the left side and through sheer brute strength pulled us out of the predicament. If he hadn't we surely would have been dashed against the bridgehead, thrown in the water and drowned.[217]

The destroyed bridge whose detritus threatened their lives was the very one Hemingway had watched being bombed in April.

On 15 November, a parade in Barcelona bade farewell to the international volunteers, who no longer served a significant military role but whose withdrawal did serve the Republic diplomatically. Hemingway and Gellhorn watched. "That evening," Gellhorn's biographer writes, "in their hotel room, she heard Hemingway, leaning against the wall, crying. It was the only time she ever saw him cry. 'They can't do it!' he was saying. 'They can't do it!'"[218]

Hemingway arrived in New York on 24 November, and by early December was back in Key West. Barcelona fell on 26 January 1939. On 15 February, in Havana, he began writing *For Whom the Bell Tolls*.[219] Madrid fell on 28 March. The war was over.

TWO

Style, Politics, and the NANA Dispatches

Hemingway wrote thirty-one dispatches for NANA.[1] The secondary sources habitually judge them inferior journalism. Carlos Baker's biography, for example, complains that the dialogue was "so heavily stamped with personal mannerisms as to be of doubtful authenticity." Baker sees a "curious monotony in his stories of battles and bombardments," a gratuitous use of graphic imagery "to shock his readers," and "a note of triumphant boastfulness" in reporting proximity to danger. He also faults Hemingway for "often hint[ing] he was alone when in fact he was usually with Martha Gellhorn, Matthews, and Delmer." Hemingway lacked Dos Passos's "eye for telling details" and the "meticulous exactitude and inclusiveness that characterized the best work of Herbert Matthews and Sefton Delmer."[2]

Phillip Knightley's *The First Casualty*, the standard history of war correspondence, paraphrases Baker but with a trouncing final judgment: Hemingway's "performance as a war correspondent was abysmally bad." But Knightley goes beyond "technical" dissatisfaction to moral condemnation. Not just "unjustifiably optimistic"—an excusable offense—Hemingway's reporting was "unforgivable" in its "total failure to report the Communist persecution, imprisonment, and summary execution of 'untrustworthy elements' on the Republican side, when he knew this was happening and when disclosing it might well have prevented further horrors like this."[3]

Such criticisms in the final analysis might bear out. As Scott Donaldson writes, Hemingway advanced the Republican cause in his dispatches by eliciting "the deepest possible feelings of horror and of sympathy for the victims" of the Madrid bombardment; his "undue optimism" often "ignored loyalist defeats and exaggerated the importance of its victories"; and "he repeatedly called attention to the participation of Italians and Germans on Franco's side."[4] It may also have served as a recruitment tool for American volunteers. Nevertheless, I think it a worthwhile exercise to attend a little more studiously to Hemingway's dispatches and their context. I don't necessarily intend to reverse the general opinion of the correspondence, only to achieve a better and more sympathetic understanding. Herbert Matthews's reporting for the *New York Times* will serve as a convenient comparison for two reasons. First, because both Baker and Knightley use Matthews's journalism as the standard of excellence to pass judgment on Hemingway's; and second, because the two worked practically side-by-side, seeing and reporting on many of the same events.

In fact so closely did they work together that NANA sometimes complained that the *Times* was not buying Hemingway's pieces because they resembled Matthews's,[5] and at one point Matthews's own editors at the *Times* suspected him of plagiarizing Hemingway. A note from one of Matthews's editors, Raymond McCaw, provides, in two columns, seven quite similar passages from Hemingway's Aragon front dispatches of 13 and 14 September with Matthews's of 14 September, with a penciled note at the bottom: "a deadly parallel if you ask me."[6] Edwin James, the managing editor and McCaw's boss, eventually agreed with Matthews's defense: "It is quite apparent that you did not file any duplicate of the Hemingway story, or vice versa. As I understand it, the similarity arose from the fact that you both went to see the same show and saw it at the sametime [sic], under the same conditions."[7]

Matthews's dispatches ring of Republican bias as much if not more than anything Hemingway ever filed. The *Times* received many letters to the editor complaining about Matthews's undisguised politics, which also gave serious concern to some of his editors. His description of the May 1937 Republican infighting in Barcelona is a striking example of how his news veered into propaganda and shows just how much he passed along the government's version of events. The government's "BLOODLESS TRIUMPH FOUGHT WITH RECOGNIZED WEAPONS OF DEMOCRACY" turned out to be blatantly false, as the government and the "COMMUNISTS [WHO] DISTINGUISHED THEMSELVES" resorted to violent suppression. His blaming the uprising on the anarchist Confederación National del Trabajo, or National Confederation of Labor (CNT) working as Franco operatives parrots the government's and the communist party's public position, even though both charges—that the anarchists precipitated the events and that they were under Nationalist direction—were also false. His dispatch's optimistic close also equivocates the political reality: "NEW GOVERNMENT HAS TAKEN POWER WHICH APPEARS TOVE CONFIDENCE VAST MAJORITY SPANIARDS IN LOYALIST TERRITORY AND TIS HOPED WILL GAIN EQUAL CONFIDENCE ABROAD STOP VIOLENCE AND REVOLUTION BEEN REPUDIATED AND NEW AND FAR HOPEFULLER PERIOD SEEMS BEGINNING."[8]

The *New York Times*, knowing full well the one-sided coverage of a correspondent writing from one side of the conflict, had a reporter on both sides: Matthews with the Republicans and William Carney with the Nationalists. Each got his facts right (or wrong) as often as the other, their editors concluded;[9] and they inspired about the same number of letters of complaint.[10] Furthermore, Matthews's dispatches received a great deal of substantive editorial revisions. One of Matthews's Teruel reports had to be cut for length, as McCaw informed James: "This bird sent 2844 words on the same facts which Hemingway covered much better in less than half that number. I wonder if Matthews thinks the paper is thriving, and that cable tolls do not matter a damn. Of course, it had to be cut for space anyway."[11] McCaw most likely refers here to Matthews's dispatch corresponding to Hemingway's "The Attack on Teruel,"[12] though his account of the fall of Teruel is also much longer (and more long-winded) than Hemingway's, and just as personal in terms of describing the dangers he faced. Indeed its length allows him to share even more of the action he endured.

Raymond McCaw held a general if perhaps overzealous disagreement with Matthews. It's also clear that McCaw's charges bear some validity—that any responsible editor could have easily and reasonably taken issue where McCaw did. One of the more interesting examples concerns the Matthews piece on Guadalajara. Because he saw evidence on Franco's side of only Italian forces, he only reported Italians. But the *Times* editors heard conflicting reports about the nationalities involved, including the possibility of German troops on the battlefield (McCaw telegram to Matthews, 17 March 1937). They thought it prudent, from this confusion, to begin the article by saying that the rebel soldiers were reported to be mainly Italians and then to change nine references to "Italians" to "Rebels," "the foe," or "Insurgents." When Matthews saw the published piece, he wrote a strenuous objection. In some instances the editors changed paraphrased quotations from his sources. One large paragraph omitted by the editors stressed the first-hand nature of the information, and Matthews underlines the key words: "All day, at every place we stopped and no matter whom we talked to or what we saw, there was only one label—Italian. The dead bodies, the prisoners, the material of every kind, the men who had occupied Brihuega and then fled were Italian and nothing but Italian." Here and elsewhere in his original story, Matthews emphasizes the "personal knowledge" of its information.[13]

Yet Matthews did not report on the foreigners fighting for the Republic—it was in fact the Italian Garibali Battalion that routed Franco's Italians—an omission that historians eager to prove an editorial anti-Republic bias themselves omit. We might surmise government censorship, though Matthews would not cable news of "CENSORSHIP STRICTER"[14] and "BAN ON MENTIONING INTERNATIONALS INCLUDING AMERICANS INSTITUTED TODAY" until July.[15] Perhaps he cautiously self-censored or politically self-censored for the same reasons the government would eventually ban mention. Still, his stridency about the deemphasizing of foreigners on one side is striking given his knowledge of their contribution to the other side. For this reason, too, and his omission of other nationalities on the insurgent side, it seemed only fair to his editor "to stand on the statement that the majority of the Rebels were Italians and let it go at that"[16]—and to name only the Italians in the accompanying boldfaced map caption. A reasonable decision.

Throughout his correspondence to his editors and his several books, Matthews maintained a passionate defense of his eyewitness journalistic standard, a position those close to him understood. "Matthews never believed anything he had not seen with his own eyes," Joris Ivens wrote. "He never saw his job as reporter as one that permitted him to sit in his hotel and read the handouts of the War Ministry."[17] Sidney Franklin recalls that some writers wrote their pieces before arriving in Madrid and came only for the "legitimacy" of the Madrid dateline.[18] And Matthews hated, on principle, having his name attached to an article that violated the integrity of his witness (though he appears to have violated his principle for the Barcelona dispatch). The only way to achieve objectivity, for Matthews, was to acknowledge each reporter's own subjective perspective. Writing to his publisher, Matthews argued that "the full documentary value" of his coverage was lost when the editors altered his submissions for "the apparent necessity of giving more or less equal space to both sides."[19]

As with Matthews, so too Hemingway. Indeed the commitment to subjectivity fit quite well with Hemingway's modernist aesthetics. If Hemingway focused the dispatches on his perspective—on his own experience dodging artillery—he did so to meet this standard as well as to fulfill professional expectations. NANA approached him, after all, for his name and personality as much as for whatever he would write. Before he even left the States, NANA pitched him to potential publications, sending out a promotional release with text to be used alongside his forthcoming dispatches and suggesting they include a photograph: "Mr. Hemingway's assignment is to get both from the bombed towns and bombed trenches the human story of the war, not just an account of the game being played by general staffs with pins and a map."[20] NANA also released each individual dispatch with a one-sentence "precede" about the "famous" or "noted" author. Ernest Hemingway was not writing as Herbert Matthews, ace reporter; Hemingway was writing as Ernest Hemingway, famous author of novels and stories well-known to be drawn from his own experiences.

That he understood this to be his assignment is further evidenced by a cable Matthews sent to his *Times* editors on 9 April 1937, concerning the loyalist attack: "WORKED CONJOINTL WITH HEMINGWAY TODAY HE SENDING EYEWITNESS DESCRIPTION WHILE EYE SENT GENERAL STRATEGY."[21] When a year later the *Times* asked NANA to ensure that Hemingway's reports differed from those of Matthews, NANA complied by asking Hemingway "to emphasize color rather than straight reporting" not necessarily out of dissatisfaction with Hemingway's reportage as Baker contends,[22] but to increase the chance of selling to the *Times* and indeed to ensure the spirit of NANA's original arrangement with Hemingway. Far from dissatisfied, NANA wrote Hemingway at the end of August 1938 a letter of agreement for his coverage of "a general European war" should it break out, "written in your colorful style."[23] (Hemingway was in Paris, on his way to Spain for the last time during the war.) When Edmund Wilson criticized the selected dispatches reprinted in *Fact*, Hemingway wrote him, "I was paid to write what are called 'eye witness' accounts . . . what is called, or was asked for as 'color stuff.' Most of such stuff is faked. Mine was not. It was straight reporting and the personal stuff was what had been asked for by the editors." Wilson's estimation was also based upon *Fact*'s inclusion of "The Old Man at the Bridge" story from *Ken*, not a news dispatch at all.[24] Speaking at Carnegie Hall before the showing of a rough cut of *The Spanish Earth*, shortly after his first trip to Spain and so very much in the context of his wartime work, Hemingway defined the writer's problem as "project[ing] [what is true] in such a way that it becomes a part of the experience of the person who reads it."[25]

Personal, anecdotal journalism had been Hemingway's signature style from his earliest days filing reports, in the early 1920s from Paris, when his editor at the *Toronto Star Weekly* "encouraged . . . what Hemingway did best: write about himself in the act of being a reporter."[26] How could he expect that NANA would expect anything else, if indeed NANA did expect anything else? In the Spanish Civil War he at least maintained his eyewitness posture; in the Second World War, however, he wrote himself into the war effort. His first piece, about D-Day, begins, "No one remembers the date of the Battle of Shiloh. But the day *we took* Fox Green beach was the sixth of June, and the wind was blowing hard out of the northwest."[27] His venue, too—*Collier's* magazine—further contributed to the storylike nature of the Second World War stories—not to mention the stories and involvement he couldn't write about, armed and running around France as more of a free agent than his guerilla-hero Robert Jordan ever was (though he began to transform these experiences into fiction in several unpublished stories). In wartime China in 1943, filing articles for Ralph Ingersoll's short-lived *PM* New York afternoon daily, Hemingway did not even care to be called a news reporter.[28]

It should be mentioned that Hemingway and Matthews enjoyed a great friendship and working relationship. Hemingway usually brought Matthews, who did not always have a car, on his excursions.[29] When Matthews left Madrid for a break in mid April 1937, he had already arranged to have Hemingway provide coverage to the *Times* through NANA. For one thing, Hemingway did not have to worry about Matthews as a rival for the history books. He could endorse his friend's book, *Two Wars and More to Come*, and praise him as "the ablest and the bravest war correspondent writing today" who "when the fakers are all dead . . . will be read in the schools,"[30] because Matthews posed no threat to Hemingway's own chances to be read in the schools. The only beef that Hemingway ever expressed he really reserved for Matthews's editors, for not wanting his Teruel street-fighting story and for cutting references to himself in Matthews's Teruel dispatches so that it appeared only Matthews had been there.[31]

As for Hemingway's neglecting to name everyone with him for every story, the *Times* cutting of his name suggests that such exactitude was hardly a priority. A paper had no incentive for announcing the fact that a competitor's correspondent stood beside its own to see and report the same events. NANA changed at least one vague Hemingway "we," which admits to the presence of others, to "this correspondent"[32]—we can hardly fault Hemingway for working in the spirit of his employer's standards. Do readers care that Matthews, Delmer, Gellhorn, and others were there? The story's effect and the limited word count also weighed against such roll calls. One editor chose not to clutter the dispatch on the great retreat across the Ebro with all the names of the American International Brigade volunteers Hemingway encountered, an omission of content far more serious than that of omitted correspondent names.[33] Hemingway often gave the names of the reporters with him, such as at Teruel; nor was he the only reporter to sometimes neglect to do so. Martha Gellhorn, for example, used a vague "we" and singled herself out as the primary participant in some of her stories. This book commits the same offense—frequently I name some or all of those with Hemingway at a given moment, but not always. One could never be sure of finding and verifying that information, information only tangentially relevant to a study of Hemingway's writing.

By using first-person reportage, Hemingway—and Matthews and Gellhorn and most of the group covering the war—were operating solidly within convention. William Stott, in *Documentary Expression and Thirties America*, calls this first-person *participant observer* technique "the most common sort of documentary reportage in the thirties" that worked "by vicarious persuasion: the writer partook of the events he reported and bared his feelings and attitudes to influence the reader's own."[34] Stott also observes another technique to enable documentary reportage to "talk to us, and convince us that we, our deepest interests, are engaged," in the use of the second person: "Thirties documentaries constantly address 'you,' the 'you' who is we the audience, and exhorts, wheedles, begs us to identify, pity, participate."[35] His examples include Dorothy Parker's Spanish Civil War writing and Hemingway's 1935 "First-Hand Report on the Florida Hurricane." A number of Hemingway's NANA dispatches employ the second person as a way of bringing the reader along for the ride.

Hemingway's dispatches used personal pronouns more artfully than is generally recognized. "A New Kind of War," which William Braasch Watson notes as having been "written with more care and imagination" than its predecessors[36]—"on the verge of becoming a story rather than a news dispatch"—begins in second person: "The window of the hotel is open and, as you lie in bed, you hear the firing in the front line seventeen blocks away."[37] He takes "you" outside, to see the damage and the dead from the bombing. "Someone makes a joke about missing teeth and someone else says not to make that joke. And everyone has the feeling that characterizes war. It wasn't me, see? It wasn't me."[38] The tension between the first-person and second-person pronouns—the movement toward identification with "you" and the insistence that "it wasn't me"—continues in the next line. Here the reader is at once still in the narrator's shoes, but strangely distanced from the narrator through biographical tidbit and, at the same time, asked to see himself in the enemy: "The Italian dead up on the Guadalajara weren't you although Italian dead, because of where you'd spent your boyhood, always seemed, still, like Our Dead."[39] It is worth quoting at length this dispatch's transition to first person:

> After the shell that lit on the sidewalk in front of the hotel you got a beautiful double corner room on that side, twice the size of the one you'd had, for less than a dollar. It wasn't me they killed. See? No. Not me. It wasn't me anymore.
>
> Then in a hospital given by the American Friends of Spanish Democracy located out behind the Morata front along the road to Valencia they said, "Raven wants to see you."
>
> "Do I know him?"
>
> "I don't think so," they said. "But he wants to see you."
>
> "Where is he?"
>
> "Upstairs."
>
> In the room upstairs they were giving a blood transfusion to a man with a very gray face who lay on a cot with his arm out looking away from the gurgling bottle and moaning in a very impersonal way. He moaned mechanically and at regular intervals and it did not seem to be him that made the sound. His lips did not move.
>
> "Where's Raven?" I asked.
>
> "I'm here," said Raven.[40]

The piece simply could not have sustained the second person for the remaining five pages. More significantly, for this deeply personal exchange between the writer and the faceless, eyeless soldier, Hemingway could not hide in the rhetorical device of the second person. In the process, he effects a reversal of the usual pronoun game; instead of identifying with the all-embracing "you," we leave that trick behind and become fully attached to the narratorial "I" as ourselves, as we might not have been had the article begun in the first person. And even as the narrator identifies himself by name for the only time in any of the dispatches—"Hemingway," and later "Ernest"—[41] as decidedly not ourselves. We do not say, *It isn't me.* The historian Hugh Thomas notes "the refreshing candour" of Hemingway's naming himself "in the world of the International Brigades, where no one's name seemed to be truthfully given."[42]

A year later Hemingway's "Tortosa Calmly Awaits Assault" resists admitting the city's imminent fall. Yet it does so anyway, by subtly alluding to the wartime rhetoric of sacrificed blood irrigating the earth and rejuvenating Spain. Such rhetoric was common during the war, appearing in speeches, print, and poetry. Many of the poems in Cary Nelson's anthology *The Wound and the Dream: Sixty Years of American Poems about the Spanish Civil War* join in the Spanish and international chorus's general connection between Republican soldiers and the land, and the particular singing of their dead nourishing the land.[43] We find such language in La Pasionaria's farewell address to the International Brigades, her epilogue to *The Book of the XV Brigade*, and in Hemingway's famous eulogy "On the American Dead in Spain": "For our dead are a part of the earth of Spain now and the earth of Spain can never die. Each winter it will seem to die and each spring it will come alive again. Our dead will live with it forever."[44] The Tortosa dispatch implies the deaths of many Republican soldiers in its final paragraph's description of newborn onions:

> The artillery was picking up a little now. Two came in at a fairly useful place and as the smoke blew away ahead and settled through the trees, you picked an armful of spring onions from a field beside the trail that led to the Tortosa road. They were the first onions of the spring and peeling one I found they were plump white and not too strong. The Ebro Delta has a fine rich land, and where the onions grow, tomorrow will be a battle.[45]

The echo is quiet, and perhaps unconscious, but there nevertheless.

The opening boastfulness of "American Veterans Tell of Escaping Insurgents" should be taken somewhat ironically. The dispatch begins by announcing that for "two days we have been doing the most dangerous thing you can do in this war. That is keep close behind an unstabilized line where the enemy are attacking with mechanized forces." Then, a few pages later, we learn about the American survivors of the spring 1938 Nationalist offensive that took Bob Merriman and eventually reached the Mediterranean Sea. Reading about these survivors creeping through enemy camps, stepping on a sleeping German soldier's hand, sprinting "across an open field toward the Ebro bank and being sniped at by artillery controlled by an observation plane overhead" and then "the desperate swimming of the Ebro" naked, we are tacitly asked to place the correspondent's plight in due perspective.[46] This story certainly escapes the charge of a monotonous battle and bombing scene; its switch from apparently boastful to awestruck witness feels almost deliberately self-conscious. Other choice self-ironic moments come in the dispatches of that quiet pre-Teruel fall of 1938. The one titled "Hemingway, Covering War, Tells of Brush with Death" has little to report from Madrid other than the new aftershave brand he is trying. In "Loyalists' Drive Seen Progressing as Planned," he writes that "Shells are all much the same and if they don't hit you there is no story and if they do you won't have to write it."[47]

Hemingway's dispatches are sometimes monotonous because his war was usually monotonous—as wars are most of the time. It should also be kept in mind that scholars reviewing Hemingway's NANA dispatches one after another do not relive the original reading experience. Hemingway wrote dispatches sporadically, papers did not run all of his dispatches, papers edited and cut them, and readers read at least a couple of papers' worth of other articles in between. He told Edmund Wilson as much in defending himself against Wilson's critique of the selected (and heavily edited and cut) dispatches reprinted in *Fact* without his consent: "If you are being paid to be shot at and write about it you are supposed to mention the shooting. . . . But I do not go in for re-printing journalism."[48]

If we can in this way better understand his style, and at least explain it if not excuse it, we similarly ought to try to contextualize—and perhaps excuse—the moral problem. The two issues here are the specific condemnation of Hemingway's silence about Republican atrocities and the general question of biased reporting (the latter of which has already partially been addressed).

Hemingway knew, as Donaldson writes, that mentioning the atrocities "would arouse anticommunist sentiments back in the States and effectively undermine any possibility of American intervention."[49] It is also doubtful that reporting them would have stopped them. But reporting Republican atrocities from Spain was not possible for the simple reason that all dispatches went through a government censor.

Matthews cabled his editors from Paris in May 1937 to tell them that "censorship does not permit us to say when the 'telefonica' is hit. So whenever you see reference in my despatches [sic] to 'an important building in the center of the city' or words to that effect, the cable desk can know that it is the telefonica."[50] As already noted, by July he would cable "CENSORSHIP STRICTER" as the ban on mentioning internationals went into effect.[51] Virginia Cowles's memoir confirms the aggressive censorship, observing that it limited journalists to exactly the kind of material Hemingway wrote about:

> There were frequent attempts to "beat the censor" by employing American slang expressions, but this came to an end when a Canadian girl joined the staff. The International Brigades were not allowed to be publicized; no reference could be made to Russian armaments, and buildings and streets which suffered bombardments could not be identified.
>
> It was only in the realm of the human interest story that the journalists had a free hand. They could describe bombardments to their heart's content.[52]

Hemingway and everyone else—to reserve incrimination for Hemingway is hardly just. No correspondent covering Republican Spain reported suspicious imprisonments and disappearances by government agents.

Hemingway, through Joris Ivens and *The Spanish Earth* project, had better access to military leaders and other officials than most. Had he been able somehow to report such activity, he would have lost that access and would probably have been kicked out of the country. His fame would have likely prevented his own disappearance, though he still worried, especially as so many of such crimes on the Republican side occurred from free agents. When Jasper Wood printed the anarchist FAI (Federación Anarquista Ibérica, or Iberian Anarchist Federation) banner in the book version of *The Spanish Earth*, Hemingway expressed his anxieties bluntly in a letter to Jasper. It is hardly "petulant," he scolded, "not to wish to be shot."[53] Hostility in the Republic against the anarchists ran high; after the Barcelona May Day conflict, the government's Foreign Minister (del Vayo) told U.S. Ambassador Claude Bowers that the "anarchist revolt throughout Catalonia [was] not only expected but welcomed as an opportunity to liquidate the anarchists who have been hostile from the beginning."[54]

It is possible that Hemingway's dispatch stating that "not one friend . . . has been executed or is missing"[55] was his clever means of reporting the rumors and indeed the general fact while being technically truthful and evading the censors, as in this very dispatch he acknowledged the presence of a censor after a bombardment. Matthews, on the other hand, never found a way to mention the censors or admit even the possibility of people gone missing in the Republic. Peter Moreira has observed that in a 1943 dispatch Hemingway related a remark by a British officer about the Chinese Nationalist government's being "hopeless on the offensive" because censorship "prevented American reporters from actually saying that the Nationalists wouldn't attack, surmising that by telling this anecdote Hemingway could sneak such a judgment into his reports."[56] In Spain, the censors, the eyewitness standard, his own safety and continuing ability to report the war, and, yes, his passionate support of the government, contributed to his decision. He could have written about government abuses from the States, but then could not return to cover the war and support the cause—a justification other journalists, those who did not return after the spring of 1937, did not enjoy. In his mind, too, knowing what he heard of fascist atrocities, any reportage that lessened the government's chances of victory through killing hopes of increased international aid would have led to more deaths at Franco's hands than the much smaller number inspired by fifth column paranoia.

(Hemingway's *Ken* magazine attack on Dos Passos over the Robles affair, and its insistence that Robles received a fair hearing and must have been a traitor, came in the summer of 1938, the desperate summer after Hemingway witnessed the successful Nationalist drive to cut the Republic in half, the summer he wrote his most unjustifiably optimistic dispatches in his hopes that Spain might survive until, and be saved by, the general war, and the summer he wrote the despairing introductory remarks to the Quintanilla book. The loose-cannon nature of the article can be better understood in this context. I also suspect Hemingway of overconfidence in his confidences—that he truly believed his government and communist party contacts kept him truthfully informed.[57])

The explanation that Hemingway did not write about Republican atrocities because he was saving it for his fiction I find unsatisfying.[58] Caroline Moorehead, in her biography of Martha Gellhorn, describes the climate for the Madrid correspondents that first spring: "And so, day by day, the correspondents walked a thin and nervous line between truth, evasions, and propaganda, telling one another that though it was not all right if things were made up and presented as true, it was acceptable to describe what you wanted, provided it was true and provided your readers were aware of your position."[59] My own sense is that they did not walk the line quite so nervously; their passionate commitment, along with their principles of position disclosure and the eyewitness standard, made that walk relatively easy.

The problem of *committed journalism*, even sixty years later, has not been resolved—as anyone paying attention to the media and world affairs well knows. One person's truth is another person's propaganda. Certainly, as Knightley notes, reporting from "the heart" affects one's judgment.[60] Yet to attempt "balance," per the edits to Matthews's Guadalajara piece, betrays one's believed truth. Furthermore, the kind of reporting done by the correspondents with the Republic—committed, one-sided, optimistic, heroic, human interest work by embedded writers—would be practiced widely and without reserve during the Second World War. Such narrative journalism, with roots in Louisa May Alcott's "Hospital Sketches" series published in the *Boston Commonwealth*, and more immediately in 1930s social documentary writing whose "essence" is "not information,"[61] anticipated postwar new journalism's adoption of novelistic narrative technique for nonfiction which culminated with such wartime books as Norman Mailer's *Armies of the Night* and Michael Herr's *Dispatches*. Hemingway's "A New Kind of War" falls in this line of development, as does his next NANA dispatch, the only one filed from New York, "The Chauffeurs of Madrid." Written a few weeks after the anarchist clashes with the government in Barcelona, the piece not-so-subtly allegorizes the Republic's path to victory, from the dwarfish, good-natured provincial Tomás, to the incompetent but brave anarchist David, and finally to the "tough," "efficient," "brave," and punctual twenty-year "union man" Hipolito. "You can bet on Franco, Mussolini, or Hitler, if you want," Hemingway concludes: "But my money goes on Hipolito."[62]

Today we might categorize these pieces under the awkward umbrella term *creative nonfiction*. That term certainly fits the mixed bag of nonfiction narratives and commentaries Hemingway published in *Ken*. These pieces are essays, not journalism, several of which directly appeal for support for the Republic, and most of which really deal with the approaching world war. *Ken* wanted "precisely the kind of opinion articles he could not write for NANA."[63] His article "The Cardinal Picks a Winner" shows a photo of a row of dead children from Barcelona and another one with Nationalist officers saluting and Catholic officials with raised hands, apparently making the fascist salute as well. He ends ironically: "So I *don't believe* the people shown in the photo can really be making it. I would rather prefer to think that the photograph was faked."[64] When Hemingway argues in "A Program for U.S. Realism" that the United States should stay out of the next war except to stuff its pockets through arms sales, one has to wonder, given his call and the democratic nations' failure to save Spain, if we are to sniff sarcasm here.

The language of the dispatches, with their corrective intent against Franco's propaganda, does risk propagandizing. Hemingway's optimism and antifascism certainly colored his correspondence work. His criticism of the anarchist and POUM militia for their inactivity on the Aragon front, for example, sounds a lot like the Spanish Communist Party's.[65] But unlike Matthews, Hemingway limited his reports within the Republic to military matters. Hemingway may have generally condemned the anarchists in his nonfiction, considering their activity as hampering the war effort, but he never repeated the accusation of their collaboration with the rebels, as Matthews had done. And when Hemingway commented on the Barcelona crisis, he referred only to the government—not to the communists, as Matthews had done.[66] Nor did he write articles asserting the limited role of the communists in the government, or explaining Spanish anarchism, also as Matthews had done.[67]

During one of Hemingway's stateside breaks between trips to Spain, his children asked if he was a "tool" of Stalin, an accusation tossed by a schoolmate who, presumably parroting his or her parents, probably understood the term no better than Hemingway's children.[68] A tool of the Republic, perhaps. But of the Spanish Communist Party? Of the Comintern?

The Spanish Communist Party (PCE) enjoyed a large measure of popular support and political clout. Its militia, the Fifth Regiment, the only military unit that had bothered to prepare for the rebellion, all but saved the Republic in those first months, first by helping stop the initial Nationalist advance on Madrid through the Guadarrama and second by its role defending Madrid. The Comintern-organized International Brigades and Russian tanks and planes and their operators also came to Madrid's aid that fall and winter. As the Madrid front stabilized and the war stretched on, the PCE led such essential homefront efforts as providing for refugees, sewing uniforms, and supplying food to workers. Because of its organization and fame, its military attracted new recruits regardless of political affiliation. Given the Republic's understandable distrust of former regular army officers, it seemed welcoming to those officers, many of whom were actually rather conservative.[69] And it drew youth (and others) less out of political conviction than from a natural attraction to the new party on the scene, and one associated with vague ideas about Soviet modernity—especially after the socialists and republicans had so thoroughly disappointed many people's hopes.[70]

When Hemingway arrived in Spain, "The communists stood for a disciplined, left-of-Centre, bourgeois regime, capable of winning the war, with private industry limited by some nationalization, but not by collectivization or workers' control."[71] As Helen Graham writes, "there was increasingly little that we would commonly identify as 'communist' in the content of either the wartime PCE's political discourse or its cultural policy, which was liberal democrat through and through." It upheld the right to private property and it rejected class revolution (in accord with the VII Comintern Congress of 1935), thus bringing frustrated middle-class constituencies into the fold alongside its traditional working-class membership. "What was radical (i.e. new or even 'communist') about the PCE in the war was not the content of its policies but its organizational techniques. Indeed by marrying the two, the wartime PCE would thus become the best republican party Spain had ever known."[72] Many if not most new Spanish communist members, given illiteracy rates and the lack of a real communications infrastructure, probably had at best a sketchy understanding of traditional communist principles. When Robert Jordan explains homesteading to his Spanish comrades (whereby American settlers could earn private property from the government by a period of successful farming on it), Agustín appreciates it as a progressive agrarian policy that indicates some measure of communism in the U.S.[73]

The Spanish Communist Party was not particularly communist. Nor did it ever fully control the government. It wielded a good measure of influence, to be sure. But that very influence also assured that other parties in the Republican government actively resisted the PCE. As a general rule, whenever Republican decisions dovetailed with the Soviet or PCE agenda, they legitimately addressed Republican wartime survival. Frequently the two acted on their own, such as the PCE and the Comintern's suppression of their internal enemies in Barcelona in May 1937. (As Cary Nelson understates the case, "a negotiated, rather than murderous, solution to differences among the Spanish Left would have benefited everyone."[74]) But it's also true that after May 1937, as Hugh Thomas concludes, "it was the Republican state which was at war with the nationalist state rather than revolution against rebellion."[75] And "once the Soviet Union had begun to offer support to the Republic, the main medium of Soviet-Spanish relations shifted to diplomatic channels broadly construed" instead of through the PCE or even the Comintern.[76] Republican politics were chiefly Republican politics.

In military affairs as well, the number of Soviet advisers never exceeded eight hundred in Spain, and they served "predominately a subordinate, technical role" as "engineers, interpreters, and technicians of various kinds and not least the pilots and tank drivers." Conflicts between Republican officers and Soviet advisors occurred, though not as a result of "a fundamental disagreement over military strategy" or any desire by Stalin "to control the Republican war effort."[77] Hemingway's Soviet advisor Golz in *For Whom the Bell Tolls* is decidedly not in command.[78] Additionally, Nelson finds that by their own accounts Soviet advisors attached to the International Brigades were driven primarily by an antifascist motivation.[79]

In brief: the Republic was not communist; the communists were not communist; and the Comintern and Soviet Union did not interfere decisively with Republican affairs. Hemingway may have been a tool of the Republic, but not of Stalin. The most well-informed of parents of his children's classmates had good reason to be suspicious. For the duration of the war the U.S. government itself wrestled with the question of PCE and USSR influence over the Republic.[80] Russia did provide aid and personnel. Many among the Spanish left's leadership clung to revolutionary language to keep the faith superficially with their traditional supporters even as they had shifted to the right, and the American volunteers (especially in the beginning) often came from the Communist Party USA ranks and with CPUSA funding, as the International Brigades had been a Comintern initiative. And thus in *For Whom the Bell Tolls* Jordan felt the crusading zealotry for communism not among the Spaniards or even at the Soviet's gathering place, Gaylord's, but at the International Brigade headquarters in Madrid.[81]

Hemingway's friendships with Gustav Regler, Joris Ivens, and Mikhail Koltsov might have tilted his politics toward communism (or socialism), but chased down with a healthy dose of realism. Regler, an exiled German communist fighting for the Republic and for socialism, viewed the war as an idealist and a skeptic: "I had been told that a special Soviet mission had arrived in Madrid. The good Russia had arrived; would the diabolical Russia follow?" He worried that the "shameful . . . Russian prisons" would see replication in Spain even as he hoped for a "true Socialist" world there.[82] The Comintern labeled *The Great Crusade*, his 1940 autobiographical novel about the war, "anti-Soviet."[83] As for Koltsov, a Hemingway letter from 1952 about his relationship with Koltsov recalls language from a passage about Koltsov's fictional avatar Karkov in *For Whom the Bell Tolls*, and thus evidence of the person and the character's oneness in Hemingway's imagination and of Hemingway's perception of the relationship: "He knew I was not a Communist and never would be one. But because he believed in me as a writer he tried to show me how everything was run so that I could give a true account of it."[84] We can probably trust that Hemingway, as Jordan tells Karkov about himself,[85] took his news from more than simply party-line presses;[86] we can also probably trust that Koltsov, like Karkov, parodied the ridiculousness of Communist propaganda.[87]

Ivens, as we will see in the next chapter, also had begun to have artistic reservations about his Comintern and Soviet affiliation. And he never controlled Hemingway. Hemingway did not follow Ivens's suggestion to write a dispatch on the significant role of the political commissars in the Republican military,[88] even though that would have meant featuring his brave new friend Regler. I disagree with William Braasch Watson, who considers Hemingway's decision "of less interest here" than Ivens's "assured control and confident command."[89] For one thing, it strikes me that Ivens gave a friendly request, not a command: "Could you write in one of your articles about the great and human function of the political commissar on the front?"[90] And if it was a command, doesn't his thwarting of Ivens's presumption have more significance? Either way, Hemingway's declining to write the article is of great interest as evidence of his relative independence and sensitivity to what might appear as propaganda. The commissar system began with the communist Fifth Regiment and then applied to the new Popular Army. A unit commissar's mission was to educate the troops on the cause, to maintain unit morale, to advise the commander on the condition and treatment of the soldiers, and to serve as a conduit of information from the soldiers to the commander. Regler carried out his duties accordingly. Others, like André Marty and Vittorio Vidali ("Carlos"), educated through execution and repression.[91] Eventually anxiety over communist influence led the government to dismantle the commissar system.

Hemingway also, in a letter to Jack Wheeler at NANA justifying his work, wrote about declining to send "a summing-up story as people might think it propaganda no matter how true and did the entry into Lerida for that week's story on April 29th [1938]."[92] That story ends: "Anyone who thinks the war is over in Spain is a fool or a coward. A great fighting people who are for the first time being led by generals who are of the people, who are not fools, nor traitors, will not be defeated that easily. But she must have planes and guns; and she must have them at once."[93]

Jay Allen of the *Chicago Tribune* characterized the second wave of correspondents to hit Spain, including Hemingway, Matthews, and Delmer, as having practically no "political beliefs" compared to the first wave.[94] Hans Schoots writes that while Ivens "thought in the unambiguous categories of Communist politics," Hemingway "did not embrace any single concept."[95] Sidney Franklin believed Hemingway feigned his communist sympathies, "Otherwise they would have thrown him out."[96] I see no reason to doubt Hemingway's retrospective summary:

> There were at least five parties in the Spanish Civil War on the Republic side. I tried to understand and evaluate all five (very difficult) and belonged to none. . . . I had no party but a deep interest in and love for the Republic. . . . In Spain I had, and have, many friends on the other side. I tried to write truly about them, too. Politically, I was always on the side of the Republic from the day it was declared and for a long time before.[97]

With the Republic and against fascism.

If anything, as Allen Josephs and others have argued, he idealized a minimalist, libertarian-friendly government. "A writer is like a Gypsy," he wrote before the war, in 1935, to his Russian translator Ivan Kashkin (and the namesake of Robert Jordan's predecessor in *For Whom the Bell Tolls*). "He owes no allegiance to any government. If he is a good writer he will never like the government he lives under. His hand should be against it and its hand will always be against him. The minute anyone knows any bureaucracy well enough he will hate it. Because the minute it passes a certain size it must be unjust." Hemingway also explicitly disavowed communism, "because I believe in only one thing: liberty." The letter was published in the *Soviet Literature* journal in 1962, with an amusing headnote framing Hemingway as a "class-conscious" friend of communism despite sometimes "sharing the prejudices of his class." The headnote's assessment in some ways, however, rings true: "As for the state, the practices of the anarchists who found themselves in power in Republican Spain and especially in Catalonia, had opened Hemingway's eyes to the real meaning of the 'state-minimum.' And

Hemingway expressed himself in favour—admittedly during war—of stoutly disciplined opposition to fascism."[98]

There is no reason to believe that the war changed his opinion, and in fact good reason, given his knowledge of the government's occasional repressive tactics, to believe otherwise. Like so many others during the war, Republican Spaniards and outsiders, Hemingway accepted the communist party as the only means to the material support, unified state, and disciplined military necessary to defeat Franco. Had the Republic been slightly more vigilant by mid July 1936, and had England, France, and the United States materially supported the capitalistic, democratically elected government, the rise of substantial domestic and international communism in Spain might have been forestalled.[99]

Hemingway went to Spain to see the war himself and to support the Republic through his ambulance fund. The paychecks from NANA helped; the fundraising from *The Spanish Earth* helped even more. Whatever propagandistic streak colors the dispatches pales in comparison to the documentary. The filmmaker, Joris Ivens, was well-established in European communist circles. The documentary genre then and now has occupied a slippery position between the extremes of impossible-to-achieve empirical nonfiction and of the outright fictionalized. Evaluations of Hemingway's journalism are too often informed by knowledge of *The Spanish Earth* and the *Ken* essays to the detriment of the journalism. And the very nature of the slippery documentary genre may enable the film to escape opprobrium. It wasn't reportage; it was altogether something else. But for that matter, Hemingway's dispatches weren't purely reportage either, and if not *altogether* something else, still something else, and should be reckoned with accordingly.

II

THE SPANISH EARTH

THREE
Making the Film

The earliest extant document regarding *The Spanish Earth*'s inception is a cable from Joris Ivens to cameraman John Ferno dated 12 December 1936: "Magnificent opportunity can you come to Spain January February poor wages important film telegraph answer Joris."[1] Four days later Ivens received $350 for the project,[2] presumably from Archibald MacLeish. Around the same time Ivens wrote Ferno a two-page letter describing the film as "a kind of documentary" that will focus on village life for a family with "two sons at the front, one son with the fleet, and mother, daughter, and one son in the village."[3]

On 18 December, Ivens drafted a plan for going forward. In addition to securing Ferno's agreement, he had already wired to meet André Malraux in Paris at the beginning of the year to help get started. Ivens's immediate to-do list included obtaining letters of introduction, credentials, cash, and some equipment. The plan named a few possible "money-contacts" (including Upton Sinclair, Theodore Dreiser, and a couple of Hollywood names), deferred to Archibald MacLeish for organizational information, and estimated a budget of ten thousand dollars. The plan concluded with the following rationale: "In the work for the Newsreels-Companies for the short film we saw that they have nothing of the real life and fight in Spain, and are selling it very expensive, and second, they closed their Library of Spain-material (will be even more in future). It is necessary and important to make our own pictures in

Spain with good chances for a large release in America."[4] This "short film" was in fact the origins of *The Spanish Earth.*

In November, Ivens and his editor (and future wife) Helen Van Dongen were in New York working on a project funded by the Rockefeller Foundation. In the meantime, a group called Film Historians, Inc. produced a thirty-minute film, *Spain—A Fight for Freedom,* by borrowing from and rearranging available newsreel material from the Spanish government. Van Dongen, who would become most known for her editing talent through working with people like Ivens and Robert Flaherty, put together a number of films of her own, including this one. As the film's distributor, Tom Brandon, recounts, Van Dongen "edited it and really did all the actual physical selection, compilation and supervised the recording. . . . The purpose was to summarize the story of the background of the revolt against the Republic."[5] John Dos Passos, possibly with MacLeish, provided the original commentary.[6] But a thirty-minute film was not viable for theaters, so Brandon added a second film about the war, a forty-minute Russian documentary called *No Pasarán!,* and distributed the two films for theatrical release under the program title "Spain in Flames."[7] The somewhat graphic and even "gruesome"[8] pro-Republic two-film program premiered at New York's Cameo theater on Thursday, 28 January 1937.[9]

Most commentators then and now discuss "Spain in Flames" as a single film, and as no copy has survived we cannot know the extent to which the two films were presented as a whole. At least two newspaper notices recognized the two "halves," under the titles "Fight for Freedom" and "No Pasarán," and properly attributed the first to Republican cameramen and the second to Soviet cameramen.[10] To Hemingway's biographer Carlos Baker in 1965, Brandon wrote that no print exists any longer for *No Pasarán!* but that "one can be dug up on the other part."[11] Brandon, a member of the Workers Film and Photo League, started Garrison Films in 1932 to promote "independent film-makers working in the public interest," such as his league's films, Soviet films, other socially conscious films, and even a few Hollywood films.[12]

The two films showed footage from King Aflonso's abdication to the bombing of Madrid.[13] As the bombardment began on 29 October, Film Historians, Inc. could not have had anything to work with before early

November. According to Ivens's biographer, Hans Schoots, the work did indeed begin that fall. As Ivens recounts:

> After watching a particularly painful session in the cutting-room, and listening to the sponsoring committee complain about results, I remarked that it would be cheaper and more satisfactory in every respect to make such a documentary film on the spot, instead of being at the mercy of newsreel costs and newsreel attitudes.
>
> This resulted in another meeting at which Archibald MacLeish, then editor of *Fortune*, proposed a new plan: to complete the present film, now entitled *Spain in Flames*, with a minimum of additional time and expense, and then to raise a new fund to send me to Spain to make a film there.[14]

The understandable confusion of the film and program titles aside, the idea for *The Spanish Earth* occurred between mid November and 12 December. Hemingway would not be in New York until 13 January, returning to Key West three days before the opening of "Spain in Flames."

During these ten days, Hemingway may have worked on the commentary for one or both parts of "Spain in Flames" with the help of Prudencio de Pereda, an aspiring American writer of Spanish descent who had initiated a pen-pal friendship with Hemingway in 1934. De Pereda worshipped Hemingway; his own fiction was a pale imitation of his literary hero's. He had written several quite eager letters in the closing months of 1936 trying to arrange a meeting during Hemingway's next trip to New York. Hemingway apparently invited de Pereda's assistance on the *Fight for Freedom* script. Afterwards, and almost two weeks into the film's opening run, de Pereda wrote a long letter to Hemingway about meeting him, about his own going-nowhere writing career, about the war, and about the long lines for tickets to see the film: "'Our' picture is doing marvelously. . . . It goes without saying that the stuff you did for it is the best there. The second part is a great deal better than the first. Even using some of my lines did not hurt it any. Boy, did I feel thrilled!" He recollects with enthusiasm being with Hemingway in the hotel: "When you were working on that picture script at the table on the second morning and I was sitting and watching you, I felt like going up and putting my arms around you in a friendly way, but I did not because we don't do very sincere and honest things or say the honest truth all the time in this god-damned society."[15]

A manuscript of subtitles does exist, titled "Madrid in Flames," for a film photographed by Soviet cameraman A. Karman and distributed by Amkino. It is written on stationery from New York's Barclay Hotel, where Hemingway usually stayed, and in what appears to be Hemingway's hand and in the style of his *The Spanish Earth* commentary.[16] Watson thinks it is Hemingway's original written narration for "the second part of *Spain in Flames*"; his note that "this second part of the film has been lost"[17] matches what Brandon says about *No Pasarán!* Yet it's not entirely clear what this manuscript is, because Soviet filmmakers Roman Karmen and Boris Makadeev made a film called *Madrid in Flames.* It could be a transcription (translation?) of that film; a differently titled transcription (translation?) of *No Pasarán!*; or an entirely new, non-Soviet narration for *No Pasarán!* or for *Madrid in Flames*. Might *Madrid in Flames* and *No Pasarán!* be the same film? Karman and Karmen the same person? The manuscript's style follows the heavy-handed melodramatic convention of most documentary and newsreel voice-overs of the era.

To Carlos Baker twenty-seven years later, de Pereda wrote that a previous commentary existed and the film "was ready for distribution in the U.S. just before Hemingway left on his first trip to the Spanish Civil War, but Ernest put his full impact on it with his own words, changes of sequences, and omissions. I don't recall whether there was any screen credit other than Ernest's (certainly the most wanted)."[18] De Pereda is rather inconsistent, as this passage suggests revisions by Hemingway and another sentence recognizes assistance he received, yet the letter also insists on Hemingway's sole authorship of both *Spain in Flames* and *The Spanish Earth*—astonishingly in the latter case, given that de Pereda wrote the first draft and Ivens had significant directive input. Moreover, Hemingway did not receive, and emphatically did not want, any credit for "Spain in Flames." Tom Brandon writing to Baker could not remember if Ernest helped on that first film with Film Historians, Inc. One would think that if Hemingway rewrote the narration at the last minute before release, the distributor would remember it in addition to Hemingway's enthusiasm for it and "fighting for the right to show it."[19] On opening day, MacLeish wrote a letter to "Jerry" about the film, citing participation by Ivens, Van Dongen, and Dos Passos, but not Hemingway.[20] Even odder, the *Chicago Daily Tribune* review credits Hemingway with actually performing the narration.[21] It's remarkable that neither Brandon nor de Pereda nor any one else reports this, especially when de Pereda claims to have initially suggested that Hemingway record the narration for *The Spanish Earth.*[22] It's possible that the *Tribune*'s writer caught wind of Hemingway's doing the narration and misunderstood his role.

Probably Dos Passos (perhaps with MacLeish) wrote the narration for *Spain—A Fight for Freedom,* and after Brandon added the Soviet-produced *No Pasarán!* to the program Hemingway wrote or revised its narration at the last minute. This would account for de Pereda's gushing about the film's second part, which has his own contributions—the second part being, as the reviewers tell us, the material shot by the Russian cameramen. We can attribute MacLeish's silence to Jerry to the decision not to publicize Hemingway's role. The day before the film's premiere, MacLeish cabled Hemingway to assure him his association with the film would not be disclosed so that his endorsement on advertisements would appear impartial.[23] Hemingway, a month away from leaving to cover the war, may also have hoped to maintain a public impression of political objectivity. Word about his involvement did get out, prior to the *Tribune*'s review; the day before de Pereda's letter, MacLeish wrote to assure Hemingway in Key West that the reviewer who outed his and Dos Passos's participation in the picture did not learn about it from Brandon or anyone else directly involved.[24]

The Spanish Ambassador Fernando de los Rios provided a foreword to "Spain in Flames" (or its first part?)[25] which in New York ran for three weeks at the Cameo followed by single event showings at the Mecca Temple (Anti-Fascist Committee),[26] the American People's Center,[27] and the Y.M.H.A. (North American Committee to Aid Spanish Democracy).[28] In Chicago, it played for about five days at the Sonotone.[29] A New York reviewer found the narration "a bit annoying,"[30] though the *Tribune* reviewer who credited Hemingway did not: "The English spoken narrative is delivered with quiet lucidity by Ernest Hemingway. Such a relief—his delivery—after the bombast, floweriness, and dreadful punning so many film commentators compel us to live through."[31] The film also ran into political obstacles in the form of bans by New Brunswick, New Jersey; by the governor of Pennsylvania; and by Waterbury, Connecticut. Ironically given the program's antifascist message, in New Brunswick the sheriff, the judge of the Court of Errors and Appeals, and the district deputy of the Knights of Columbus felt "exhibition of the film would constitute a violation of the so-called Anti-Nazi Act."[32] In historically Quaker Pennsylvania, the governor cited the film's encouragement of young men to fight and possibly die overseas, though some suspected Catholic influence behind his decision.[33] The Knights of Columbus, clergyman, and "several Italian societies" were responsible in Waterbury.[34] The Pennsylvania ban, which made the American Civil Liberties Union's top twenty list of "major acts of repression,"[35] was eventually overturned in court.[36] This December 1937 reversal would have effectively denied the state's ban a week earlier of *The Spanish Earth*.[37]

Hemingway's introduction to *The Spanish Earth* most likely began when he was reworking the "Spain in Flames" narration in late January. MacLeish's letter to "Jerry" on opening day notes, "Hemingway has joined the group concerned with the full length Spanish film and will write the dialogue if things go as anticipated."[38] It's possible that Hemingway agreed to the idea when he first got to New York or even before, as articles in the *Times* and the *Tribune* on 17 January link Dos Passos's travel plans to Hemingway's.[39] Dos Passos queried Hemingway about the latter's plans on 1 February: "Could you let me know fairly soon if anything definite comes through about this picture—as I would like to plan my future accordingly."[40] MacLeish's letter of assurance on 8 February about the leaking of Hemingway's connection to "Spain in Flames" also asked after his plans, "so that we can arrange about the dialogue on the long picture. You don't mind our announcing that you are going to do dialogue on the long picture? It will help."[41] By the time he met Ivens in Paris in early March, Hemingway was fully on board and the production company, Contemporary Historians, Inc., was in business.

Ivens himself had arrived in Europe at the beginning of the year with a plan in hand. On 23 December, he and MacLeish fleshed out the initial idea, which the next day MacLeish turned into a brief treatment a few pages in length. As MacLeish wrote to Lillian Hellman that day, from his office at *Fortune* magazine, "I am afraid it contains my ideas a bit more than it should because I remember last night's discussion pretty much in the terms of what I was trying to say." He informed Hellman that on the boat to Europe Ivens would have the treatment which she could "tear into at your leisure."[42]

The treatment called for the film to open in a village on the road to Valencia as King Alfonso flees Madrid by car in the middle of the night. A landowner's family, including "his soldier son, his priest son," and military officers, a money lender, and others, respond to the king's abdication with "trepidation"; the commoners, including a doctor, a pharmacist, the schoolmaster, and union field, factory, and railroad laborers, express some confusion but also hope. Then the sequence turns "at last to our family, a family of peasants, ignorant of the significance of the event but touched by the excitement."[43] The next sequence covers two years and observes tensions rising between the workers and villagers on one side, and the landowner and military post on the other. Efforts to build a new school and dig an irrigation system "create conflicts between the new proposals and the old property rights"—those "new proposals" being the Republic's agrarian reform and secularized public education initiatives.[44]

During the building of the school, the family sends one of its sons to fetch a tool from the landowner where he "stumbles upon a cache of rifles in a granary of the house." The rifles are German. The film shows the viewer a Berlin meeting of "Spanish officers and Nazi officials. We glance at Italy, perhaps at Portugal. We follow these rifles into the hands of the fascist group in the village, who drill with them." Fighting breaks out: "Our family, against its will, is drawn into the fighting. The father is killed, the house is burned." The rest of the family flees the village for Mardrid, where it realizes that the village's struggle "is part of a great struggle which has shape and purpose." The son joins a militia and marches out of Madrid back to his village: "The film ends with the recapture of the village schoolhouse, still roofless, the boy, rifle in hand, on the walls he has helped to build, understanding now the significance of what he was building."[45]

MacLeish's Christmas Eve letter to Hellman explores how they might craft letters seeking financial support. The rhetoric MacLeish recommends is corrective: "We are trying to correct the rebel propaganda which has filled American papers. . . . We have no propaganda purpose save this one anti-propaganda purpose." Specifically, and to allay concerns that siding with the Republic means endorsing communism, MacLeish wants to rebut what he regards as the rebel's successful characterization of the war in the oversimplifying terms of a fascist struggle against communism:

> The fact is, of course, that there are so few Fascists that the Fascist leaders have been forced to depend upon Moroccans, Germans and Italians. The further fact is that there are only between forty and eighty thousand Communists in all Spain, including Barcelona, and that the great majority of the Popular Front is made up of such non-radical elements as Basque nationalists, who are Catholic, Republican groups and the like.[46]

The presence of communists and anarchists within the government, he notes, is a matter of democratic necessity given the effectiveness of these groups.

The desire to inform the American public of the situation's political complexity was admirable, especially his hope to disentangle the strong associations of Catalonia (Barcelona) with communism and the Republican cause with anti-Catholicism. Oddly, the film he envisioned would have depoliticized the war: "For this purpose we plan to make and show a moving picture which will pick up a characteristic village and a characteristic family in that village and show the background and impact of the Civil War in terms of the actual life of the most characteristic element of the people."[47]

On Saturday, 26 December 1936, Ivens and Hellman boarded the *Normandie* along with the ninety-six young men forming the first contingent of the Abraham Lincoln Battalion,[48] arriving in France on New Year's Eve.[49] The American volunteer soldiers for the Republic had been organized by the Communist Party of the United States of America (CPUSA) and, according to Cecil D. Eby, funded through "'front' organizations like the North American Committee to Aid Spanish Democracy, whose members in most cases would not know that they were supporting the battalion, much less that the CPUSA was whistling the tune that both of them danced to."[50] The volunteers belonged either to the CPUSA or the Young Communist League (YCL), and they provided various destinations other than Spain to the authorities.[51] Though they were supposed to maintain their many fictions, and their eighteen-year-old assistant commander patrolled the decks breaking up clusters of six or more men, "it must have been perfectly clear to everyone aboard ship who they were and where they were going."[52] Ivens and Hellman must have known with whom they were traveling, and perhaps the volunteers' leadership knew of either or both of them (they may have all shared a funding source). The men defied orders to behave themselves in other ways, drinking heavily and consorting with the "statuesque girls of the Folies Bergères"—"bourgeois parasites" according to their commander: "The seamen, if their tales contained even a grain of truth, broke sexual records with the girls on their crossing."[53] Once in France the men were rushed to the train station, where they joined other international volunteers on the way to Spain, their travel organized by the French Communist Party.[54]

Ivens spent his time in Paris getting organized and securing his relationship with the Spanish Republic through the embassy. The Spanish filmmaker Luis Buñuel, an acquaintance whose work included the 1934 social documentary *Land without Bread* and who belonged to L'Association des Écrivains et des Artistes Révolutionnaires, was serving as the Republic's Minister of Propaganda in Paris. Ivens agreed to provide a copy of the footage to Buñuel for inspection at the embassy's expense, probably as a concession for gaining government support.[55] From the embassy Ivens would have received the necessary safe-conduct papers as well as (probably) permission to meet with military commanders and political operatives and to obtain material and technical support from the union-operated Madrid-Film company.[56] An undated draft for a wire to MacLeish reported "most favourable possibilities and help from Government."[57] Hellman meanwhile had caught pneumonia and returned home instead of accompanying Ivens and Ferno to Spain.[58]

Ivens and Ferno shot their first footage at Valencia on 21 January. According to his not-always-reliable memoir, Ivens realized immediately that MacLeish's treatment would not work:

> This is the sort of documentary script you might imagine can be filmed—only when you are very far away from the war-torn country of your script. . . .
>
> How could we ask people who had fought in the fields and in the trenches around Madrid to help reconstruct the atmosphere of King Alfonso's abdication? These people were too deeply involved in their fight to think about how a typical village had behaved before the war. We felt shame at not having realized this. One could not possibly ask people who were engaged in a life and death struggle to be interested in anything outside that struggle.

Moreover, Ivens discovered that while the government permitted him some access to military leaders, it lacked an effective agency for information or propaganda for substantial assistance: "There was neither informal nor organized propaganda into which a subtle half-fictional, half-documentary film could be fitted."[59] The propagandistic intent for the film is here clearly admitted—as is, however, the fact that the crew would be more-or-less on its own in producing and distributing the film. Gellhorn's account of the correspondents' situation accords with Ivens's of his filming. With no public relations officer or any other entity tending to the press, "It was very much a do-it-yourself war . . . we'd get some petrol, run to taxis . . . we just sailed around. We would either hear with our ears something was going on, or we'd hear by rumour that there was a push or a battle or something, and we just got to it." They didn't even have identity cards.[60]

Ivens and Ferno drove to Madrid on 22 January, where they continued filming and familiarizing themselves with the situation and the players. In those four weeks, through 17 February, they accomplished a good deal of filming, among other things, of the evacuation of civilian populations from Madrid to Valencia; of Enrique Lister's first Mixed Brigade, then southwest of Madrid; of University City with artillery shelling of the clinic; of the removal of art from the Duke of Alva's Palace of Liria museum; of exercises by the CNT militia on the grand boulevard; of barricades around Madrid; of the Garibaldi battalion; of the hospital in Valencia; and of an aerial bombardment of the nonmilitarized village of Morata de Tajuña.[61] The people fled the village, and after the bombing Ferno filmed even more as they returned:

> The women looked bewildered, their hands over their bellies in the agony of shock—not yet knowing what had happened. We filmed them not realizing that we were being brutal but feeling we had to get those pictures. . . . We found two women picking up a baby. We saw other women unconscious of their movements, simply holding handkerchiefs over their eyes. We filmed some dead. Women looking from a window. Little kids playing with parts of a rifle.[62]

A couple of weeks earlier, on 26 January, they had filmed a "grand meeting" at a movie theater, the Salle de Goya, where a number of prominent Republican leaders had gathered to celebrate the incorporation of the many organizational militias into a unified Popular Army. Gustav Regler was there, and spoke, as were Vittorio Vidali, or "Carlos," the political commissar of the fifth regiment; Pietro Nenni, political commissar of the Garibali Brigade; José Díaz; Cayetano Redondo Aceña, the mayor of Madrid; Dolores Ibárruri, or "La Pasionaria," the charismatic woman and communist party member who had become a symbol for the Republican defenders; and Francisco Antón, commissar of the Army of the Center, secretary of the Madrid communist party, and Ibárurri's lover (younger by twenty years).[63]

Ivens and Ferno also spent three days in February filming the fighting for the Valencia-Madrid Road toward Arganda, in the early days of the battle of Jarama, and the fighting that *The Spanish Earth* captures as the climactic battle for the Arganda Bridge, just south of (and closer to) Vaciamadrid on the way to Arganda (and Fuentedueña and eventually Valencia). The Nationalists' offensive began on 6 February, and for the next three days they fought to cross the Jarama River. According to a Soviet paper,[64] on 8 February the Nationalists captured a bridge across the Manzaneres to the north of the Jarama (west of Vaciamadrid) that the Republicans recaptured the next day. This is probably the action described by Regler in his memoir, when "the Moors descended from the plateau in the south-east . . . and crossed the Manzaneres to cut off the Arganda bridge and the road to Valencia"—so they occupied an area north of the river between Madrid and the Arganda Bridge, "very near to the Valencia Road" according to the Soviet paper, without actually winning the bridge or the road. "During the night that followed the disaster, Pacciardi and his 'Garibaldi' battalion drove the Moors back and secured the road to Valencia."[65]

Ivens's shooting chronology puts him and Ferno in this vicinity on 10 and 11 February, the dates of a fight for yet another bridge, this one across the Jarama south of the Manzaneres and west of the Madrid-Valencia road. This fight commenced when a unit of Moors knifed the French sentries to death around dawn allowing the Nationalists to seize the Pindoque railway bridge.[66] The republicans tried to blow the bridge with previously stationed explosives, but it rose a few feet and settled back down. The Italian Garibaldi Battalion stopped the Nationalist advance though apparently did not recapture that bridge (less likely it was the event described by Regler). Ivens's notes indicate the filming of the "Garribali" battalion in formation. For a second time, the Nationalists failed to win the Arganda Bridge or seize the road. Ivens and Ferno returned to Arganda on 17 February, at the time of another Republican counterattack.[67] The final film most likely compresses these several days into what feels to be a single action, drawing on all of this footage and probably representative footage filmed elsewhere.

Back in Paris in late February, Ivens showed some of his developed footage (of roughly twelve thousand meters) to a select group, where he told this story about one of the scenes caught on film while under fire:

> We were on the front. They had to attack a position which put us under continuous gunfire. A [grenade] explodes behind us on the inhuman short distance of 5 yards. We could not film an exploding [grenade]. It is impossible that any cameraman can film an exploding [grenade] on such a short distance and instinctively when bombs and shells exploded in our immediate surrounding—also this time—we brought the maybe protecting piece of metal that our camera was, before our face.
>
> A second later we look and see that the commander of the Garribaldi-Brigade is wounded in the face. I throw him from behind

> my low shelter my handkerchief. To go to him was impossible on account of the heavy firing by the fascists. Pietro Nenni, political Commissar of the Italians of this Brigade is next to the commander and bandaged his face and then the commander raises and calls to his men: "Avanti!" and his troops storm forward.[68]

This scene—we see the bandaging and the bandaged commander directing his troops in *The Spanish Earth*—most likely occurred during the battle for the bridge on 11 February. That battle involved the Garibaldi Battalion and Ivens's shooting summary for that day includes a note for "Commandant Garribaldi" followed by an illegible word that could be *grenade* or *gunshot.*[69] The wounded commander was Randolfo Pacciardi, a dashing Italian who would later develop a fancy for Martha Gellhorn.[70]

Hemingway, not landing at Havre until after the first week of March,[71] happened to miss this first screening.[72] It's also probably the case that the negatives left Paris for New York before he had a chance to view them in Paris. Ivens telegraphed MacLeish on 26 April that he was shipping them "next week" aboard the *Queen Mary,* which left on 3 March and arrived in New York on 9 March, passing Hemingway going the other way.[73]

Hemingway's first experience filming *The Spanish Earth* occurred at Guadalajara shortly after he and Ivens landed in Spain at Valencia. (Ferno probably left Paris ahead of them.[74]) They got to the battlefield soon enough to at least obtain shots of the Italian dead and of the scattered letters to which his dispatch refers. These are the dead in the two photos identical but for Hemingway's presence; these are the dead who thought they were earning extra money for minor police action in Ethiopia. Ivens's stories of meeting villagers behind the lines inspired Regler "to show him the front at once." Regler recalls Ivens telling him that "you and the peasants will be the heroes, you, the nameless, and they who until yesterday were landless." And he began filming:

> He filmed the bursting of shells from a dangerously short distance, and said that he intended to follow these with explosions of a different kind, which were to make it look as though the shells in this war had tapped new springs, causing water to flow through land

> that for centuries had been neglected by its wealthy landowners. The owners were gambling away their money in Hendaye [France], and Ivens intended to go there and film them as they were, overfed and weary with idleness. He was still not afraid of plain black-and-white. "The world *is* black and white!" he said. "Look!" And he produced photographs out of his case of peasants kissing the soil that was at last to be rendered fruitful again—seared and wrinkled faces now wreathed in a new smile. "Faces like the earth itself."[75]

If Ivens ever filmed the fat cats of Hendaye, no such scenes made the final cut. And assuming Regler's memoir fairly accurate in spirit and detail, it reveals an early vision for interweaving the war and the irrigation narratives, and even the kind of language the film would employ.

The next morning Ivens showed Regler "a picture of the open space in front of a hotel, under a bright sun. Beside a black hole in the plaster a man lay with his face to the ground in a dark pool." Ivens told Regler what he already knew, that the Nationalist army "deliberately only shoot one shell a day into town . . . to keep everyone in a state of fear." His comment that "Hemingway will explain it" must refer to the American writer's dispatches to the outside world. "And now I'm going to photograph the peasants, over there behind Arganda. Perhaps I shall be able to get some who dare to come out and do their ploughing at night. That will be another symbol of the dirtiness of this war—ploughing in secret, as though it were a crime!" In Arganda's town hall, Hemingway met with a group of "demoralized" soldiers, the French survivors of the defense of the Madrid-Valencia road (the Arganda Bridge). "They recognized him at once as one of themselves. He started by offering them a flask of whiskey. Then he asked about the battle." Afterward, "they invited him to accompany them to the bridge" that led back to the front line. They wanted others to see them return to the fight of their own accord. They headed off, some rifleless. "They passed in straggling formation through the entrance to Death Alley. They would not let him march at the head of the column; he followed them as though he had just been drafted."[76]

Snow and sleet had turned the battle of Guadalajara into a cold, muddy mess. It was still bitter when the film crew showed up; Hemingway ate the raw onions he carried in his jacket pockets, to Ivens's and Ferno's displeasure, though they helped him polish off his whiskey flask every day by late afternoon.[77] In a short letter wired to MacLeish in late March or early April, Ivens reported, "These few days weather conditions bad," so it had been "only possible [to] film quiet front Italian casualties." He then proposed producing two films—one with the material sent aboard the *Queen Mary*, which "could be released in middle April, and village picture as second picture middle of May."[78] On 7 April, MacLeish rejected the idea. He had seen the initial footage and believed the film's potential "MUCH TOO GOOD" to be "CUT INTO SHORTS." He was "CERTAIN HEMINGWAY AND DOS CAN SUPPLY SOME SORT CONTINUITY" to help Ivens turn the initial footage and the new material into a "FEATURE LENGTH PICTURE ON HIS RETURN STOP DOS SHOULD ARRIVE IMMEDIATELY."[79]

For the next five weeks, Ivens, Hemingway, Ferno, Dos Passos, Franklin, and their sundry drivers and occasional hangers-on filmed the rest of what would become *The Spanish Earth*. Not only was Hemingway a good grip, "carrying anything that had to be carried" and "taking orders willingly," he also helped Ivens in "talking over how to film a battle" and "with what you might call the general strategy of the film."[80]

In short order, spring hit with a vengeance. In the heat, Hemingway later wrote, "you ran with cameras, sweating, taking cover in the folds of the terrain on the bare hills. There was dust in your nose, and dust in your hair and in your eyes, and you had the great thirst for water, the real dry-mouth that only battle brings." As they filmed the combat west and south of Madrid, he worried that Ivens and Ferno "would be killed if they kept on because they took too many chances," and his own "moral problem was always to get clear how much you were holding them back from necessary and just prudence, based on experience, and how much was simply the not so pretty prudence of the burnt monkey who dreads hot soup."[81] Gustav Regler and Werner Heilbrun continued to provide assistance. Dr. Heilbrun, with his "slanting smile, the cap cocked on the side, [and] the slow, comic Berlin Jewish drawl," supplied food and gasoline and ran them to the action, and "when all the rest of us were dead with sleep, Heilbrun would do his work; the work he did so well, so intelligently, so painstakingly, so delicately and skillfully, and always with the languid air of doing nothing."[82] Heilbrun became in death the hero of Hemingway's two post-film commentaries, "The Heat and the Cold" essay and his remarks at fundraisers after showing *The Spanish Earth*.[83]

Sidney Franklin's fame as a bullfighter made him a perfect factotum, enabling him to secure "gasoline, passes to the front, and transportation for the crew when all other methods failed."[84] George Seldes, who thought Franklin "funny but really stupid" and so a strange "bosom pal" for Hemingway other than his slavish devotion, nevertheless acknowledged his utility: "Hemingway returned from the Int'l Brigade front one day telling us what terrible scenes he had witnessed in the hospital. There was not a sharp hypodermic needle available, the wounded were suffering inhumanly. Hem asked Franklin if he could get some hypodermic needles—Franklin replied he would get some if any existed—if he had to steal them. And he got them, and Hemingway went back to the front and delivered them."[85] Gellhorn also helped the care effort by transporting blood to battalion aid stations in a station wagon and by writing letters for the wounded.[86] During this second round of filming, the crew also shot more shelling and life-goes-on scenes on the streets and in the trenches of Madrid, as well as the village scenes from Fuentedueña.

In a July 1937 interview Ivens credits Ferno with discovering Fuentedueña.[87] The village fit their plans because of its location along the strategically important road from Madrid south to Valencia (the new capital of the Republic) and because the villagers had only recently acquired the land from the landlords and were preparing to irrigate it for the first time.[88] Much of their time the crew spent familiarizing themselves with the villagers and gaining their trust simply by hanging around, at the inns for example, "learning more than just their names and the names of their kids." Dos Passos, the only member of the crew who spoke Spanish, played the critical role of facilitating communication.[89] And while some of the shots captured scenes as they happened, a number were "re-enacted," even invented. Julian, the film's peasant protagonist, an actual young man from the village serving in the defense of Madrid, appears in the final film as a very nearly fictional character.

The reenactment of Julian's return from Madrid "naturally developed into a whole real scene of Julian's homecoming, with three generations meeting him in front of their home, and Julian's little brother calling his father from the vine field." But they were not real at all; Ivens admits that some of the shots "seemed a little stiff and awkward."[90]

The final film would move away a great deal from the treatment MacLeish composed after brainstorming with Ivens back in New York, primarily in ditching the historical trajectory. But it preserved the focus on a rural family, including the villagers' undertaking of an irrigation project. Around this time, probably the second or third week of April after the filming at Fuentedueña was underway—and perhaps even later than that—a very short new outline emerged. The new vision captures the essentials of the final film, including "collective work on an irrigation project," the young man's returning on leave and his training the village boys, and the general "parallel between the irrigation project being completed and the fighting for independence, the freedom of that earth." This one-paragraph plan does not name Fuentedueña or Julian, but it does place the village "25 kilometers" away from the front—the same distance as Fuentedueña—and it provided the "continuity" that enabled a single feature film.[91]

Ivens and Dos Passos departed Madrid on 25 April. The next day Ivens wrote Hemingway from Valencia. He asked Hemingway to "look after" Ferno and Franklin, who he hoped had only two or three more days of filming to do in Fuentedueña. He also expressed his concerns about Dos Passos, who was making a lot of noise about the Robles execution. "He is running here for the same cause as he did in Madrid—it is difficult. Del Vayo [Alvarez del Vayo, Minister of Foreign Affairs] spoke to him about it. Hope that Dos will see what a man and comrade has to do in these difficult and serious wartimes."[92] Dos Passos remained, however, a supportive member of the film team. When Ivens asked him to keep any interview comments about the picture to a "minimum," and proposed to write the "dialogue and talk in the film" with Hemingway, he was agreeable. On 28 April, Ivens wired from Paris to stress the necessity of getting shots of the Lincoln Battalion.[93] He sailed aboard the *Ile de France* for New York on 5 May.[94]

Presumably Hemingway spent some time his last week in Spain

filming with Ferno and Franklin. He and Gellhorn left the first week of May and let Ferno wrap up,[95] getting to New York on 18 May, where Gellhorn caught up with Ivens to assist with the picture and where Hemingway eventually joined them. But first he needed to spend some time with his family.

Ivens took a break from piecing the film together to visit the Hemingways in Key West for a few days from 30 May to 3 June. He and Hemingway then headed back to New York together on 3 June to make an important engagement: Hemingway's first public speech and the first public viewing of the film in progress, *The Spanish Earth*.

Friday night, 4 June 1937, at Carnegie Hall, "some 360 U.S. novelists, poets, critics, and journalists, and several times as many onlookers" gathered at Carnegie Hall for the second National American Writers' Congress organized by the League of American Writers.[96] Ivens accompanied Hemingway from Key West and perhaps played a role in getting him on the agenda, though there is no evidence that he orchestrated the whole affair, as some biographers have claimed.[97] Gellhorn, who gave her own speech the next day, wrote to Eleanor Roosevelt her amazement that the hall was "jammed" and "3500 and more turned away at the door," all just "to hear writers."[98] Among those 360 were Van Wyck Brooks, Carl Van Doren, playwright Marc Connelly, Archibald MacLeish, journalist Vincent Sheean, Donald Ogden Stewart, Walter Duranty (*New York Times* correspondent in Moscow), John Gunther, Thornton Wilder, Earl Russell Browder (of the Communist Party), Joseph North (editor of *New Masses*), Anna Louise Strong, and Muriel Draper. Sidney Franklin also made it, as did Prudencio de Pereda and a future Abraham Lincoln Brigade member, Alvah Bessie, whom Hemingway would meet during the 1938 spring retreat across the Ebro. (In 1950 Bessie became one of the "Hollywood Ten" blacklisted by the House Un-American Activities Committee.)

Hemingway arrived late for his speech on 4 June—about ten o'clock p.m.—and waiting backstage to follow Duranty muttered to himself, "Why the hell am I making a speech?"[99] Then he stepped on stage. One witness described Hemingway's intense nervousness, observing both his sweat and his impatience for the applause to be done: "It was magnificent. As if everyone had taken him into their arms—truly a companion in arms in the fight against fascism. How could this fight be lost now, with Hemingway on our side? Thousands must have felt this way—he was a man to be loved."[100]

Paul Romaine's enthusiasm for Hemingway and estimation of his influence was shared by others, including Prudencio de Pereda, who called his idol's performance a "triumph." To de Pereda's recollection "it was the speech of the meeting. The audience had come for Ernest; he was there for them. He lapped up the warm acceptance." Hemingway was nervous and his presentation somewhat awkward, as even de Pereda acknowledged, but "all that just seemed to tone him up."[101] The American supporters for the Republic gathered at Carnegie had clearly not given up hope. "When men fight for the freedom of their country against a foreign invasion," Hemingway said that night, "and when these men are your friends—some new friends and some of long standing—and you know how they were attacked and how they fought, at first almost unarmed, you learn, watching them live and fight and die, that there are worse things than war."[102]

The reporter covering the showing of the film for *Time* couldn't resist cutesy editorializing:

> Because it was a congress of writers, everything was a little disorganized: the film began unwinding before Ivens had introduced it, and it was only after some difficulty that Chairman MacLeish managed to get it stopped. The sound had not been put into the picture, so occasionally through the hot silence the ghostly voice of Photographer Ivens would be heard saying, "At this point you would hear machine guns." But also because this was a congress of writers, they filled such gaps with their imaginations, responded with enthusiasm to some brilliant photography, much of it taken under fire, of the shelling of University City, and of Madrid streets, and an air raid on Morata.[103]

The next day Hemingway retreated to Bimini, and de Pereda wrote to congratulate him on his "great speech last night! God damn it, hombre, you've got everything!" And in a postscript, he asked to help in whatever "menial" way on the picture, even offering to pay Hemingway for the "privilege."[104] I doubt Hemingway took any money, though he and Ivens let de Pereda write the first draft of the commentary.

The second and third weeks of June were quite busy in New York. Ivens and Helen Van Dongen, with Gellhorn's help, cut the majority of the film and maintained communications with Hemingway. On 15 and 16 June, Tuesday and Wednesday, Ivens sent him two telegrams, the first promising editing recommendations for the commentary to be sent the next day and the second reporting the news from the *Times* of Lukács's death and Regler's grave wounding.[105] He wrote his detailed thoughts about the film on Thursday. De Pereda had already completed his draft. Ivens's rejection of de Pereda's treatment of the earth "as a kind of symbol before republic came" refers to a passage in de Pereda's script:[106]

> The first note to be expressed in the picture is one of hard, dry barreness, that was the characteristic of the monarchy and the near-dead first Republic. We show this in the hard, grey, lumpy earth. We show this, too, in the hard, wind-swept face of the peasant faces. We are going to show through this picture how change had been wrought. . . . In the first scene, immediately after the commentator in English has said, "The Spanish face is hard, is dry," we show how the faces break into conversation, the hardness softens into a flow of speech.[107]

That flow of speech subtly corresponds to the coming flow of water through the irrigation project and the symbolic rejuvenation of the land, the people, and the country. Ivens's suggestions for the opening at this point change very little of de Pereda's effect: the two peasants still talk in Spanish; they still talk about the necessity of supplying food for the war.

The final film loses this conversation and will not mention the war for several minutes. Hemingway's revisions to de Pereda's typescript, at this stage, are in kind. In many respects he simply recasts the language. As an immediate example, Hemingway changes de Pereda's opening two lines, "The Spanish earth is hard, is dry" and "The Spanish face is hard, is dry," to a single line: "In Spain the earth is dry and hard and the faces of the men who work that earth are hard and dried from the sun."[108] The rest of de Pereda's draft reveals any number of similar recastings—Hemingway's revisions look more extensive than they actually are, for while he rewrote much of the commentary, he left some of it alone, and most of his rewrites preserve some of the language and much of the spirit of de Pereda's effort. Of course, de Pereda was fitting his narration to a first draft of the visual sequence, and he was also trying to write like Hemingway (a task his imitative fiction prepared him for) based, as he says, on his experience with Hemingway on "Spain in Flames."

Neither de Pereda's extant draft nor Ivens's letter go much farther than the speeches in the Salle de Goya scene; Ivens closes by promising the rest of his comments the next day and requesting word of when he will receive Hemingway's final version: "All my recording plans depend on it, all our tempo."[109] On 18 June, Gellhorn wired to press Hemingway to come soon, for three days, as the film was behind schedule.[110] The next day Ivens reported having completed the editing and pleaded to Hemingway to fly up Monday, 21 June.[111] An undated missive from Hemingway to Gellhorn asks her to tell Ivens that he would indeed be on hand that Monday.[112] Meanwhile, MacLeish was trying to sell unused film segments to raise more money.[113]

The first round of recording took place on 22 and 23 June.[114] MacLeish brought in Orson Welles to speak the commentary. At age nineteen, Welles had starred in MacLeish's 1935 play *Panic* and two years later as the announcer in his radioplay "The Fall of the City," and MacLeish had helped arrange financing for Welles's upstart Mercury Theatre.[115] MacLeish would also have been responsible for recruiting the composers Marc Blitzstein and Virgil Thomson, both of whom were politically sympathetic and both of whom worked with Welles at the Mercury.[116] Welles once told an interviewer that he and Hemingway came to blows during this work, because Welles thought some lines "pompous and complicated" and told Hemingway as much. And because Welles was involved with avant-garde theater, Hemingway "thought I was some kind of faggot and said, 'You—effeminate boys of the theatre, what do you know about real war?'"

> Taking the bull by the horns, I began to make effeminate gestures and I said to him, "Mister Hemingway, how strong you are and how

> big you are!" That enraged him and he picked up a chair; I picked up another and, right there, in front of the images of the Spanish Civil War, as they marched across the screen, we had a terrible scuffle. It was something marvelous: two guys like us in front of these images representing people in the act of struggling and dying . . . we ending up by toasting each other over a bottle of whiskey.[117]

De Pereda denied that the quarrel happened, though his denial is not completely convincing, especially in the context of his rose-colored perspective of Hemingway.[118] Apocryphal or not, it's a great story. Hemingway was back in Florida by 29 June, though probably earlier.[119]

Welles's wasn't the only voice recorded for the film. A list of "Needed spanish voices" has names written for most of the "characters" in the film, including three speechmakers at the Salle de Goya: Díaz, La Pasionara, and Lister.[120] That Vidali, Regler, Nenni, and the Málaga delegate do not appear on this list is explained by the fact that, according to Ivens's shot notes, they spent part of the day after the event in a Madrid sound studio[121]—thus their voices in the film are probably authentic. Various budgets also include line items for actors in Spain, France, and New York.[122] The production team also arranged to have sound effects made for everything: different kinds of weapons fire, different kinds of explosions, shattering glass, tank and truck movement, soldiers hustling up a staircase, splashing water, sirens. Irving Reis directed this process. "Two nights ago," Gellhorn wrote to Eleanor Roosevelt, "we worked with three sound engineers in the lab at the Columbia Broadcasting, and we made the sound of incoming shells with a football bladder and an air hose and fingernails snapping against a screen, all tremendously magnified and it sounds so like a shell that we were scared out of our wits."[123] An earthquake effect from the film *San Francisco* was run backwards to mimic a bombardment, and "Shell explosions that actually take one-fifth of a second we stretched out five times as long."[124]

The days for Gellhorn, Ivens, and Van Dongen were long and exhausting and stretched into weeks. A master print of the final film was ready on either 2 or 3 July. Even after that date Gellhorn and Ivens continued their efforts to secure special screenings and to land a major distributor. Gellhorn tried and failed, for example, with NBC and Columbia. But through her friendship with the Roosevelts she secured a dinner and private showing at the White House on 8 July, the first time anyone outside its creative team saw the complete film.[125]

President Roosevelt said nothing for several minutes, then offered that the film "holds up well even without a story," which Ivens thought "showed a good instinct for documentary films." He asked about the performance of the French and Russian tanks, about Brihuega, and other military details. Afterwards he expressed his liking for the film but also his inability to comment publicly on it.[126] Ivens and Gellhorn both concluded that the president sided with the Republic, but the international and national situations prevented him from taking even humanitarian action.[127] He did suggest that more attention be paid not just to the republicans' "fight for the right to their own government, but also for the right to bring under cultivation those great tracts of land which the old system forcibly left barren."[128] His wife apparently shared this concern; that night already back in New York, Gellhorn wrote to tell Mrs. Roosevelt that Hemingway and Ivens "were impressed that you and Mr. Roosevelt said to make it stronger—that's what it amounted to—by underlining the causes of the conflict."[129] And the next day in her regular column Eleanor Roosevelt wrote that the filmmakers "presuppose too much knowledge on the audience's part of old world conditions."[130] According to Ivens, Lillian Hellman shared this objection, but the desire for "wide theatrical release" led them to avoid overdoing the "political" or "educational" information.[131] Ivens, Hemingway, and Gellhorn also realized that they needed to rely on the film's visual impact—the faces of desperation, the bombings, the maimed, the dead. They were following a decade's worth of photographic social documentary based on the principle that talk bores and images inspire.

On Sunday, 11 July, Ivens, Hemingway, and Pauline flew to Hollywood for several engagements set up by Ivens, including a private affair at the home of Frederic March on Monday, a screening to a full house of 3,500 at the Philharmonic Auditorium on Tuesday, and later in the week at the homes of Joan Crawford (and Franchot Tone), John Ford, and Darryl Zanuck.[132] March, who the following year would narrate Ivens's China documentary *The 400 Million*, invited a number of friends to his home theater, including Robert Montgomery, Luise Rainer, Silvia Sidney, Miriam Hopkins, Lewis Milestone, Alan Campbell, Dorothy Parker, Fritz Lang, Anatol Litvak, Ernst Lubitsch, Lillian Hellman, King Vidor, Dashiell Hammett, Arthur Kober, Errol Flynn, Joan Bennett, Donald Ogden Stewart, and Lionel Stander.[133] F. Scott Fitzgerald was there. Dudley Nichols, who would draft *The 400 Million* commentary, was probably also there. After the film, Ivens gave the speech Hemingway had written. Sixteen of the guests contributed one thousand dollars each, enough for sixteen ambulances. One guest who did not pay, Errol Flynn, snuck out a bathroom window.[134]

The other business conducted in Los Angeles was the recording of a new narration. Few if anyone cared for Welles's. Gellhorn bemoaned that the "awful voice . . . mangle[d]" Hemingway's "beautiful" writing;[135] apparently the Roosevelts hadn't like it either.[136] Hemingway purportedly said that "every time Orson said the word 'infantry' it sounded like a cocksucker swallowing,"[137] and he offered to pay for a new recording despite the fact that the film and the ambulances had already financially drained him.[138] If anything, Welles's narration was understated, a perfectly articulated and simple reading, yet the very smoothness of his voice may have indeed worked against the message of the film. As Ivens reflected, "There was something in the quality of his voice that separated itself from the film, from Spain, from the actuality of the film."[139] It did not evoke the working class and the rough nature of Spanish life but the other end of the class spectrum—the cultivated, the rich, in a word: the enemy.

De Pereda claimed to be the first to suggest that Hemingway record the narration, even before Welles had been recorded. Having heard Hemingway read it aloud several times, he didn't imagine Welles could improve upon the original.[140] Helen Van Dongen remembered thinking that Welles's voice "wrecked the film" and asking Hemingway to read his own narration. "'If you can write it you can read it,' I told him. He did, and it was wonderful."[141] Ivens, whose memoir does not mention de Pereda a single time, credited other Contemporary Historians—Hellman, Parker, and Herman Shumlin—with the idea.[142] Hemingway had two other motivations: time and money. In

Hollywood they had the use, for two days, of a Paramount recording room at no cost.[143] The opportunity was there. Taking the time to find the right voice for the right price of the simple privilege of doing it was not really an option. The film had to be ready for its commercial premier on 20 August at the 55th Street Playhouse in New York.[144]

Ivens and the Hemingways were back in New York from Hollywood by 17 July. After taking Pauline to Key West, Hemingway returned through New York on his second trip to Spain. He missed opening night by six days.[145]

From beginning to end, the creation of *The Spanish Earth* was a collaborative process.[146] Ivens clearly steered the group. On 10 June, with the editing well along, MacLeish wrote to Hemingway asking his support for naming Ivens the president of the board, a position MacLeish held at the time only nominally. For MacLeish, Ivens was running the show and ought to have his authority formalized, particularly for the purpose of arranging for the film's distribution: "The corporation so far as I am concerned is Joris Ivens, Inc., whatever we choose to call it."[147] Hemingway objected to the book version, for one reason—as Jasper Wood noted on the second printing—because "it gives him credit for a film the credit for which should go to Joris Ivens and John Ferno."[148]

Yet Ivens himself recognized Hemingway's contribution beyond mere gruntwork to the filming process in the spring. When he left in late April, he left Hemingway to supervise Ferno and Franklin, and in writing to Hemingway gave them some latitude to respond to the dynamic situation.[149] Hemingway wasn't in New York for all of the cutting and editing that June, but when present he was, according to de Pereda, the heart of the project, "it was he who gave it the wonder touch."[150] Even as an inflation of Hemingway's direct role, de Pereda's view still speaks to the energy, the spirit, the cohesive element that Hemingway brought to the group. De Pereda's letter to Hemingway during the second World War, requesting a recommendation for transfer to the Army Signal Corps to help produce documentaries, suggests either the extent of his exaggerating imagination concerning Hemingway, the extent of his fawning, or the real possibility that Hemingway and Ivens collaborated on somewhat more equal terms than is generally supposed:

"They're doing unusual work with film and all the fine documentaries they do—their best work—derive principally from the real innovations that you put into THE SPANISH EARTH. I keep getting pleasant surprises whenever I see one of them and notice all these great new things about them and then think back to when I saw you make them for the first time in any film."[151]

De Pereda wrote the first draft of the commentary. Yes, he and Hemingway were following Ivens's cutting of the film draft, and Ivens certainly provided guidance and feedback. Still, their work was theirs and must have influenced the way Ivens and Helen Van Dongen thought about the picture. We've already seen that Ivens generally accepted the opening dialogue and focus. Van Dongen, by all accounts a superior editor and Ivens's technical collaborator, would have had her say, too. Hemingway watched the rushes several times and worked with her as well as Ivens as he prepared the narration.[152] As one film historian has written, Ivens and Van Dongen "worked on equal terms as joint creators, a collaboration which has been one of the most fruitful in history."[153] Van Dongen took credit for pouring over the footage and discovering the link "between the labourers in the field and the soldiers whom their labour fed."[154] If it's hard to imagine the confident Martha Gellhorn keeping her thoughts to herself during those long June days in New York, Van Dongen in a later interview didn't remember Gellhorn being around much at all.[155] Dos Passos had fallen out of favor with Ivens over the Robles affair—"keep Dos Passos out" Ivens scribbled on the back of a telegram from Hollywood prior to the fund-raising trip[156]—but he was a cooperative presence during the editing and an important collaborator back in Spain. He not only served as translator between the crew and the villagers, and surely added his two cents about the filming, but he also participated in discussions about the film's main message, by his account convincing the others that "instead of . . . a blood and guts picture we ought to find something being built for the future amid all the misery and the massacre." The group "settled on an irrigation scheme being put through by a village collective."[157]

Had he made this suggestion back in December, when a village irrigation project first appeared in MacLeish's treatment? Had he pressed the point in the spring, perhaps after MacLeish's insistence on producing a single film (an insistence that reveals a great deal about MacLeish's weight in the collaboration)? Does he misremember or exaggerate his role? Stephen Koch derides his contribution as "some innocuous footage" that "wasn't much, but it was something other than war."[158] Hardly inconsequential bits of footage by which Ivens appeased Dos Passos, the irrigation project was there from the beginning and is in fact the very lynchpin of the film. We learn about it before we see any fighting, the film climaxes with its completion as a symbolic result of the military victory, and the issue of irrigation was one of the historic bases for the conflict between the peasants and the landowners. "For 50 years we've wanted to irrigate, but they held us back," Hemingway intones for the Spanish peasants in the opening sequence. According to Ivens, he and Hemingway incorporated the Roosevelts' advice to strengthen the historical nature of the conflict by having Hemingway's narration emphasize the word *they* "hatefully."[159]

John T. McManus tells a different story in his *New York Times* review. According to McManus, Ivens initially wanted to focus on "the relation of a people to their agricultural life, and the determination to maintain that relationship in a state of war," a plan that "has been thrown off balance" by the war story. He blames the Contemporary Historians, Ivens's "employers," who have used Ivens's "product as they see fit. They have used it as a violent outcry against fascism. Ivens might have made it lasting art as well."[160] I don't know McManus's source for this version of the story. Perhaps Ivens told this tale to scapegoat his collaborators for the anticipated criticism of the film as propaganda; perhaps the tale is just true enough—true enough anyway to support an argument about the film's collaborative nature. Another *Times* article from the fall of 1937 credits Hemingway with the commentary and MacLeish and Hellman with the "story-pattern."[161]

Ivens in his memoir tells the story of watching the editing of *Spain—A Fight for Freedom* and observing that a better film could be made. From his observation, Ivens says, MacLeish proposed just such a film.[162] Hellman also names MacLeish as the source of the proposal,[163] and Hemingway credits MacLeish as both "the great originator" and the one who chose the title.[164] It is at least safe to conclude that *The Spanish Earth* initially emerged as a collective venture.

Koch would have us believe otherwise. To his book *The Breaking Point: Hemingway, Dos Passos, and the Murder of José Robles*, many professional and lay Hemingway scholars owe a debt of gratitude for reminding us of Joris Ivens's deep connection with the U.S.S.R.-backed Comintern. According to Schoots's biography—on which Koch draws heavily—the left-leaning Ivens first solidified his commitment to organized communism in the late 1920s, when he joined the Association for People's Culture (in Dutch the Vereniging voor Volkscultuur), "a subsection of the Dutch division of International Red Aid, a support organization linked" to Comintern.[165] Ivens's indirect Comintern bosses in the early to mid 1930s were Willi Münzenberg and the Mezhrabpom Studio. (Münzenberg would later be present in Moscow to support the Comintern's idea of recruiting from outside Spain to create the International Brigades.[166]) From April 1934 to January 1936 Ivens lived in Moscow. He moved to the United States in February 1936, where he "regularly [sent] reports back to Mezhrabpom" and "kept the Soviet film company Amkino . . . informed of his activities."[167] Furthermore, the North American Committee for Spain, to which Hemingway and company supplied ambulances, was "a branch of an international committee that had been formed, once again, by Münzenberg in Paris."[168]

From these facts Koch fashions a dramatic tale of Ivens with marching orders from Moscow (however indirectly issued) targeting Dos Passos, forming the Contemporary Historians, and eventually bagging the great prize of Ernest Hemingway. "Dos was still exploitable," Koch writes. "Dos was famous. Dos looked independent. Dos brought in people like MacLeish. And by using Dos and MacLeish together, the Comintern thought it just might hit the jackpot. Hemingway. . . . Ivens reeled him in with the utmost care."[169] Yet beyond the general relationship Ivens had with Comintern organizations and functionaries, there is little evidence of such a deliberate scheme, even if, as Watson surmises, Ivens delayed his return to Spain in order to receive Hemingway in Paris.[170] I admit that Koch knows far more than I do or ever will about Comintern operations, and I sympathize with Koch in that anyone trying to puzzle together Comintern activities must rely to some extent on an imaginative piecing together of circumstantial evidence. Indeed, as the quotation about reeling in Hemingway adumbrates, the great problem of *The Breaking Point* is its novelistic style that plays a little loose with available facts and sources in its hope for a good read. It dramatizes rather than reports. In many cases Koch novelizes his history using as his historical sources already fictionalized novels.

For example, the account of Josephine Herbst's conversation telling Hemingway about Robles's death, particularly the characterizations of Hemingway's glee at the prospect of confronting Dos Passos and her own pleasure in orchestrating it, appears exaggerated and does not consider other accounts, not even that of her own diary. Her memoir portrays Herbst as agonized over her knowledge of Robles's death, and from one tentative line, "Perhaps he agreed with too cheerful a readiness,"[171] Koch spins two paragraphs:

> It was Hemingway's turn to put down his drink. Josie thought he looked almost *too* cheerful. He was beaming. He thought Josie's little plan *splendid*.
>
> Josie smiled too. Her own back was completely covered. Either on her own or in collaboration with a senior Soviet propaganda agent [the Spanish official Alvarez del Vayo], she had quietly and discreetly handed the exact weapon she knew he was looking for. And then, just as quietly and discreetly, she had shown him how to use it.[172]

Neither one of them smiled in Herbst's telling, and her two pages Koch melodramatically stretches into six. Other biographers and literary historians report Hemingway's dismay at having to report the news of Robles's death.[173] Perhaps partial to Hemingway, a reading of him as performing a dear friend's painful duty nevertheless warrants its due. At the luncheon later that day, where Hemingway supposedly revealed the news to Dos Passos, Herbst watches Hemingway from another table—according to Koch—"glowing with confidence and cruelty" as he spoke with Dos Passos and "hitting with all his sadistic fervor."[174] Yet nothing in Herbst's memoir or diary supports this characterization. The diary in fact tells a different story than the memoir. Instead of a private conference with Hemingway where the two hatch their plan to tell Dos Passos, Herbst writes: "Go to Hem's room. Stand around. Few drinks. Dos comes in. Has found out Robles executed. Wants to investigate. Discuss with Hem danger of D investigating. R bad egg given fair trial—give away military secrets." Diary shorthand aside, the conversation seems quite reasonable. At the luncheon itself, the diary presents Hemingway and Dos Passos as practically allies: "Glib talk going on and Hem & Dos really finding out something."[175] This story is a far cry from Koch's version, or any version that has Hemingway delivering Dos Passos the news at the luncheon.[176]

The issue at hand, however, is the authorship of *The Spanish Earth*. In the summer of 1937 Ivens had planned to return to Spain and even make a second film for the cause,[177] but as Schoots notes, a letter from Ivens to Hemingway of January 1938[178] does seem to indicate that he received a "change in assignment" sending him to China.[179] But we cannot easily conclude that he had been assigned to make a documentary about Spain. Indeed, the available evidence points to an opportunity seized rather than a job tasked. He was in the United States and in New York, reporting to various Comintern-associated agents, at the right time and place. Such a distinction perhaps splits hairs, especially with people working under the Comintern's motto, *everything for the party, but nothing in the name of the party*. It's quite possible that Ivens appointed himself Hemingway's personal commissar.[180] Yet Moscow and the Comintern exerted minimal direct influence over the making of *The Spanish Earth*, and there is reason to believe that while Ivens held fast to his leftist ideals and used the film to advance them, he sought a manageable artistic independence from Moscow.

At some time while in Spain, Ivens consulted with *Pravda*'s correspondent and Stalin's friend Mikhail Koltsov, who would become Karkov in *For Whom the Bell Tolls*, and Vittorio Vidali ("Carlos"), an Italian Comintern agent and the man rumored responsible for the mass of executions in Madrid the previous fall. Exactly when these conversations occurred is not clear. The subject of the film probably came up more than once with Koltsov. Schoots believes they took place shortly after Ivens and Ferno arrived in Madrid the first time (late January or early February),[181] but the narrative order of Ivens's memoir places these conversations much later, in the spring—after Hemingway arrived, after the discovery of Fuentedueña, and indeed after much filming had already been completed. Yet the memoir's chronology is rather confused. He writes, for example, that Dos Passos worked with Ivens and Ferno in February, leaving around the time Hemingway arrived, when in fact Dos Passos was not in Spain at all until mid April, after Hemingway's arrival; the memoir's ordering suggests too that the filming of the bombing of Morata happened after Hemingway joined the crew, though it actually had happened before he had even left the States. And in this chronological confusion he presents the revised one-paragraph plan right after the discussions with Koltsov and Vidali such that the narrative order suggests a much stronger connection between their advice and the film's focus and message than is probably the case. Ivens actually uses those two conversations simply to transition from the filming to the arranging processes, and to typify the "contrasting attitudes" offered by the several people "who talked with us about the general problems of the film."[182]

By way of the actual transition, Ivens writes, "Out of these talks came this outline."[183] I have dated this outline to the second or third week of April (if not even later) because of its references to Fuentedueña and Julian and its apparent heeding of MacLeish's instructions to incorporate the new village footage into a single feature film. The memoir's narrative order and language and the actual chronology matter in regard to questions about the film's collaborative authorship and its potential fictionality. As far as anyone knows, Ivens might have talked casually about the film with Vidali in January in the Madrid recording studio, and with Koltsov in the presence of Hemingway at Gaylord's in the spring. Per Ivens's memory and willingness to disclose, Koltsov thought the film should show "the happiness of laughing people wanting to live . . . the relationship between the bistro and the barricades . . . and also the continuance of normal life."[184] Vidali wanted a more politically obvious film:

> Madrid is defended by all the people—workers, peasants, the middle class, intellectuals. They defend a democratic parliamentary Republic and the independence of Spain. You could compare it to the Civil War in the United States. We should show the activity of the children's organizations. We should show how Moroccans come over from the fascists to the people's side. Definitely show the workers' living quarters—and the "steel brigades" in the factories.[185]

Their different approaches suggest how little the message was controlled by outsiders, and the final film expresses a little of both, obeying neither in its focus. As for others with whom they consulted while in Spain, Ivens's memoir names Werner Heilbrun and, oddly enough, Sidney Franklin, but we can safely suppose a few other specific people: Gustav Regler, Hans Kahle, General Lukács, André Malraux, Enrique Lister, Ilya Ehrenburg, Wenceslau Roces (not to mention whoever he showed the first footage to in Paris in February[186]). Ivens did not write the outline immediately after consulting the *Pravda* journalist and the Italian Comintern brute; rather, the outline emerged after all sorts of conversations and after a good deal of filming. A later emergence of this outline also decreases substantially the fictionality of the final film. It absolutely bears fictional elements, but the later emergence reveals Ivens's teams' effort to adapt their story to their encounters rather than impose a story concocted beforehand (as many documentaries did).

The Soviet Union and the Comintern, in the late 1930s, were changing in ways no more agreeable to Ivens than they were to Regler. According to Schoots, a document housed at the Central Party Archives in Moscow confirms that Ivens belonged to the Communist Party of Holland (CPH) from 1931 to 1936, but "was not an 'activist,'" and a CPH acquaintance "believed that, in contrast to the usual practice, Ivens was not part of a cell—the basic party unit in a factory or neighborhood—and was thus an outsider within the party."[187] In 1934, following the party line, he publicly renounced modernist avant-garde practices and adopted Socialist Realism.[188] Yet he was living in Moscow at the time, where he still lived when "the run-up to the great terror of 1936–1938"[189] began, arriving in the United States as the purges really got underway:

> Ivens himself did not get anywhere as a filmmaker in Moscow. . . . His activities for the International Communist movement, and especially his status as an employee of Münzenberg's Mezhrabpom Studio, had lured him into a position of dependency. His films were being screened for Communist audiences or not at all, and he was economically tied to the movement. On top of all of this, his friends were dying in the Gulag. . . . With his departure for America, Ivens traveled to freedom. Fifty years later he summarized the situation by

> saying: "Of course, the poor in the United States had a hard time, but as a filmmaker you at least didn't get letters of instruction and you could do what you liked."[190]

Ivens and Van Dongen arrived in the U.S. in February 1936,[191] and by the summer "his efforts to get a film off the ground in the United States suggest he was not at all too anxious to return to the USSR."[192] The Soviets shut down Mezhrabpom Studio a month before Franco and the other generals rebelled, and began "reining in" Willi Münzenberg,[193] who in 1940 "was found dead under a tree in the South of France with a noose around his neck."[194] Boris Shumyatsky, Stalin's chief of the Soviet film industry from 1930 to 1937, was executed as a traitor in 1938. Others of Ivens's Russian colleagues were killed, disappeared, or ostracized.[195] In this environment how could Ivens not feel conflicted in his allegiances? In this environment, how could Ivens not accept an assignment to do a film in China? Especially if it afforded him the opportunity to pursue the kind of work he found so satisfying with *The Spanish Earth*. A film he always insisted was antifascist, not procommunist.[196]

Much of his initial attraction to Soviet film in the first place was for its avant-garde nature, which he and so many others of his generation conceived of as an aesthetic protest to superficial and standardized commercial films and connected to a political protest against capitalism.[197] Revolutionary art became revolutionary art. When he arrived in Moscow in 1931 he declared to a daily paper, "Here I can work the way I want to. Being here gives me a new lease of life both personally and artistically."[198] In the 1930s the Soviets began restricting experimental, intellectual, and individualized artistry—an artistic spirit like Ivens's must have balked. As he articulated in 1931, "a documentary film requires the development of the personality of the filmmaker, because only the personality of an artist separates him from commonplace actuality, from simple photography. A good filmmaker stands in the middle of the matter, in the middle of reality. . . . With other films, this realistic as well as important criterion to estimate the personality of the filmmaker at its true value does not exist."[199] The suspicion Regler felt toward the Soviet Union while serving in the Spanish Civil War led to full-blown dissidence "around 1939" such that the German Democratic Republic—Soviet-bloc East Germany—"erased" him from history and demanded that Ivens cut his scenes from *The Spanish Earth*.[200] Ivens acceded, most likely only to ensure that the film could still be seen in the GDR.

Schoots insists that Ivens "remained absolutely faithful to the party,"[201] and while his socially and politically committed films bear this fact out, we might qualify that absoluteness. He continued promoting communism as well as Soviet-American friendship. At the beginning of the second World War, he wrote to MacLeish, who was then working for the federal government under Roosevelt, with ideas about documentaries to support "our government;"[202] over the next few years in the U.S., he worked on such war films as *Our Russian Front*, *Action Stations!*, *Know Your Enemy: Japan*, and *The Story of GI-Joe*. In his personal life, Ivens found himself committed to two relationships, one with his new wife from his old life, Helen Van Dongen, and the other with an American woman, Marion Michelle. The balancing of these commitments and the strange independence achieved by nature of the dual commitments strikes me as analogous to his balancing of Russian communism and Western artistic freedom. With *The Spanish Earth*, Ivens negotiated the demands of his social passion, his artistic control, and his organizational loyalties. I'd like to think that he repeatedly insisted on his role as the source of the film's idea as much to separate himself from his Comintern handlers—both for the sake of a potentially suspicious American audience and for his own self-definition as an artist—as from the Contemporary Historians and in particular Hemingway, who shared the spotlight with Ivens in all publicity and reviews and who decidedly was not present at the film's conception.

Ivens's published account of meeting Hemingway in a Paris café that March, with Hemingway not yet involved in the film, we can perhaps attribute to a poor memory or to unclear writing: "We had a lot of drinks and Hemingway said that if there was any way he could help he'd be glad to do it. . . . Hemingway was on his way to Spain as a correspondent for NANA."[203] The manuscript draft notes read, "There met Hemingway. Who was not in from beginning. He was going to Spain for American Newspaper."[204] The same basic story—that Hemingway said he was on his way to Spain as a reporter—Ivens repeated in a 1981 interview.[205] Perhaps Ivens was unaware of Hemingway's agreement to contribute the dialogue until that moment. Perhaps, to a reader who accepts Koch's version of the larger story, the passage covers up Ivens's months-long campaign to recruit Hemingway as an unwitting Comintern agent. (The draft notes are actually accurate in reporting Hemingway's absence at the very beginning of the project; Ivens's omission of Hemingway's connection to the film upon arrival in Paris could be a simple matter of neglect, or of Ivens the memoirist perhaps having trouble reading his own sketchy notes.)

Ivens's writing implies that he introduced the film project to Hemingway in Paris and tells us that he informed the somewhat naïve American about the great fascist threat to Europe, presenting himself as the top dog. To credit Ivens with converting Hemingway to a conviction about "the disastrous effects of the U.S. nonintervention policy"[206] strikes me as giving Ivens too much credit and Hemingway not enough. The issues of fascist intervention and democratic nonintervention would have been known to anyone following the war, much less Hemingway, especially given his work on "Spain in Flames." Watson notes that the "Madrid in Flames" manuscript—which he believes Hemingway wrote—includes commentary about Madrid's "being burned by Fascists of both Germany and Italy" and "is not just an anti-war film." As Watson rightly concludes, "Hemingway did not need Joris Ivens to convince him that the war in Spain was 'the first test of fascism in Europe.'"[207] Indeed Ivens in the 1981 interview admits that he let Hemingway draw his own conclusions.[208] Similarly, Hemingway, a more-than-able military historian, hardly needed the communists to convince him of the necessity of a unified military command structure. Nor did he need the communists to foment in him a distrust of the anarchists and other more radical leftist groups, as the Republic had been distrustful of them years before the communists became a party to be reckoned with. Hemingway had been taking full note of the government's struggles with them.

Never a dupe, Hemingway knew full well just how far left his American Contemporary Historian compatriots leaned, and if he hadn't known Ivens's history before arriving in Spain, he would have received his first lesson upon arrival, walking around Brihuega talking with Ivens and Regler. Or at the Gaylord Hotel, where Ivens introduced Hemingway to Koltsov and other Russians. "I didn't keep any secrets from him," Ivens told Watson in an interview.[209] Gellhorn's letters to her lover in June 1937, about Ivens becoming the group's president, tell us a great deal. In one she jokes that the hammer and sickle is her new letterhead graphic and appreciates Hemingway's anarchist youth; in another, she calls communists "sinister folk and very very canny."[210] Hemingway had in fact tried to prevent this reorganization, wiring MacLeish from Bimini: "KNOW HOW HARD YOUVE WORKED UNREWARDEDLY BUT HOPE YOU WILL RETAIN PRESIDENCY HISTORIANS EVEN THOUGH BURDENSOME FEEL POSSIBLY UNWISE JORIS SERVE PRESIDENT DUE FOREIGN CITIZENSHIP LACK BUSINESS LEGAL EXPERIENCE YOU AND HE SHOULD KNOW ABOUT THIS THOUGH PLEASE READ HIM THIS WIRE REGARDS PAPPY."[211] In an interview decades later, Gellhorn recalled that their circle of foreigners in Spain mimicked the Spaniards in using the phrase *la Causa* to describe the Republican dream, but "with a certain amount of happiness and irony, because none of us were given to rhetoric."[212] And that's a healthy detachment from the good-hearted republicans, not the sinister communists.

After Ivens packed his bags for China, Hemingway accused the "Third International" (Comintern) of giving up on Spain.[213] Ivens's own letter to Hemingway of 28 January 1938 about the new assignment (written en route to China with Ferno and Capa), with his references to "my people," confirms that Ivens had previously opened up to Hemingway about his official affiliations. One choice line about the China project demonstrates Hemingway's awareness of his role, Ivens's ongoing effort to define himself first and foremost as an artist, and the two men's candor with one another: "I feel like a good fun artist! You know you are the propagandist."[214] That in August 1937 Ivens wrote letters of recommendation for Hemingway to two communist friends, to Wenceslau Roces of the Republic's propaganda ministry and to the editor of the French Communist Party, telling them that Hemingway will show them the film and asking that they help him, seems hardly remarkable.[215] Ivens was headed to China, leaving *The Spanish Earth* and the Spanish cause in Hemingway's hands. Ivens simply wanted to give his friend and compatriot whatever connections he could to promote the film. In that January letter, Ivens wrote about the difficulty of leaving Spain behind, of not knowing Hemingway's plans, of trying to get a silent copy of the film to Wenceslau Roces in Spain, and of other efforts to distribute the film throughout Europe. He also offered by correspondence to set Hemingway up "with one of our leading people." If this is an offer to hook Hemingway up clandestinely with a communist agent,[216] the offer reinforces the two men's level of familiarity, Ivens's affiliations, and his openness, but reveals nothing about Hemingway's politics or susceptibility to influence. As Schoots supposes, "Ivens's confidences [in this letter] might have gone a little too far."[217]

As Peter Moreira has shown, Hemingway's dispatches from China and his intelligence reports to Washington placed his favor with the Nationalist Kuomintang instead of the communists. This pro-Kuomintang position was in keeping: If in Spain he had backed the communists as the best chance for defeating fascist Franco, in China he backed Chiang Kai-Shek's Kuomintang as the only power capable of defeating imperial Axis Japan and as the legitimate government, in both cases despite the less palatable aspects of the supported cause (i.e., the regrettable if inevitable wartime brutality): "Chiang Kai-Shek was the man to ensure that China remained in the war."[218]

To Carlos Baker, Prudencio de Pereda once wrote about seeing Ivens in 1939 or 1940 after the latter had recently spent time with Hemingway: "The continued friendship with Ernest was no surprise to either of us."[219] I sense the two as having become quite close, each admiring the other's talent and dedication to his art, his bravery, and even his energy and charisma. When Ivens didn't see Hemingway as much as he would have liked after that summer of 1937, he wrote touchingly about his disappointment.[220] *The Spanish Earth* is Ivens's film, but he respected Hemingway and allowed him to be as much a collaborator as anyone, even Ferno and Van Dongen. He wanted Hemingway to join the China film project not because he could manipulate him. He could have manipulated any left-leaning American writer. He wanted Hemingway because of the professional understanding and the deep camaraderie they had developed.[221] They had worked hard to limit the film's commentary to keep its blatancy from interfering with the visual impact while saying what needed to be said. It was minimal, if not as minimalist as Hemingway's stories. Hemingway knew it was propaganda. He knew that it delivered more than a hint of communism. He also believed that the film was ultimately about preserving the Republic against fascism, about respecting individual liberty and dignity. He believed it was a film about the Spanish people. For him, it was always about Spain.

FOUR

The Film and the Book

"This Spanish earth is dry and hard and the faces of the men who work that earth are hard and dried from the sun."[1]

The six-reel, fifty-two-minute documentary *The Spanish Earth* tells the story of the rejuvenation of the land through the efforts of hard-working villagers and the Spanish Republican soldiers. The plot works circularly: While the fight against the enemy saves the land and the people, it is the land and the people who sustain the fight against the enemy. The film's first seven minutes refrain entirely from visually presenting the war while the commentary mentions it twice, to establish Fuentedueña's role in supplying food. First the narrator, somewhat casually, voices the thoughts of the villagers; then he quite explicitly makes the village essential to victory: "The village is on the Tago River and the main highroad that is the lifeline between Valencia and Madrid. All food for Madrid comes on this road. To win the war, the rebel troops must cut this road."

The six reels function as chapters in terms of organizing the presentation into units, though the transitions from one reel to the next are invisible to filmgoers. The first reel focuses on village life—the men and boys headed to the fields, the women staying behind to do laundry and pick up bread. The Republican war posters above the racks of bread loaves and the narration's references to supplying food to Madrid further connect the village to the war. Shots of villagers transporting food to Madrid establish a visual continuity throughout the film, as all travel from the village to Madrid moves right to left across the screen, and all travel from Madrid to the village left to right—a continuity that generally matches the orientation of the film's occasional maps showing the village to the southeast—lower right—of the city. The transition from village to war, and from reel 1 to reel 2, shows a man beating flat the bed of the new irrigation ditch as the distant thundering of artillery joins and eventually replaces the thudding of his mallet.

Reel 2 responds to reel 1 by focusing on life at the front. Soldiers trudging to battle echo the workers on their way to the fields as the commentary in both reels draws attention to their faces. This initial battle sequence highlights the artillery duel on the plains before Madrid, with shots of soldiers carrying ammunition, firing the cannons, and observing and directing the action.[2] The war scenes here are generally characteristic of those elsewhere in the film, of men talking and planning and watching and marching, with the real action barely visible on the horizon. Though we see no tanks yet, Virginia Cowles's description is apt: "I was surprised to find how banal war became from a distance. Against the wide panorama of rolling hills the puffs of smoke were daubs of cotton and the tanks children's toys. When one of them burst into flames it looked no bigger than the flare of a match. Against the great sweep of Nature, man's struggle becomes so diminutive it was almost absurd."[3] The narration connects the front to the village only once, and crudely: "The villagers of Fuentedueña hear this noise and say, 'Our guns.'" More subtly, soldiers working on and in the trenches reprise the villagers working on the irrigation ditch. A scene showing soldiers carrying ammunition crates in and out of a cave contributes to the earthiness of the film. The camera then takes us to the front, to the more routine life of soldiers reading the paper and enjoying a shave in a mobile barber shop, accompanied by the same peppy and folksy march music that had accompanied the daily life of villagers in reel 1. Soldiers operating the propaganda loudspeaker and learning to disassemble and assemble a rifle also contribute to the texture of the routine. Scenes of troops getting and eating their chow remind us, even if unconsciously, of where it came from. (A very brief shot of a man carrying the food container follows him moving from right to left, the Fuentedueña-to-Madrid direction.)

Reel 2 climaxes with the fight for the clinic at University City, in the northwest corner of Madrid. The battle is closer, more urgent than in the earlier artillery fight. Men hustle up stairs and through shot-up buildings; soldiers fire machine guns and rifles through windows and smaller openings; the camera catches a spent casing jumping out of a rifle chamber, and lingers on a machine gun's muzzle. The cinematography in this segment is the most interesting of the film, with stark contrasts between dark building interiors, where the action occurs, and the framed daylight, signifying the enemy's position, glaring forcibly through.

Reel 2 then moves us toward the Julian storyline by concluding with his letter home to Fuentedueña and even creating a kind of suspense: "Papá, I will be there in three days. Tell our mother." Julian's role is, per Ivens's plan, to "personalize" the larger story, in this case the connection between the rural communities and the war. Viewers today, I hazard to generalize, mostly find that Julian depersonalizes the experience for the viewers through his obvious, abstract, rather impersonal, duly and dully symbolic presence. Indeed before his entrance, there are two moments in reel 2 of far more emotional pull. The first is perhaps the most powerful piece of Hemingway's commentary, introducing us to a bearded man in the scene during the fight for the clinic, Commander Martinez de Aragon: "Before the war he was a lawyer. He was a brave and skillful commander and he died in the attack on the Casa del Campo on the day we filmed the battle there." The second emotional moment is all Ivens, as the camera shows a lone soldier gazing out a window and out of frame to the right and then pans left to take in, first, a full mirror, and then the shattered remnants of another mirror with one fragment reflecting the building outside the window: the building is occupied by the enemy and is the endpoint of the man's stare.

The majority of reel 3 takes place at the Salle de Goya meeting with excerpts from the speeches by Lister, Vidali ("Carlos"), Díaz, Regler, and La Pasionaria. Preceding the meeting, in the first scene of the reel, a company has assembled "to elect representatives to attend the big meeting." Reel 3 moves from the meeting back to the trenches by a right-to-left dissolve from La Pasionaria to a loudspeaker, implying her speech's broadcast over the trenches, across no man's land, and to the rebels. The loudspeaker then encourages Nationalist soldiers to desert. Back in the trenches we see Martinez de Aragon, an unsettling image of a man we probably did not expect to see again that baldly communicates the film's suspension of chronological fidelity. The narrator draws our attention to the Moors and the Spanish Civil Guards fighting for Franco, joining the Spanish military rebellion in trying to impose itself on the people. The rebellion would have ended months earlier were it not for the support of Italy and Germany. Julian's battalion heads home on leave (left to right), with shots of the men walking interspersed with shots of the living rooms of Madrid homes visible through the missing walls and shots of artwork being removed from the Duke of Alva's bombed palace to be taken to safety.

Reel 4 presents Madrid in the disquieting state of war. Civilians help build barricades and stand in long queues for food. Mixed in with trolleys, trucks, and pedestrians are moving images of ambulances and a man carrying a coffin on his back. Bombardment takes the life of—the narrator informs us—"a bookkeeper on his way to the office at eight o'clock in the morning." The depicted evacuation of Madrid, while logically following the bookkeeper's death by indiscriminate bombing, seems to violate historical chronology. Ivens and Ferno had filmed the evacuation as soon as they got to Spain in late January, when Franco's Nationalists were still seriously advancing on the capital. The footage of normalized Madrid probably came later, perhaps even in the spring with Hemingway—after, in fact, life in wartime Madrid had normalized. President Azaña's speech to the Cortes in Valencia is followed by, and thus associated with, a villager issuing instructions for work on the irrigation project's pump house. Scenes of village leaders discussing the project, drawing maps, and building the house reflect by contrast and connection similar military scenes, particularly the surveying of the land from the heights, albeit with houses going down instead of up. The end of the reel again uses Julian as the personalizing thread, as he arrives home by truck (traveling from left to right).

Reel 5 builds toward the film's culminating battle. Julian arrives home and begins drilling the village boys, who we know will grow up to fight for Madrid because we next see "a future shock-battalion" of men drilling in Madrid. An imagined parting from his wife of a soldier on his way to battle ironically deemphasizes the danger to him: "'Take care of the kid,' he says. 'I will'—she says, and knows she can't." The next dead bodies shown, a couple of minutes later, are indeed those of two boys who, we are told, were collecting shell fragments. The film then moves to an unnamed village to show the approaching enemy bombers and the results of their mission: the damaged buildings, dead bodies, and survivors—including two small boys in Republican uniforms. Ivens and Ferno caught this moment in February at Morata, though some viewers might infer Fuentedueña because the film does not name the village. (The three explosions in reel 5, in Madrid and Morata, come from footage Ivens shot "from a dangerously short distance" during combat filming elsewhere.[4]) The sequence continues with a shot of a downed rebel plane from Germany, filmed on a different day and somewhere else, and then with images of the dead Italian soldiers from Brihuega, communicating a moral comeuppance for their sides' killing of the innocent. As Ivens's memoir states, the bombardment sequence ends with "the accusation against the enemy," the "preparation for the counterblow, and then the blow itself."[5] According to Van Dongen, the downing of the German plane was the only footage to appear that Ivens's crew did not film.[6]

"The Rebels attack the Madrid-Valencia road again," reel 6 begins. "They have crossed the Jarama River and try to take the Arganda Bridge." The editing visually pairs the battle for the bridge with the building of the elevated and final portion of the irrigation system. The soldiers and tanks, apparently headed to the battle, we see marching and driving in all directions, the usual pattern disrupted in the moment's urgency. The battle itself occurs only at the edges, as it were: the "undramatic movement" of infantry walking (to quote the film itself), and tanks and trucks apparently getting into position to fight; leaders talking; and shells exploding either so far in the distance or so close to the camera that they do not seem a part of the story. In the story "Night before Battle," Hemingway describes the tanks as "small mud-colored beetles" followed by "toy men."[7] The images probably come from several filming occasions to create the onscreen battle. Nenni's applying a dressing to Pacciardi's wounds Ivens and Ferno filmed their first trip, at the bridge battle. (We get a number of glimpses of Pacciardi in reel 6, a somewhat lanky man wearing a short-billed skull cap with a single star, and also a couple of bespectacled, bereted Nenni.) But some of the tank and infantry movement, and the ambulances at the medical evacuation point, would have been shot in the spring with Hemingway and probably Heilbrun. Hemingway almost certainly has a cameo appearance in this scene, quite briefly and in profile right in front of the camera. Saving the Republican injured until the last battle of the film bolsters the message of the sacrifice necessary for the new day—with the Republican victory to save Madrid, water flows through the irrigation channel at Fuentedueña: "This is the moment that all the rest of the war prepares for, when six men go forward into death to walk across a stretch of land and by their presence prove—this earth is ours." The final images cut from an anonymous Republican soldier firing his rifle to the waters flowing in the same direction. Such "daring cutting" between the fighting and the irrigation, as Ivens reflected two years later,

> has nothing to do with pure symbolic editing, such as you sometimes see in Russian films. Suppose you see a man in prison and suddenly he becomes happy and you see apple blossoms. That is all very well, but it is purely symbolic cutting. I am trying very hard to convey my point, because it is so important. This kind of cutting is not just symbolic, because it goes much deeper than that. It is part of the theme of the film. It is optimism.[8]

I suspect that many audiences today would find *The Spanish Earth* slow and undramatic. In 1937, however, some viewers very much appreciated the film. Hemingway's commentary and narration, while a bit heavy-handed to our ears, fit the style and tone of the day, no more overdone than Norman Corwin's world war broadcasts a few years later. The *New Yorker* raved that "no film yet has come so close to the people and the places of its interest" and that "so expert and beautiful is the photography, accomplished with the most rudimentary resources, that the film would seem to abolish the need of a studio and studio accessories forever."[9] As undramatic as much of the war footage was, few had ever seen war filmed that closely before. The bombardments of civilian populations in Madrid and Morata were filmic firsts. The *New York Times* considered Hemingway's "terse, powerful" narrative less impressive than the film's "compelling" and "irrefutable" visual argument;[10] three months later another *Times* article called the film "a masterpiece of beautiful and simple cinematic statement, making its points conclusively by artful implication."[11] Other reviewers were turned off by its propagandistic message, thinking it undermined the artistic effort; one saw it as neither artistically interesting nor politically compelling.[12] Still, the National Board of Review of Motion Pictures named it one of the year's ten best foreign films, and it quickly became a text studied in film societies and film classes.[13] In 1964, documentary filmmakers at the Mannheim Film Festival voted *The Spanish Earth* one of the twelve best documentaries of all time.

A few film historians count *The Spanish Earth* as a landmark in the evolution of the documentary. For one thing, it represents how during the Spanish Civil War the medium in general "flourished" and came into its own as a means of recording and influencing current events.[14] For Thomas Waugh, the film registers as the "prototype for a central tradition of cinematic understanding of our era that has endured to this day and the iconography and the politics of which have changed amazingly little."[15] José Manuel Costa also accords it such prominence:

> The practical and conceptual experience of *The Spanish Earth* can in fact be seen, metonymically, as a decisive point in the larger development of Documentary. By now, for the first time, Documentary was taking shape as a new *form*, where the personal authorship itself, no matter how strong it was, worked and expressed itself under new rules, demanding a new analytical frame. . . . The strong, assertive, visual construction of the avant-garde, or the straightforward constructivist mood in the use of the camera and in montage were displaced into a personal way of confronting and penetrating an evolving situation.[16]

In other words, while shooting *The Spanish Earth* Ivens and crew, "for the first time in the practice of non-fiction cinema," had to work out his conception on the scene while confronting his dynamic subject. In Spain "the enemy was co-director" Ivens often said, and through this film the documentary form became "*the* representational mode that structurally has to integrate another source of control, and that is actually built upon that confrontation, or simply, on partial *lack of control.*"[17] Ivens himself was quite aware (or at least quite hopeful) of his project's potential, cabling to MacLeish in February 1937 his belief in the film as a "new artistic form."[18] For the rest of his life he ranked *The Spanish Earth* as among his best and most important works.

When Ivens began his career in the 1920s, documentary was very much the avant-garde of film as it has arguably remained to this day. For the early documentary artists, fictional film was limited to the conventions of fiction, especially the staged performances on which it drew, and was bound to commercial and mass market appeal. As simply another kind of stage, a means of reproducing and distributing tried-and-true performed fictions for a larger audience, fictional film by its nature could not take advantage of what was unique to its medium: the ability to study real objects in and over time, to capture the aesthetics of movement, to explore inner truths through exterior examination, to explore the relationship between representation and actuality, and indeed to communicate the artist's own self. The formal and epistemological issues fit squarely into the larger modernist project of the era. Ivens's 1928 *The Bridge* begins, after one shot of the bridge, with Ivens holding his camera in profile and turning to face us. Around this time he also attempted to design a camera "to imitate the movements of the human eye."[19] For Ivens, "The documentary film in the current state of affairs, is the best way to find the road to true film. There shall be no danger of its descending into theater, literature, music hall, in a word everything that is not film."[20]

Early documentary artists worried less about defining their medium in nonfictional opposition to fictional film than as a means to aesthetic experimentation. Per Ivens's definition, "On the one hand you have fiction or acted films, on the other hand you have the newsreel, and between those two you have the area covered by documentary film."[21] It most resembles the art of nonfiction writing, its possibilities comparable to nonfiction writing's range, from literary journalism to poetic investigation and expression. Initially Ivens valued the documentary for its unique aesthetic ability to study form and movement. Ivens's 1928 eleven-minute short *The Bridge* is to film what William Carlos Williams's 1923 "The Red Wheelbarrow" is to poetry: a visual study through motion rather than an imagist still life through words. We see some of this in *The Spanish Earth*, especially in reel 2's attention to the mechanics of weaponry, to soldiers moving through space, and to the interplay of light and dark. Ivens's early imagistic aesthetic achieved the abstract in its absolute concreteness, and it approaches Walter Pater's mantra of all art aspiring to the condition of music. Then, in the late 1920s and early 1930s, Ivens joined the Soviet documentary movement, and aesthetics took a back seat to the proper political message. About his early peopled documentaries, such as *Song of Heroes*, Ivens's comments reveal something of how he worked at that time: "It is only on location where the right material is chosen that matches the plan's directives. . . . It is here that the organization of the directives is placed into the context of the found live material."[22] While he does not create a detailed script for a film as most of his peers did, he nevertheless conceives the film before the filming, choosing what he films and arranging it, even "reconstruct[ing] events and facts," according to the plan. This contructivist approach precludes a film from becoming "a mere recording of events."[23]

The difference between the method he describes here and the method of *The Spanish Earth* five years later is the degree—in this case a significant one—to which the director privileges the plan or the live material, whether fitting the material to the plan or adapting the plan to the material. While today we might experience the film as a dysfunctional conflict between newsreel reportage and scripted nonfiction, for some film historians *The Spanish Earth* delivered a productively creative tension that advanced the documentary art forward. Ivens's struggle to reconceive the film as he experienced the war while filming it perhaps correlates with what Bill Nichols has described as the "existential" challenge for the viewers of any documentary in the reconciliation of the film's version of reality with their own understanding of reality.[24] Its formal flexibility (or generic range) and this existential challenge contribute to the troubles we have in defining the documentary and in evaluating individual documentaries. In a 1938 article, the *New York Times* film critic Frank Nugent offered several definitions only to conclude that "it is child's play to blast any one of them sky high";[25] in a 2008 article, the *New York Times* film critic A. O. Scott observes that a documentary's "engagement with reality is at once impossible to miss and difficult to define" and writes about "semi- or quasi- or crypto-documentaries."[26]

Thus two documentarists as closely in sync as Joris Ivens and Helen Van Dongen can disagree as to whether Robert Flaherty's *Nanook of the North* is a documentary—Ivens says yes, Van Dongen no. And as Van Dongen admits for all of us, "I have never been able to define precisely where propaganda begins and art is left behind."[27] A legitimate function of the documentary is to present a perspective, *one* point of view. As Van Dongen has said, "If I know that something is wrong I tried, through film, to send out warnings and make people think about what was happening."[28] Early twenty-first-century examples of this issue are Michael Moore's documentaries, and even more interesting the 2008 television miniseries *Generation Kill.* Based on a nonfiction book which itself was a reworking of *Rolling Stone* reportage pieces by an embedded journalist during the 2003 U.S. invasion of Iraq, *Generation Kill* is something like dramatized or reenacted nonfiction that communicates a definite political message against the war—the degree to which the film accurately documents the Marine unit's general attitude isn't known. Does such a film count as propaganda?

Thomas Waugh describes *The Spanish Earth* as a "cinematic hybrid" of the "newsreel" filming of public events, the "spontaneous" filming of the happenings around the camera crew, and the "mis-en-scène" filming of staged shots using real people on actual location. And as Waugh reminds us, the documentary's evolution is more complicated than an easy leaving behind of scripts for the uncertainties of firsthand encounters; indeed "the general trend" from the 1930s onward moved to "greater use of mis-en-scène" staging of shots.[29] John Huston's 1946 *Let There Be Light* is a perfect example. For today's audiences the employment of Julian is the least artful aspect of *The Spanish Earth.* The reenactments and creative enactments of his story, his role as an emblem instead of a person, risk the fictional even though Julian really was a soldier from Fuentedueña and even though what we see is a version of more-or-less actual events by the actual people. Documentaries commonly used nonactors to play themselves and 1930s and 1940s spectators would not have read these scenes as fiction.[30] Techniques for presenting the real in early documentaries covered the spectrum, and in most cases one knowingly accepted the reality presented. But for this twenty-first-century viewer, the introduction of Julian breaks the spell. Julian adds a real, linear story at odds with a fully associative presentation in which we would not mind chronological violations and images from separate events brought together.

For Ivens, an event should be reenacted if the film crew missed when it happened or "to obtain higher technical and artistic qualities for the film"—if the lighting was poor or the person not sufficiently clear in emotion or action. "Should repeating scenes and re-enactment in documentary film be tolerated? Does it harm the honesty or integrity of the film?" Ivens asks, and then answers: "In order to express the truth, such scenes should be directly related to the central ideological theme, should be typical and characteristic for the situation, and should be acted convincingly, possibly by the same people at the same place of the original scene."[31] If an original scene ever even took place. Brian Winston's useful spectrum of documentary intervention and reconstruction includes both "re-enactment of the typical" and "enactment of the possible" (albeit toward the fictional end).[32] How would we characterize the scene with the soldiers electing representatives to attend the Salle de Goya meeting? Ivens does recognize that dramatizations of the real of whatever kind enter "dangerous grounds . . . closing in on the fiction film" and "risk obtaining false notes in our film" and thus losing the spectator's willingness to believe.[33] Yet it is worth repeating that the risk of sounding a false note, and the balance a director must strike, is historically contingent. General sensibilities change.

The Ivens letter's reference to himself as the artist and Hemingway as the propagandist matches, and perhaps even jokingly alludes to, the *New York Times* review:

> Mr. Ivens' camera argues gently and persuasively, with the irrefutable argument of pictorially recorded fact. . . . By comparison with

> the picture's commentary, written and presented by Ernest Hemingway, the camera would seem to be mightier than the pen. Hemingway's narrative is, of course, superb. It is terse, powerful, and at times informative; but it is vengeful, bitter and unreasoning. In its contemplative way, the film argues its point much more effectively. Its technique is that of the film document, but Hemingway's narrative makes it definitely a propagandist effort.[34]

The visual argument alternates between Ivens's fondness for movement and for shooting from interesting angles and apertures, and his tender attention to people.

Some reviewers appreciated the commentary, others found it annoying. The *New Republic* found the film free of "bombast and sloganism," a work of powerful "understatement," and in terms of Hemingway's performance wanted it both ways:

> His voice doesn't come over too well, and what with his suggestion of some overrehearsed WNEW announcer in an embarrassment it isn't vintage Hemingway; but with his knowledge and quiet statement of the odds against survival, that feeling for the people of Spain which comes from his heart, the combination of experience and intuition directing your attention quietly to the mortal truth you might well have missed in the frame, there could hardly be a better choice.[35]

The Spanish Earth also innovates, I think, by setting up a tension between the visual and the verbal. This viewer anyway wants both more information and more commentary—and wants the narrator to shut up and go away. As Van Dongen explained, documentary films of the time typically used "voice of God" explanatory narratives to become "illustrated lectures" rather than films. "If you silenced the voice and screened the picture there was no film that made any sense, just a random succession of scenes which illustrated the voice."[36] *The Spanish Earth* works oppositely, giving us occasional commentary to illustrate the visual. Moreover, the sporadic nature of the commentary builds on the gap with the visual argument using the suspense of its next voicing. Waugh also sees the narration's innovative obliqueness and its "multiplicity of postures toward the spectator," as it sometimes speaks as narrator, sometimes as character or characters, and sometimes directly at the spectator.[37] Additionally, "The contradiction between Hemingway's soundtrack, existential machismo and Ivens' happily predominant sense of the heroism and commitment of daily life and of the civilian front, is responsible for much of the creative tension of the film."[38]

Van Dongen similarly resisted the typical war film sound track. "I tired of seeing so many war films which went continuously 'Bang, bang,' relentlessly, without nuances. If you do not break it down into separate parts, use silence to create effects, you are subjected to one long continuous noise which no longer has any effect and certainly has nothing to do with proper film-making."[39] The occasional use of various weapon and impact sounds effects a steady stream of surprises, and it more accurately mimics the battlefield rhythm.

Of course a film would have great difficulty reaching its audience if it presented nothing familiar in technique or content. However new its hybrid form, it did not abandon but simply recombined and revised the familiar. And if the Spanish Civil War itself was quite foreign and new, the other half of the film's story decidedly was not. The attention to heroic agrarian efforts battling horribly dry conditions and hindered by the old economic system spoke a visual rhetoric extremely familiar to Dust Bowl–era Americans. Waugh has called Ivens's Spanish "peasants . . . the first cousins of the exploited sharecroppers and drought refugees who people the photographs of the Farm Services Administration and the expose photo essays of the liberal journalistic media of the day. As early as 1934, Ivens's Hollywood friend King Vidor had in *Our Daily Bread* crafted the West Coast prototype for *Spanish Earth*, complete with collectivized workers improvising an irrigation system and a coda showing water rushing across the dry earth!"[40] The major difference is the film's "optimism," to use Ivens's word.[41] American social protest films depicted individuals as victims; *The Spanish Earth* empowers them to make a better Spain. Shots of a baby and young children after the Morata bombardment provide this sense of continuation, hope, and life.[42] Not only does the film target "mainstream culture" by focusing on the Spanish family, as Waugh observes,[43] but it also clearly depicts traditionally aligned gender roles.

In Fuentedueña only the men head to the fields while the women stay behind. We see no women taking up arms as they did the first months of the war, nor any women working outside the home in other capacities to support the war and keep things running; we hear nothing about the Second Republic's early commitment to enfranchising women. The film even plays to American racism by demonizing the Moors fighting for Franco in University City like infidels while pitying the dead Italians who thought they were headed to fight in Ethiopia.

The agrarian and irrigation story line coincided with standard Dust Bowl imagery, but one should not mistake that rhetorical appeal as the reason for the film's focus. Indeed the agrarian problem was arguably the central cause of the unrest that gave rise to the Spanish Republic and to the Spanish Civil War in the first place. As Paul Preston summarizes it, the landowners refused "to engage in expensive projects of irrigation" and "preferred instead to build their profits on the exploitation of the great armies of landless day laborers"; the Civil Guard came into being as a repressive and protective instrument of the landowners.[44] The captions to President Azaña's speech give the film its title: "We, the People of Spain, obtained the land and the right to cultivate it by democratic elections—but fascist landlords try to take our land away. Now we are forced to fight for the defense of the Spanish earth. Even in the smallest villages." The speech is veritably continued in the film by a villager in Fuentedueña: "Our irrigation project must be completed in time for the new defense of Madrid." On the other hand, this oversimplification neglects Spain's developing industrialization with its concomitant labor problems and inevitable conflict between city and country, not to mention the ideological differences between the communists and anarchists (and anarcho-syndicalists) over how to manage resources.[45] That the film expressly locates the president in Valencia, referencing what many on the scene considered the government's premature departure from Madrid, also spoke to the tensions within the Republic.

To answer worries about an anticapitalist Republican Spain, the film provides a bookkeeper killed by the rebels, and as the narrator tells us "men from all businesses, professions, and trades enlist[ing] in the Republican Army." We see bread stamped with the union label of the

UGT, the largest union in Spain—but unions aren't communist collectives. To answer worries about an anti-Christian Republican Spain, the film lingers on a statue of a priest beside and above a wire defensive barrier, integrating him into the defense of Madrid (though visually this image could also blame the church for the divisiveness, for the war).

Other messages would have registered subtly if at all for many American viewers. Hemingway honestly narrates the removal of art from the Duke of Alva's palace as an act of cultural preservation in the midst of the fascist bombing campaign against Madrid. The images also communicate a rupture between the Nationalists' professed ideology of traditional culture and their willingness to risk destroying the artifacts of that culture. While elements of the Republican left would have interpreted the removal as a legitimate act of cultural appropriation, monarchists and others on the right would have interpreted it as looting. Both sides would likely have recognized the target of the act: the Duke of Alva, or Alba, had been involved in anti-Republican propaganda in London since 1932,[46] and during the war he served as Franco's agent in London, receiving thousands of telegrams from Franco trying to control the international story,[47] passing along information obtained about arms shipments to the Republic,[48] and giving land to pro-Nationalist peasants.[49]

Soldiers reading newspapers and writing letters (including Julian) attested to what Anthony Beevor considers "the most important achievement of the republican government of 1931–3," namely "education and reducing illiteracy."[50] During the war the Republic continued to push education on its citizens and its soldiers. In a 1981 interview, Gellhorn remembered seeing grown adults, young and "sometimes quite old," learning to read and write in the "painfully shallow" trenches.[51] On 27 April 1937, Josephine Herbst recorded a visit to a school for soldiers in her diary:

> Very eager to come. Learn to read & write. Some learn in 4 days. Others in 2 weeks. . . . Begin books in pencil, soon graduate to ink. The map of Europe on the wall. Learn rudimentary culture. All sitting with eager attention—big men sunburned & the teacher eager. . . . Men writing, perhaps home. The slow thick start. Can't handle

> pencil. Then skimming along. Domingo, the boy who wrote so well. Some never had written a letter—others knew a little, how to write name. Often 75% did not know how to read or write before.[52]

The following fall Paul Patrick Rogers recorded a similar entry in his diary, from Valencia:

> Went to visit schools in the barracks. They have them also in the hospitals factories, & trenches. . . . In Madrid alone there are 800 such schools. People of all ages attend and study everything from the ABCs through anatomy to art. . . . Schools near front often camouflaged. . . . Theater groups organized. The instructors fight as well as teach. . . . These schools began on May 1st. By June 22 there were 507 maestros in the trenches, and 2000 today. . . . There are contests between groups, regiments, etc., in essays, studies, pictures, & like. Prizes given usually in Goods & money. Essays and articles winning are also published.[53]

We should recall that MacLeish's original treatment for the film ended with the recapturing of the village's new schoolhouse, the young soldier standing on the walls he helped build and finally understanding what it was all about. The inference here is the Republic's aggressive efforts to replace the Catholic school system with its own secular one, a fact that only an aware viewer might have understood. The reform was both an honest separation of church and state and a deliberate move to wrench the citizenry free of the church and its ties to the landed establishment. The other implications here are that the teaching missions established in 1931 to bring basic literacy, books, and cultural and civic training to the people could be regarded as paternalistic, and that the enlightenment message lacked "resolute, coherent and costed policy of practical social reform" with material support. In other words, the people "needed bread and medicine, and we had only poems and songs in our bags."[54]

The film deliberately obscures the fact of international assistance for the Republic. We see French Renault and Russian T-26 tanks, but are not told what they are. "Government" soldiers marching through streets toward the end of the film, supposedly on the way to defend the bridge, might belong to the International Brigades—it's impossible to know. We aren't told that Italians fighting for the Republic beat Italians fighting for Franco at Guadalajara or that Italian volunteers are saving the bridge. Hemingway's commentary does introduce Gustav Regler as "one of the fine writers of Germany who came to Spain to fight for his ideals," though does not mention any of the speakers' communist affiliation. The film refers to the international support for the rebels, however, several times. When the camera shows the writing on the Junkers downed by government pursuit planes, the narrator tells us that he "can't read German either."

The portrait of an amateur army would have appealed to an American audience's myth of its own reluctant militancy, with soldiers who have never held a rifle learning to reassemble one and men from all walks of life volunteering to fight and being pitted against the "professional" Moorish soldiers. This was a true enough story, but a more complicated one. To garner sympathy and confidence for support from abroad, the Republic needed to show its military as built of amateurs yet honed for victory. The film struggles a little with that difficult dual presentation and chooses to emphasize what Waugh calls the "unsoldierly" (as opposed to the perfect military formations in Riefenstahl's Nazi Germany).[55] Scenes of youth and new soldiers drilling, while intended to indicate their transformation into mature disciplined professionals, reveal the shortage of arms, ammunition, and wisdom for conducting meaningful training. Per George Orwell, who experienced this training firsthand after arriving in Spain in December 1936:

> The so-called instruction was simply parade-ground drill of the most antiquated, stupid kind; right turn, left turn, about turn, marching at attention in column of threes and all the rest of that useless nonsense which I had learned when I was fifteen years old. It was an extraordinary form for the training of a guerilla army to take. . . . Yet this mob of eager children, who were going to be thrown into the front line in a few days' time, were not even taught how to fire a rifle or pull the pin out of a bomb.[56]

The film's drilling youth is unintentionally representative—among Orwell's motley militia forces on the Aragon front, "quite half of the so-called men were children . . . of sixteen years at the most."[57]

Two weapons fielded by both sides, especially on the stagnant fronts, were the megaphone and the loudspeaker. The loudspeaker shown in *The Spanish Earth* may have been the one which appeared in the spring of 1937 outside Madrid to battle the enemy's megaphones, described in Cecil Eby's *Comrades and Commissars*: "The Republicans drowned out their enemy when they brought up a public-address system so vast that it had to be transported by two trucks, the first containing electrical equipment and a bulletproof room for the announcer and the second supporting the speaker, an apparatus twenty feet long and six feet wide at it's mouth." Eby calls it "a demonic contraption [which] frayed the nerves of friend and foe alike as it blared forth endless surrender harangues, interspersed with recordings of 'Ave Maria' so loud that the individual words were lost in the ear-splitting decibels."[58] Regler titles his chapter on Guadalajara and Brihuega "The Battle of the Loudspeakers." As Orwell notes, on the Aragon front in early 1937 also "the real weapon was not the rifle but the megaphone. Being unable to kill your enemy you shouted at him instead."[59] Annoying and ridiculous, the apparatus effected some desertions on both sides, as Eby and Orwell acknowledge.[60]

The Salle de Goya's gathering celebrated "the uniting of all military regiments into the new brigades of the People's Army," a necessary consolidation of forces for effective command and control. Yet this restructuring never managed to solve the old problems completely. Militia units were placed in command structures, not disbanded and reintegrated at the individual soldier level. Old loyalties, rivalries, and real political differences persisted. Orwell reported that "the only changes that had actually taken place were changes of name. . . . The fact that the militia troops were also, on paper, Popular Army troops, was skillfully used in the Press propaganda. Any credit that happened to be going was automatically handed to the Popular Army, while all blame was reserved for the militias."[61] Harsh disciplinary methods essentially impossible in the volunteer, horizontally structured political militias became quite possible in a traditional hierarchical army, and the militias were generally less supplied and less regarded than the regular Popular Army units.[62] The move to a unified army brought the entire military increasingly under the influence of the communist leadership; the move also furthered the challenge of maintaining the nonprofessional, citizen-soldier image. The film's phrase "government militiamen" (as they carry art to safety) is a telling historic oxymoron.

What Arthur Coleman reads as the film's depiction of "a fundamentally agricultural and romantically primitive society,"[63] Waugh describes as "an iconography of flesh versus steel, rifles versus planes, the earth below versus the sky above."[64] We see rebel planes but no Republican ones; the only enemy bodies we see are the dead ones restored in death to the earth. The medical evacuation sequence is aptly placed after the battle for the bridge toward the end of the film as a visual version of the rhetoric of sacrificed blood renewing the land and the nation. Their blood becomes the water that irrigates the land at the end. The carrying of wooden troughs for the canal alludes to the carrying of wooden coffins in Madrid earlier. Wounded soldiers and civilian coffins aside, the fact that no dead Republican soldiers appear in the entire film advances its optimism.

Unlike in the battle footage, the camera closes in and lingers here because it can. Heilbrun's cooperation assured the film crew's access. This sequence has received no critical attention, yet audiences would have never seen its like before either. And compared to the bombardment of civilians, it documents an equally significant development in warfare:

> One series of innovations in the republican army in the winter of 1936–1937 would ultimately affect the rest of the world. These were the changes in the treatment of war wounds . . . and fractures by immediate surgery; the stitching of the edges of the wound; and the protection of the injured part, and the giving of rest to the patient, by extensive use of plaster of Paris. These changes meant bringing the surgeon to the patient and not, as was usual in the First World War, the patient to the hospital.[65]

How much of this revolutionary care took place at this scene is unclear; it had begun in Catalonia and took some time to spread to the rest of the army. We do not know if the limited treatment on screen is conducted by doctors or medics, nor the extent of treatment prior to loading the wounded on the ambulances. Hemingway, a veteran ambulance man and wounded passenger from the First World War, must have taken great personal interest at this site. He also had the immediate interest of his sponsorship of American ambulances for the Republic. If not outright inspecting his own donations, he would have been assessing the situation. And he and Ivens needed those images at the end of the film for their fund-raising events to segue to their personal appeal for money as they related the suffering the wounded endure without the luxury of proper ambulances—describing the scenes unseen and the sounds unheard in the film—and all but blame those who do not give money for some soldiers' slow deaths.[66]

Ivens's joy shines through in two telegrams of late August 1937 from New York to Hemingway in Paris (en route to Spain): "PICTURE BREAKING PLAYHOUSE RECORD"[67] and three days later "SPANISH EARTH BROKE ALL BOX OFFICE RECORDS OF THEATRE STOP SENDING YOU REVIEWS."[68]

Success at the 55th Street Playhouse and the great reviews in the *New York Times* and the *New Yorker* only somewhat mitigated the disappointment in the failure to win over a major distribution company. Tom Brandon's Garrison Films, the distributors of the "Spain in Flames" program, working in conjunction with Prometheus Pictures, eventually placed the film in three to four hundred theatrical and special showing venues nationwide. One newspaper article claimed the film grossed $100,000,[69] a figure which seems excessive unless it counts donations in addition to box office earnings.

Ivens attended a showing at the National Press Club in Washington on 25 August for an audience of several hundred diplomats, journalists, and others. Gerald G. Gross's brief review in the *Post* the next day is probably the harshest on record and accords with what a general audience today would likely say: "The six-reeler is frankly Loyalist propaganda, has some good camera shots, is dull for long stretches, contains little of a 'horror' nature (as most had expected) and, in sum, amounts to about 6,000 feet of war news-reel clipped together."[70] The state of Pennsylvania disagreed and on 15 September 1937 banned the film "on the ground that it contained scenes too gruesome for public exhibition,"[71] though politics was probably the real reason. In

December, the Common Pleas Court decision reversing the ban of "Spain in Flames" would also have freed *The Spanish Earth*. The Bureau of Police and Fire of Providence, Rhode Island, banned it for criticizing the "friendly powers" of "both Italy and Germany."[72]

The film had more censorship trouble in England.[73] The censor's office delayed the scheduled 23 October London premier and did not permit its release until 8 November[74] after cutting all references to German and Italian intervention except one easily overlooked line: "Government pursuit planes shoot one Junker down." As with France, Great Britain maintained its commitment to nonintervention and could not admit even to itself the extent to which future Axis nations were violating the European pact. If the British reviews held at the Joris Ivens Archives are representative, they were overwhelmingly affirmative. Even those dismissive of its leftist politics appreciated the film as film. The *Observer*, for example, called it a "scorching piece of propaganda, . . . a Red picture, a propagandist picture, but, before all other things, it is a good picture. Whatever your political beliefs may be, you must find some beauty in it, if it's only the beauty of simple things felt simply and simply said."[75] The *Daily Telegraph* and the *Evening News* also recognized the propaganda but praised the film anyway.[76] It's interesting to speculate on the film's reception had it not been cut. I suspect the reviews would not have changed much; the cutting of German and Italian support removed a detail of the message, not the message itself. Basil Wright wrote two gushing reviews. In *World Film News* he praised Hemingway's work as "the best commentary in the history of the sound film" and says that Ivens's "sense of film-making, gives this film a quality of greatness"[77]—though in the *Spectator* he did complain about Julian as striking the film's "one false note."[78]

The *Liverpool Post* expected the two themes "to meet and merge in a single triumph, and somehow it is not there—the film peters inconclusively away, and so it does not leave any very definite propaganda message in the mind of the audience. And in a film made as definite propaganda this must be counted as a weakness."[79] Nevertheless, it judged the photography and composition of the battle scenes as "astonishing." The *Manchester Guardian* considered it "the best film in London."[80] Both the London *Times* and the *New Statesman* characterized the commentary as romantic but generally effective;[81] the latter publication said that in the film "war seems to be like a macabre, untidy, unamusing picnic."[82] Others found the concise commentary quite powerful.[83] One observed the film's lack of political education and its focus on daily life such that

> it is not very clear what this war is about. . . . No one should expect to find in SPANISH EARTH either a fierce war picture or a violent piece of controversial propaganda. What Ivens and Hemingway have done is to focus a finely handled camera on the background of daily life behind the Madrid lines, where an army of young men has to be hastily improvised while there are so many mouths to feed. Hemingway's terse commentary is exceptionally well done.[84]

Similar troubles cumbered the film elsewhere. Ivens had to fight the censors in Holland; France planned to remove close shots of corpses, and Cuba backed out of its contract.[85] In January 1938, Ivens worried the film was already dated.[86] Arguably it was outdated before it was ever shown; the situation in Spain had changed severely between April and July 1937. Of course the film's relevancy truly ended with the war in April 1939. It became a dusty relic six months later, when Hitler invaded Poland.[87]

As for the Contemporary Historians, Inc., within a week of the Hollywood trip and about a month before opening night, the corporation drew up papers to dissolve itself and donate all assets to the Emergency Ambulance Committee. Hemingway, MacLeish, and Dos Passos signed them, leaving signature spaces for Lillian Hellman, Louise Eaton, and Osgood Field Jr.[88] They never finalized the disbandment. Instead, by November Herman Shumlin replaced MacLeish as president, with Dos Passos, William B. Osgood Field Jr., Hemingway, Ivens, MacLeish, and Anita Marburg as directors. Most likely Ivens's reassignment to China drove these organizational changes—MacLeish had written Shumlin on 12 October for a financial statement, which he hoped to use as he tried to raise funds for Ivens's film on China.[89] In January 1938 Ivens and perhaps others again considered liquidating Contemporary Historians, Inc. "The organization, as such, is really of no consequence," wrote Rollin Dart to Hemingway.[90] But they decided they still needed the legal entity for conducting business with the distributor.

The group formed a new company for the China film. On 28 February 1938, the *New York Times* announced the new corporation, History Today, Inc., its plans, and its members: MacLeish, Hellman, Luise Rainer, Clifford Odets, Shumlin, and Ivens.[91] No Hemingway (or Dos Passos). By the middle of March, Shumlin still hoped Hemingway would agree to serve on the board.[92] Ivens meanwhile, from January to June, wrote several letters practically begging Hemingway to join him.[93] Hemingway never officially signed up.[94] It is possible, however, that he later doctored the commentary. Once again, MacLeish, with Hellman and Ivens, wrote the initial story vision for the documentary that would become *The 400 Million* (1939), one remarkably similar to the initial vision of *The Spanish Earth*.[95] In 1943, Hemingway wrote de Pereda after the release of the movie adaptation of *For Whom the Bell Tolls*: "Dudley Nichols, in spite of his great reputation, I think, writes terrible scripts. You may remember the awful one he did for Joris on that China picture and how [Joris] had to call in poor old Papa to rewrite it as it was absolutely hopeless and simply a rotten imitation of THE SPANISH EARTH."[96]

Ivens once wrote that Nichols's script was "revised by myself and a friend."[97] His published diary from the trip does not mention a rewriting by a friend; it does contrast Hemingway's *The Spanish Earth* commentary ("understatement") with *The 400 Million*'s ("more descriptive and explanatory"[98]). William Alexander names Ben Maddow as the possible script doctor for the draft, but he notes that Maddow himself grew "less sure about this" when presented with Ivens's account.[99] If Hemingway lied to de Pereda about rewriting Dudley Nichols's script for *The 400 Million*, it might have been an act of revenge—the context of his claim is his response to a de Pereda letter critiquing the film version of *For Whom the Bell Tolls*. Nichols wrote the screenplay.

In July 1938, Hemingway entered a vigorous epistolary dispute with MacLeish and Ralph "Mac" Ingersoll about reimbursements Hemingway felt due for money he had loaned to complete *The Spanish Earth*. Hemingway issued his harshest words to MacLeish: "I laugh at you.

But no one who keeps going to a war laughs last and I confidently look forward to your makeing [sic] me out a shit who doesn't want to give any more money for ambulances. . . . But you, Archibald MacLeish in the year 1938 with all your excellent record on the Spanish war, and it is good and I admire it, are not the citizen who has any right to make that suggestion."[100] The issue was finally put behind them, but tensions persisted for years. In any event, the film continued to find venues and generate a quite modest income. On 28 January 1939, Herman Shumlin wrote to inform Hemingway that he, Ingersoll, MacLeish, Hellman, Dashiell Hammett, and Dorothy Parker had decided to hand their earnings over to the North American Committee. He hoped Hemingway and other investors would join them.[101] Hemingway was happy to do it.

After the war, proceeds from the film went to support Spanish Refugee Aid. In 1962, Shumlin wrote to MacLeish that Contemporary Historians, Inc.—of which he was the last president—"was long ago dissolved, and, alas, I no longer have the file on it." He planned to forward the $567.50 recently received from Brandon Films, the current incarnation of Garrison Films, to the Spanish refugees.[102] In January 1971, Hellman decided to take over the handling of any income in order to send it to Ivens. Her first letter proposing the idea to MacLeish is lost, but she repeats her rationale in March: "I have a strong sense of guilt about the money that properly belongs to Ivens," Hellman wrote MacLeish. "When I was told a year ago about Ivens [sic] very bad financial state, I wanted to send my own check, but his friend says he will not take money from anybody, but that he would take money from his work. That's the only reason for my nagging at you, myself and Herman."[103] The other two agreed. "Of course Joris deserves whatever Spanish Earth brings in," MacLeish had replied in January. "It's his work and Ernest's and Ernest no longer needs royalties."[104] (Hemingway had died ten years earlier.) Shumlin even had papers drawn up passing legal responsibilities for the film to Hellman and MacLeish, to which all three parties eventually agreed even though, as MacLeish joked, "Of course I approve in so far as a man can when he doesn't know his own status."[105] By fall a final routine emerged, with Tom Brandon cutting checks to Ivens but sending them via Hellman (who received all financial statements).[106]

Ivens was quite grateful. Unfortunately, this practical solution for disposing of the proceeds did not solve the actual ownership of and rights to *The Spanish Earth*. For years Ivens let others use clips from the film so long as he approved their cause, and after Franco's death in 1975 he arranged for a screening of the film in Paris despite a lack of clarity about international distribution rights. He sometimes acted as if he owned the rights; he certainly felt the film ought to belong to him. Hellman never presumed to control rights or permissions, believed Ivens the film's proper owner, and avoided trying to untangle the legal uncertainty surrounding the film. Efforts toward "finding out where the true ownership lies . . . would be stirring up a possible hornet's nest," she wrote in 1974.[107] The situation grew increasingly complicated by the several changes to the distribution company over the years: from Garrison Films to Brandon Films, to MacMillan Films, to Audio Brandon Films, to Films Incorporated. And when Ivens contacted her about showing *The Spanish Earth* in Paris, she refrained from getting involved:

> I think it is very unwise that I get in touch with anybody about your film. . . . It simply comes down to what I have said: any decision or request, anything about the picture should now come entirely from you. . . . Sorry not to be able to help you, but I am afraid if I did it would endanger all of us, and possibly even put any checks to you in future danger.[108]

It's unclear whether Contemporary Historians, Inc. was ever actively dissolved. Shumlin may have simply dumped the files. The legal hornet's nest involved this question as well as Shumlin's personal tax problems with the Internal Revenue Service, the legality of the transfer of authority from Shumlin to Hellman, and the possibility that the estates of the corporation's deceased members held stakes.

From 1975 onward Hellman insisted that as far as she was concerned the film belonged to Ivens. After her death in 1984, her assistant Rita Wade wrote three letters directing disbursements to be sent directly to

Ivens. The last of these is dated 17 December: "It is now imperative that you send the checks directly to Mr. Ivens. Miss Hellman passed away on June 30th and this apartment is being sold and there will be nobody at this address after the end of the year."[109]

Joris Ivens died in 1989. To this day, to my knowledge, no one knows who owns *The Spanish Earth*.

But there is one more part of this story.

Rollin Dart to Ernest Hemingway, 14 March 1938: "How about the proposition of Jasper Wood I wrote you a few days ago looks OK to me want to get him started all profits to you no middle man on the deal."[110]

Rollin Dart was a Canadian aviator Hemingway met in Spain and for a few months permitted to handle his affairs in New York, such as finding a theatrical producer for *The Fifth Column* and working on the movie rights to *To Have and Have Not*. With four years in the U.S. Army Air Corps, he had hoped to fly for the Republic. Instead he first fought as an infantryman with the English-speaking 86th Brigade at Cordova, and then served in various positions—adjutant for the Lincoln Battalion, staff officer for the XV Brigade, Bureau of Operations, and training officer for the Canadian Mackenzie-Papineau Battalion.[111] He turned out to be more trouble than he was worth.[112] His early involvement in the reimbursement tiff did not help; he asked Ernest and Pauline for several personal loans; and after three months Hemingway let him go.[113] Dart returned to Spain, partly because his bungling left him few options and partly because of a scandal involving "a certain divorcee on Park Avenue."[114] Back in Spain, when Hemingway was asked by Delmer about Dart, he answered, "If I ever lay eyes on that ____ ____ of a ____, . . . I shall break every bone in his body."[115]

Jasper Wood was a seventeen-year-old kid from Cleveland, Ohio. Seeing *The Spanish Earth* in early 1938 inspired him to write Hemingway for permission to put together a book version. Initially Dart served as the go-between. He bears some fault for the book's problems. The commentary he provided did not match the final recorded commentary,[116] and Wood wanted, and Hemingway expected, photographic stills to accompany the text. "I wanted a film continuity and to illustrate the book with photographs, stills from the film," Wood wrote Hemingway a few years later. "But Dart fumbled on that part."[117] According to Wood's father, Lehman, "Hemingway's agent" sent photographs "not suitable for publication" and failed to provide better ones.[118] A more trustworthy agent who could have been kept around to oversee the project would perhaps have prevented these problems as well as others.

Hemingway's complaint to Wood, wired on 19 July 1938, reveals what Hemingway imagined for the book: "EYE WAS INFORMED COMMENTARY WAS TO BE PUBLISHED WITH PICTURES FROM FILM STOP OTHERWISE IT IS MEANINGLESS . . . WITHOUT PICTURES OR A SCENARIO DESCRIBING WHAT IS PASSING ON THE SCREEN THE COMMENTARY IS MEANINGLESS AND UTTERLY RIDICULOUS."[119] Over a year earlier, in late May 1937, MacLeish exchanged several letters with Louis P. Birk at Modern Age Books on the subject of a possible short book about the war to be written by Hemingway and to consist largely of photographs. Birk was the editor working to bring out the book of Quintanilla's war sketches, eventually published as *All the Brave*; his company sided with the Republic. Hemingway had only just returned from his first trip to the war. Birk first suggested a book of fifty to sixty thousand words and thirty-five to sixty pictures, with a healthy first run of eighty thousand paper and twenty thousand cloth copies to be promoted "on a very large scale," including radio, and promised to Hemingway "the biggest ride ever received by a book under his name." Modern Age wanted to publish the book as quickly as possible, "though it may not be ready for our first list in July."[120]

MacLeish wrote back, airing his supposition that Hemingway would not be interested in a book of that word count.[121] Birk replied by dropping the number to thirty-five or forty thousand words. Anything shorter would not appeal to the public as a full book.[122] Birk appealed directly to Hemingway on 9 June, promising mass distribution and asking after any plans he and Ivens might have for "a picture book following somewhat the same pattern as the movie."[123] But MacLeish had advised Hemingway to decline the offer, and instead of having to write another forty or fifty thousand words for a Modern Age Books edition, publish a few photos in *Life* magazine with only "brief descriptions."[124] Hemingway settled for the four-page spread in *Life* with eighteen images from the film and his accompanying captions. "The War in Spain Makes a Movie" appeared in the 12 July 1937 issue in conjunction with the film's initial screenings.[125]

Wood's proposition for a book combining film stills and the commentary promised what neither of these other opportunities did. It's quite possible that Hemingway harbored a distinct and high ambition for a book version of the film. Highbrow circles had begun not only to see the photographic image as significantly complementing the written word, but the word as significantly and artistically complementing the image. *Ken* magazine, fashioning itself as a leftist version of *Life*, employed compelling images to push its agenda, and later in the war two of Hemingway's contributions to *Ken* focused on photographs: "Dying, Well or Badly" used corpse imagery, and "The Cardinal Picks a Winner" juxtaposed a line of corpses with a line of Spanish priests presenting the Nazi salute alongside several rebel officers.[126] Throughout the 1930s, magazines such as MacLeish's own *Fortune* ran photo-essays that gave equal weight to image and word, and several book-length photo-essays—what William Stott's excellent discussion calls documentary books—also began to appear. MacLeish in fact published one of his own, *Land of the Free*, in 1938. For Stott, this trend coalesced in November 1937 with Erskine Caldwell and Margaret Bourke-White's *You Have Seen Their Faces*, a financial and critical success hailed by reviewers as "a new genre" and "a new art."[127] Had such a book version of *The Spanish Earth* appeared in July, Hemingway might have beat Caldwell and Bourke-White to this bragging right.

As Stott observes, most documentary books "had a social purpose," and two "were unabashed propaganda: Fredrick Barber's *The Horror of It: Camera Records of War's Gruesome Glories* (1932), and Laurence Stallings's *The First World War: A Photographic History* (1933),"[128] the latter of which Hemingway owned a copy of in Key West.[129] Both were about war, as would be Robert Capa's propagandistic documentary book on the Spanish Civil War, *Death in the Making* (1938). Jay Allen translated and provided the preface to Capa's book, which included photos by Gerda Taro and served as Capa's unstated memorial and tribute to her. Indeed Hemingway perhaps had in mind photos by Capa and Taro, who had a number of photographs of Spanish peasants at work as well as a large collection of combat shots that would have added to the film stills and photographs taken by Ivens and Ferno.

Stallings not only wrote an early Great War novel, *Plume*, and co-wrote (with Maxwell Anderson) a Great War play, *What Price Glory?*, he also adapted *A Farewell to Arms* for the stage and wrote this review: "Certain books . . . remain forever out of literary categories and become, according to the depth of originality in the writer, a work unto themselves. Their influence is not to be calculated. So it is with 'Death in the Afternoon.'"[130] Published in 1932, Hemingway's *Death in the Afternoon* used eighty-one photographs—a compromise from his initial two hundred, to "show what he could not describe in words"[131]—albeit the book was chiefly text, the photographs relegated to the back, and editor Max Perkins's idea for running only sixteen photos would not have entirely derailed it. With sixteen or two hundred photographs, it was still an illustrated lecture. Still, *Death* might have prompted Stallings's documentary book and could be seen to have contributed to the rise of the documentary photo-essay book.

Without photographs, Wood employed a local illustrator, Frederick K. Russell, to provide graphic accompaniment. Japser's father, Lehman, an advertising executive, suggested Russell, and Jasper went to a "Communist bookstore" to find "ideal source material" for Russell to work with.[132] A black-and-white woodcut dominates the title page for each reel and corresponds to its focus. A bearded soldier clutches a rifle for reel 2, women and older men line up for food on a village street for reel 4, a couple embrace as the man begins to turn away to head to battle for reel 5, and soldiers battle behind a wood barricade for a small arched stone bridge for reel 6. The picture for reel 3, of a large clenched fist raised against three airborne planes above, appears in a slightly modified form on the cover and communicates the film's thematic scheme pitting the natural, earth-based Republic against the hierarchical, technophilic fascists. It also leads into the image of "the clenched fist of Republican Spain" raised by those attending the Salle de Goya meeting. A final illustration, opposite the final text, completes the story visually: from a small tree withering in the sun at reel 1 to this illustration of a tall, healthy tree standing beside an irrigation ditch.

Wood also wrote a seven-page introduction and reprinted as an afternote Hemingway's *Verve* essay about the film, "The Heat and the Cold." Hemingway did not believe *Verve*'s editor, Arnold Gingrich, could grant permission for the reprint. He also objected to the introduction for being "INACCURATE IN BAD TASTE AND DOES NOT GIVE SUFFICIENT CREDIT TO JORIS IVENS."[133] The introduction begins rather grandly and strangely insultingly in its prognostication: "In *The Spanish Earth*, Ernest Hemingway has made his greatest contribution to society. In it, he gave his all and we can't really give our all but once. That is my reason for saying that in the future, he will, because of what he has given, give less."[134] Hemingway correctly critiqued its inaccuracy in treating it as his film—Wood calls Hemingway "a vital factor in the formation of Contemporary Historians," and he says that the group recruited Ivens and Ferno and that Hemingway and Ivens conceived the film's "general theme."[135] In fact Ivens was a vital forming factor, the group recruited Hemingway, and however much Hemingway may have helped Ivens integrate the two story lines together he had nothing to do with the original conception. Wood's introduction also charges that Hemingway first "faltered" in his commitment to loyalist Spain[136] and mischaracterizes the film as pacifist: "It will always be with us to remind us of the horrors of war and it will keep repeating its message over and over again. Get rid of war, get rid of war, get rid of war."[137] Though not exactly plagiarism, the passage describing the faces we see in the film derives from *Time* magazine's review with a few bits of language directly borrowed. "Not since the silent French film, *The Passion of Joan of Arc*, has such dramatic use been made of the human face," writes the *Time* reviewer.[138] And Wood: "Never before has such dramatic use of the face been incorporated into a picture and will most likely never be done again."[139]

For all of Wood's missteps in the introduction, we can still laud his gumption and recognize the missteps as those of an ambitious teenager oversure of his talent and writing himself between the same covers as his idol: "They are trying to save us and are trying to shock us out of our complacent position, but we won't listen. That is the reason for this book. To make you realize what it is all about."[140] We should also admire his speed, from receiving permission after 14 March to publishing on 15 June.[141]

His most egregious misstep was the printing of the FAI anarchist banner in the inside back cover, about which Hemingway telegraphed and wrote Jasper and his father three times.[142] Wood remembers buying the banner at the same communist book store where he found material for Russell to use and did not worry about it until he showed a copy of the book "fresh off the press" to a Communist Youth League friend. "I was not a member of the party but liked very much many of the members. But some of them never talked to me again. Of course I was persistent and did not let this disturb my relationship with most of them."[143] Hemingway insisted by telegram that Wood replace the banner with a statement disconnecting himself from the book's preparation, commenting on the introduction's inaccuracy and poor taste, protesting the FAI banner, and directing all income to be paid to Werner Heilbrun's widow, Almuth.[144] Wood's statement of Hemingway's objections, which appears on the rear lining of the book's second issue, is adapted almost verbatim from this telegram. Between fifty and one hundred of the one thousand copies of the book display the FAI banner.[145]

By early November, according to Wood, the book had paid "for itself and now is beginning to show a profit." He expected to run out by Christmas.[146]

"It would be a most interesting story if Hemingway would write a book based upon his experiences while in Spain working on the film. He has not and says he will not."[147] At least in this respect Wood's introduction was more accurate. Hemingway did not write a book based on the filming experience *per se*. But when he did write his novel of the Spanish Civil War, he gave far more than young Jasper Wood predicted possible.

III

FOR WHOM THE BELL TOLLS

FIVE

The War, the Film, and the Novel

In 1952, Veterans of the Abraham Lincoln Brigade (VALB) published *Heart of Spain*, an anthology of international writings about the war. Alvah Bessie's preface explained the decision to exclude anything by Hemingway—his "On the American Dead in Spain" had been seriously considered:

> Hemingway's talent and the support he rendered to many phases of the Loyalist cause were shockingly betrayed in his work "For Whom the Bell Tolls" in which the Spanish people were cruelly misrepresented and leaders of the International Brigade maliciously slandered. The novel in its total impact presented an unforgivable distortion of the meaning of the struggle in Spain. Under the name and prestige of Hemingway, important aid was thus given to humanity's worst enemies.[1]

Indeed when Hemingway's novel appeared twelve years earlier, many veterans and other leftists flogged it in printed reviews and publicized gatherings.

A protagonist fighting for the Republic who waffles on his politics was one thing. Vilifying the International Brigade commissar André Marty and soiling the reputation of La Pasionaria while writing kindly of a fascist lieutenant was something else entirely. The atrocities dramatized in Pilar's story of the uprising were not, for these readers, balanced by the hard statement that the rebels committed still worse crimes when they took back the town, by their murder of Joaquín's parents, brother-in-law, and sister in Valladolid, or by the gang rape of Maria and whatever other and still worse violences she suffered but won't tell.

For Milton Wolff, Robert Jordan was made for Hollywood. American guerilla squad leaders didn't have "Abercrombie & Fitch sleeping bags" but only "ponchos for both ground cover and blanket," and they had "no Marias to share their bedding."[2] (Even as a few pages earlier Wolff admits to sleeping with a "very pretty Spanish girl named Eulalia" in a hotel bed, in far shorter order and with less communication than Jordan and Maria,[3] and with Hemingway's blessing to boot; even as a number of American volunteers married Spanish girls.[4])

The Nationalists do receive their due, in addition to the spoken and unspeakable atrocities against civilians. During the mission to blow the train led by Jordan's predecessor Kashkin, a fascist officer shoots two of his own men in the back of the head to motivate the others to advance;[5] Captain Mora, the fascist officer killed by El Sordo, pulls a pistol on his men as well.[6] And soldiers and citizens of the Republic, if we can apply Ronda across the board, do not harm women.[7] On the other hand, Hemingway makes clear that leadership by gunpoint afflicts the Republican forces as well, in actual and threatened political assassinations and in Robert Jordan's fear that if he does not carry out his orders he will be shot.[8] Pablo's temporary betrayal is also balanced by Captain Mora's buffoonery—at least the republican survives.

The novel also expresses the sense of individuals more or less apolitical but caught in history and politics, who live and die accordingly, on both sides. Anselmo recognizes that the soldiers guarding the bridge are peasants fighting for the Nationalists only to prevent the execution of their families;[9] the sentries are in fact just such conscripts who prefer this boring duty to combat.[10] They do not share the rumored cold-blooded passion of Nationalist soldiery. Jordan knows he has killed scarce few actual fascists.[11] One of the murdered men of Ronda, Don Guillermo, had no money and "was only a fascist to be a snob and to console himself that he must work for little, running a wood-implement shop," and because he loved his devout wife. It was the death of this man that turned Pilar and two others against the killing spree,[12] this man who adopted his wife's Catholicism just as Hemingway did. The scout Jordan kills is hardly a real fascist but a twenty-one-year-old working-class boy, the son of a blacksmith, who hails from Navarra, the region of Jordan's favorite Spaniards. We don't learn his politics, but his sister is anti-Marxist the way Jordan and company are antifascist.[13] Fascism was often promoted by its leadership, and accepted by its supporters, as simply the antidote to communism.

Among the Republican guerillas, Joaquín's apolitical brother-in-law belonged to a syndicate only in order to work, and the Nationalists killed him for his syndicalism.[14] Andrés has enough self-awareness to realize that, were it not for their father's Republicanism, he and his brother would have fought with the fascists.[15] Rafael the gypsy, Jordan thinks, is politically ignorant.[16] Earlier Anselmo gives this same observation a bleaker spin. The gypsies, he says, understand only that they now enjoy a license to kill as they haven't had since bygone days.[17] Among the actual U.S. brigaders, too, the reasons for their participation had their idiosyncrasies:

> It would appear that among the American citizens who entered the conflict, some could be classified as out and out hired recruiting agents, whose purpose was to lead others to the scene of hostilities and then perhaps vanish; others no doubt came over due to inability to find employment and are probably not over enthusiastic under their present circumstances; others apparently were inspired by motives more or less ideological; and no doubt a section would be found whose predicament could be traced to an unscrupulous exploitation of their spirit of romance and adventure.[18]

The data for this Department of State internal letter comes from six deserters across the French border, and while undervaluing the political commitment of most U.S. volunteers, the letter speaks to the variety of impulses motivating these men (and women).

For Whom the Bell Tolls is as fair-minded as it could possibly be, especially given Hemingway's loyalties, and thus the anger and calumny. Cary Nelson, in *Remembering Spain*, rightly contextualizes the veterans' initial response: "The 1940 novel appeared at a moment when the status of loyalist Spain in American culture was still uncertain. . . . Moreover, in 1940 the Vets still hoped antifascist activity outside Spain might make Franco's reign a short one. Thus the Vets were highly sensitized to any political impact Hemingway's novel might have had."[19] They were highly sensitized to any personal impact, too: the midcentury communist panic associated with the McCarthy era had already emerged. Jordan himself even worries about his postwar prospects back home.[20] By contrast, the anti-jingoism of *A Farewell to Arms* enjoyed a decade of distance and a far more hospitable climate; Frederic Henry may have taken his cue from all the other novels and memoirs of disillusion from that war.

For some veterans, novelistic realism demanded dramatization of their courage, commitment, righteousness, noble suffering, and sacrifice. For others, it might have demanded dramatization of suffering of a different vein. Desertions began before Hemingway set foot in wartime Spain. According to Thomas D. Davis, the American Consul at Valencia, in a report dated 15 March:

> If the various statements by these deserters . . . can be relied upon, the fatal casualties among the American volunteers have been exceedingly heavy, some statements placing total casualties in the 'Lincoln Division' as high as 75 per cent. It is claimed that they are invariably used as shock troops with insufficient preliminary training and inexperienced and inefficient officers. They also said that practically all the foreign troops were ready to desert at the first opportunity.[21]

In July, another deserter reported that the original Lincoln battalion complement of 600 had been reduced to 152, "about half of whom have been killed or wounded during the last 10 days" when the government put it alongside the other American battalion, the Washington, at the front of an offensive west of Madrid. The Washington also suffered "heavily."[22] Other American volunteers would report being denied discharge at the conclusion of their contracts, the arrest of Americans who refused to be incorporated into the regular Republican army, and the "fake court martial" and execution of some twenty-five Americans "who had left the front lines to report to the headquarters for discharge because their contracts had expired." Exaggerated or not, as the State

Department official reporting this last information acknowledged, the stories spoke volumes.[23] Sefton Delmer's memoir tells the story of Milly Finckelstein, a New Yorker performing secretarial services and some news work in Spain who was widowed several times over: "The last time I saw Milly she was married to her fifth American volunteer."[24] Most histories confirm the heavy casualties, poor leadership, and nearly inhuman conditions suffered by the International Brigades.[25]

Hemingway couldn't win. He realized the difficulties of depicting an International Brigader—the inevitable, impassioned charges of inaccuracy and misrepresentation from either direction. The memories and wounds were too fresh. A solo Robert Jordan, without a uniform, afforded Hemingway the liberty of a complex character unfettered by actual unit history and politics. Creative invention was aesthetically enabling and politically prudent, yet he still couldn't win.

In its own way, the fictional *For Whom the Bell Tolls* achieves a human reality that *The Spanish Earth*, a work of nonfiction, given its design and intent, never could. The film acted as one motivating element in the creative process of the novel, as a negative example against which Hemingway wrote. Writing after the war, Hemingway found himself freed from the wartime requirement to support the Republic. More significantly, his dispatches and the film had already satisfied the need to express and support the cause. Allen Guttmann's *The Wound in the Heart: America and the Spanish Civil War* (1962) sees the film and the novel sharing a similar structure, climaxing with a battle for a bridge and then closing with the natural imagery—of "the waters rushing through the newly constructed irrigation ditch, bringing life to the sunbaked soil" and of Robert Jordan pressed against the forest floor among the pine needles.[26] The wartime rhetoric whereby dead loyalists revitalize the land for the triumphant growth of the Republic correlates Jordan's death with the film's final irrigation imagery. The novel's conceit of the fallen loyalist soldier's integration into the land was hardly original; in his postwar poem "Tomorrow's Seed" Langston Hughes iterates this language: "Man / Who fell in Spanish earth: / Human seed / For freedom's birth."[27] Yet to counter readings that see Jordan's death as futile (if heroic), the conceit gives the novel a hope for a post-Franco reflowering of Republican Spain.

Structurally, too, the film and the novel jump among story lines, in the film among the village, Madrid life, trench life, and the several battles; in the novel, as it progresses, among Jordan and the gang, Anselmo at his observation post, El Sordo's last stand, Lieutenant Berrendo, and Andrés's journey to deliver Jordan's message to the general. Such a "splitting technique," Allen Josephs reminds us, is quite unusual for Hemingway's fiction.[28] He had quite possibly absorbed this jump-cutting technique working with Ivens and Van Dongen on *The Spanish Earth*. He might also have transferred from film to page the multi-vocal narration. In the film, the narrator is sometimes the narrator and sometimes a character.

Michael Reynolds has discovered that Hemingway imported the bridge from a draft of *To Have and Have Not*, the earlier novel's cut scene of a "boatload of dynamite here reduced to what Jordan can carry on his back."[29] Generally, however, one should not puzzle too long over a bridge figuring so prominently in a war novel. Bridges are a common military objective, and they carry such blatant symbolism that they feature in any number of war narratives. Hemingway placed a bridge at the center of a couple of unpublished short pieces set in the second World War.[30] In these stories, the Germans blow a bridge that must then be rebuilt. *For Whom the Bell Tolls* even references the film's bridge battle, as Jordan wonders why the enemy did not conduct it and the Guadalajara offensive at the same time in what would have been an unstoppable move.[31] Peter Wyden believes that the Arganda Bridge "would stay with Hemingway and his readers forever" as "the [physical] model for the bridge" in *For Whom the Bell Tolls*.[32] Josephs disagrees, concluding that Hemingway imagined the bridge, including its appearance, if possibly from "some other source."[33] Physical differences aside, the film's bridge and the novel's bridge bear a certain resemblance.

Both film and novel serve up an epic. Both emphasize the one common man on whom history hinges—Robert Jordan, of course, who himself saw Anselmo as singularly critical, the last man on the end of a flank on whom so much depends.[34] In the film, we have the small squads in assault, "Where each man knows there is only himself and five other men, and before him the great unknown. . . . Six men were five. Then four were three, but these three stayed, dug in and held the ground. Along with all the other fours and threes and twos that started out as sixes." Plus the character Julian, who was supposed to be as central as Robert Jordan, but with whom the crew lost contact and so lost for the final scenes.

Other passages from the novel echo the film. Hemingway's "hateful" emphasis on the word *they* in the film's lines—"For 50 years we've wanted to irrigate, but *they* held us back" and "The bridge is ours"—become the book's "*They* have taken Valladolid. *They* have Avila. . . . *They* will never take this town. *This* town is ours."[35] Then there are the faces. "This is the true face of men going into action," intones Hemingway in the film. "It is a little different from any other face you will ever see. Men cannot act before the camera in the presence of death." Later he comments that "when they move you out in trucks, it's to a battle." In the novel, these lines become Andrés's reflection:

> Once as he passed close to a troop truck and the lights flashed he saw their faces fixed and sad in the sudden light. In their steel helmets, riding in the trucks in the dark toward something that they only knew was an attack, their faces were drawn with each man's own problem in the dark and the light revealed them as they would not have looked in day, from shame to show it to each other, until the bombardment and the attack would commence, and no man would think about his face.[36]

Similarities aside, what matters more is how Hemingway rewrites the film into the novel beyond the plot differences. How he turns it on its head.

From the spare film narrative with its simple and directed message, we get the most verbose novel of his career, with a complexity of sympathies equal to his other great works. Hemingway leaves Julian, the simple country caricature of a government soldier, far behind in his portraits of Jordan, Pilar, Pablo, and others, like Andrés, who can simultaneously feel "ashamed, empty-feeling, proud and happy,"[37] an emotional feat Julian could never accomplish. Most especially, in this regard, we have Lieutenant Paco Berrendo, the young Nationalist officer the reader can't help but admire. Through Berrendo, Hemingway instructs his reader to avoid reductive and dismissive conclusions about other human beings. As Jordan watches Berrendo's men return from killing El Sordo's gang, he spies El Sordo's automatic rifle "lashed arrogantly" atop a saddle; yet we learn in the next sentence that Berrendo "felt no arrogance, . . . only the hollowness that comes after action."[38] The Catholicism so demonized by the Republic and its proponents becomes in Berrendo evidence of humility, depth of heart, and decency. The Spanish church's traditional support of the pre-Republican social system, combined with anarchist and communist atheism, led to a de facto official atheism within the Republic observed by Hemingway's Republican guerillas—to a point. Pilar admits that God probably exists despite the official line otherwise.[39] By the end of the novel, Joaquín, Anselmo, and Maria have all prayed.[40] Anselmo's prayer follows one of Lieutenant Berrendo's by a few paragraphs, with Hemingway veritably validating the Nationalist officer's Catholicism: "He went on with the prayer, the horses' hooves soft on the fallen pine needles"—pine needles associated with Jordan throughout the novel—"the light coming through the tree trunks in patches as it comes through the columns of a cathedral."[41] This validation transpires by way of the very natural imagery generally associated with the Republic (in opposition to the fascist, Catholic, professional, mechanized, Nationalist military). As Wallace Stevens wrote of a "martyred" Republican soldier, "This man loved earth, not heaven, enough to die."[42]

Sleeping with Maria, among other benefits, helps Robert Jordan attend to his own inclination to stubborn, knee-jerk ideological attitudes and rhetoric.[43] The protagonist hasn't entirely dishabituated himself, as his later judgment of Berrendo's arrogance shows. Naturally, it was exactly the complexity of sympathies that infuriated the veterans and their fellow travelers when the novel first appeared.

More important than the "unusual" splitting of story lines for Hemingway, whose novels normally "follow one action through from beginning to end,"[44] is this multiplying of perspectives. Against *The Spanish Earth* with its godly voice-over stands a novel that mostly inhabits the subjective terrain of one voice, but which ranges through many others: those of Pilar, Pablo's horse, Fernando, Anselmo, the Nationalist guards, El Sordo, the Nationalist cavalry, Lieutenant Berrendo, Karkov, Andrés, Lieutenant-Colonel Miranda, General Golz, André Marty,

Maria, and the occasional pronouncement from an apparently omniscient view.[45] The several perspectives seem also to comment on the allegiance to the eyewitness account of correspondents like Hemingway and Matthews—a single point of view could not have both presented as much information about the novel's wartime situation and called the reader's attention to the limited nature of witnessing. (In this sense perhaps Jordan does speak to Hemingway's self-estimation—Jordan realizes more that he actually knows about the military situation, such as the real purpose of the attack and its going forward no matter what.)

The many shifts in point of view disrupt the idea of a single, Republican sympathizing worldview and underscore contests of perspective that do not depend on narrative shifts. While a monolithic hegemonic perspective would violate the ideal terms of a democratic republic, critics have long recognized that the fractiousness of Pablo's gang mimics the internecine disputes of the Republic, that the dysfunction of the one mirrors that of the other. Not to mention the distrust in the novel among bands supposedly fighting on the same side. The independent nature of Pablo's gang, its struggle over its role in the war, and its responsibility to the government and the Spanish people (which aren't always synonymous) suggest the plight of a number of political groups within the Republic, those most committed to autonomy and resistant to a centralized military (and state) as well as those who, like some of the anarchists, became state functionaries despite their own antistate ideology. We see internal Republican hostility when, for example, Agustín wants after the war to "shoot the anarchists and Communists and all this *canalla* except the good Republicans."[46] Such dysfunction first arises at the book's historical genesis, at the beginning of the war in Ronda, when tempers flare with the anarchists, and when citizens feel obliged to defend and prove their loyalty to one another often by way of violence against suspected Nationalist sympathizers with that suspicion based on the most trivial evidence.[47] You haven't seen anything, Pilar tells Jordan, unless you saw the war begin in a small town.[48]

Pilar's story of the Ronda massacre captures the historic moment truthfully if not factually. Violent retribution against a town's elite in Ronda and other sites was in fact perpetrated by outsiders[49]—by people like Pablo, from Avila. The war's madcap beginning also as often as not presented an opportunity to settle old scores, personal ones and otherwise, such as the slaughter of individual members of those bourgeois and Civil Guard who never wronged anyone, but who belonged to an historically offending class, as happens in the novel.[50] Atrocities on the Republican side against presumed Nationalist sympathizers occurred mostly at the beginning of the war, and in just such spontaneous outbreaks as Pilar describes, by civilians and civilian militias. As Helen Graham concludes, "the picture which emerges from local studies is clear: what happened in villages and neighborhoods was very often not under the control even of the *local* committee, let alone any political authority beyond that. The uncertain correspondence between the left's political organizations and coercive action in the aftermath of the coup is epitomized by the vexed term 'the uncontrollables' (*incontrolables*)."[51] Atrocities committed by the fascists, on the other hand, were systematic, sanctioned, conducted by the military, and sustained throughout the war. As Robert Jordan reflects on Maria's story of being shaved and gang raped, "I know that we did dreadful things to them too. But it was because we were uneducated and knew no better. But they did that on purpose and deliberately."[52] Even more startling, the Nationalists practiced violent repression against citizens "in places controlled by the rebels from the outset: where there was no objective military threat, no significant political resistance . . . in short, where one would be hard-pressed to find a 'war-situation' at all."[53]

Hemingway also dares to humanize the fascist's atrocity system by painting Lieutenant Berrendo as a reluctant participant. He executes no one; he kills Joaquín promptly and tenderly after making the sign of the cross only to put the dying boy out of his misery. He orders his men to decapitate the corpses only because he needs the heads as evidence.

"'*Qué cosa más mala es la guerra,*' he said to himself, which meant, 'What a bad thing war is.' Then he made the sign of the cross again and as he walked down the hill he said five Our Fathers and five Hail Marys for the repose of the soul of his dead comrade. He did not wish to stay to see his orders being carried out."[54] Counterpointed to Berrendo's horrific duty against enemy corpses is Jordan's question of taking the initiative to murder one of his own compatriots. Pablo's later betrayal by stealing away with the dynamite blasting caps perhaps retrospectively proves the practical case for his death; on the other hand, only Pablo could find the men and horses needed after the annihilation of El Sordo's band, and only Pablo could, after the battle, lead the group to safety. Everyone recognizes Pablo's intelligence. His reservations about the bridge mission are based on sound tactical judgment; Jordan sometimes shares these doubts. And the historical context should make any International Brigader pause. Starting at Jarama, which Hemingway described as an "idiotic, stupidly conceived and insanely executed attack,"[55] the brigaders had followed bad order after bad order to devastating result. As the war continued, the rhetoric of self-sacrifice became increasingly difficult to sustain. Far too many could only hope to emulate Pablo's knack for survival.

When, in *A Farewell to Arms*, Frederic Henry initiates a battlefield execution of an Italian sergeant during the Caporetto retreat, Hemingway hardly gives us time to consider the act's justification as he propels the action forward. Moreover, as Margot Norris has convincingly claimed, readers have tended to be disinclined to confront the novel's several moral challenges, preferring instead to let themselves simply enjoy the melodramatic love story.[56] Hemingway poses the same reading conundrum in *For Whom the Bell Tolls*. If we can forget Jordan's loving of Maria and swinging like Tarzan to rig the bridge, Hemingway all but demands that we mull the idea of political executions over and over—among Pablo's crew with Jordan, between Karkov and Jordan, with Jordan and himself, between Gomez and a staff officer, and between Gomez and André Marty. He also potentially encourages the reader to regret Jordan's failure to kill Pablo and to appreciate Pablo's killing the partisans recruited to help with the bridge mission in order to secure enough horses for his group's getaway and survival (especially of Maria, about whom I have more to say in the next chapter). The novel's later excoriation of Marty for his role in political murders, however justified, must nevertheless be read through the ambiguity over Pablo. Marty is a clear example of immoral excess, yet our hero, Robert Jordan, and even we readers, have already in our imaginations crossed the line.

None of which we see in the film, whose simplicity the novel doggedly denies.

In his preface to Gustav Regler's *The Great Crusade*, Hemingway writes an odd testimony:

> The greatest novels are all made-up. Everything in them is created by the writer. He must create from knowledge, of course, unless his book is to be a tour de force. There have been great tours de force too: *The Red Badge of Courage* and *Wuthering Heights*. But the authors of such books are usually poets who happen to be writing fine prose. But there are events which are so great that if a writer has participated in them his obligation is to try to write them truly rather than assume the presumption of altering them with invention.[57]

Regler's autobiographical novel came out the same year as *For Whom the Bell Tolls*. Regler had worked on it while living with the Hemingways in Key West, and Hemingway had taken time away from his novel to write the preface. The oddness of the testimony comes from its contradictory privileging of works of invention versus works of truth, its different greatness standards, and Hemingway's paradoxical position as nonparticipant and participant-observer.

Reasserting his mantra that the greatest novels come from invention, Hemingway upholds his artistic, poetic superiority. He is perhaps preparing readers for the invented qualities of *For Whom the Bell Tolls*, declining to write the war "truly" in this passage's terms, in anticipation of the criticism from veterans while putting himself and such invention in its place—he did not participate in these great events and must "assume the presumption" of creative license. Does Hemingway imagine his novel will be a tour de force? His own status as participant-observer in the war, a status reinforced throughout the rest of the preface, ambiguously and maybe anxiously marks the book's nature and potential. He surely aspired to write, as *Newsweek* would dub it, "*the* book about the Spanish war."[58]

As with the retreat from Caporetto in *A Farewell to Arms*, Hemingway did not witness the actual Republican offensive for which Robert Jordan must destroy the bridge. In creating an entirely fictional scenario for a battle he did not witness and a protagonist and a ragtag militia atypical of the International Brigade and Republican army experience, Hemingway hoped to avoid charges of inauthenticity while freeing his fiction to its own possibilities, its full epic potential. He chose a minor action in which the XV International Brigade, the one with U.S. volunteers, did not participate.

The attack in the Guadarrama Range, just northwest of Madrid, on La Granja and Segovia, intended to draw Franco's forces away from their drive to take Bilbao with perhaps an even grander strategy in mind: A month before the attack, the Republic's Foreign Minister told the U.S. Ambassador to France that "if Franco should fail to capture Bilbao he was confident that the morale of Franco's armies would collapse rapidly and he would expect Franco to be defeated by the month of July."[59] Launched on 30 May 1937, the offensive ended on 6 June with the government troops back where they started, less about three thousand men. Hemingway's novel got much of the battle right. The characters' worry, for example, that the entire effort was secondary to other military aims, simply to relieve pressure from the rebel campaign in the north.[60] And according to Beevor's history of the war, the loyalists failed "because the nationalists appeared to have got wind of what was being prepared, but mainly because the speed of the nationalists' reactions and the effectiveness of their air power."[61] In the novel the Nationalists in Segovia gossip about the upcoming government attack, and the Nationalist aircraft dominate the sky. General Golz's complaint that he never owns his attacks is also accurate; the International Brigades and the Russian advisors to the Popular Army followed the operational commands of the Spanish leadership.

The first major Hemingway biography, Carlos Baker's *Ernest Hemingway: A Life Story*, follows a 1962 article in the *Polish Review* in identifying Hemingway's General Golz as General Walter, a pseudonym for General Karol Świerczewski, a Polish-born career Russian officer.[62] Scholars have repeated this identification ever since. Walter's division, one of the three participating divisions in the battle, included an International Brigade (albeit the French-Belgian XIV), so Jordan's presence has some validity. Baker draws his conclusion that Hemingway esteemed Walter from Hemingway's portrayal of the fictional Golz.[63]

Following Baker, Jeffrey Meyers and Allen Josephs offer additional evidence. A letter to Edmund Wilson describes one incident in which Hemingway admired Walter's battlefield sangfroid;[64] a letter to Evan Shipman quotes Walter in language quite similar to Golz's about his refusal to think too much.[65] Finally, and most convincingly, a letter from the novel's Polish translator paraphrases Hemingway's decision to change Walter's name: "He was such a splendid man and a splendid soldier that I wouldn't dare to present him in fictitious situations, and put in his mouth fictitious words."[66]

Herbert Matthews called Walter "one of the ablest Communist officers sent in."[67] A memoir by Walter's adjutant, Aleksander Szurek, documents several incidents of the general's standing up to bullets unfazed by the danger, "madly" brave.[68] "I know which bullets are dangerous," he once quipped.[69] Perhaps inspiring Golz's apparent experience with wartime lovers,[70] Walter had a Spanish mistress Isabelita, whom he would introduce as "Madame Commander." According to Szurek, introducing her in front of André Marty required no small amount of bravery. Marty "did not tolerate the presence of women in the International Brigades," and affairs and even marriages transpired in secret from him.[71]

Yet some evidence challenges this identification, or at the very least challenges what Hemingway knew about Walter. Szurek, who cites Walter as Golz's model[72] and who rarely left his side during the war, mentions the general's meeting André Malraux at Gaylord's in Madrid[73] and his fondness for Robert Capa and Gerda Taro,[74] but he describes not a single encounter with Hemingway even though Szurek writes about Hemingway for several pages in another context.[75] How well could Hemingway really have known Walter? Walter's actual performance in Spain left something to be desired. His first battle as commander of the XIV International, during the Corunna road offensive in the final days of 1936, proved "a singularly inauspicious start," according to Beevor. "The nationalists decimated their ranks with machine-gun fire, mortars, and artillery. . . . Some 800 corpses were left under the olive trees and 500 men deserted the front line." One brigader, Major Gaston Delasalle, was subsequently executed after an ad hoc court martial by André Marty.[76] The Guadarrama offensive on which

Hemingway modeled his battle was equally disastrous for the general: "Walter ordered XIV International Brigade to launch a frontal attack, which left the pinewood hills scattered with corpses. Walter's cynicism was revealed in a report back to Moscow in which he wrote, 'the XIV, which heroically, but passively, allowed itself to be slaughtered over the course of five days.'" One third of the battle's casualties came from the XIV International Brigade; Walter was relieved of command.[77] When another division retreated from one of its positions, "an infuriated Walter (before he was relieved) had ordered 'the machine-gunning of those who pull back, executions on the spot, and the beating of stragglers.'"[78] Walter's outburst over Duran's retreating 69th Division saw its equal carried out in his own unit:

> And the brutality of their commanders when some of their men broke in the face of strafing by nationalist fighters was extreme. Captain Duschesne, who commanded the punishment company of XIV International Brigade, "designated five men at random and shot them, one after another, in the back of the head with his pistol in Soviet style."[79]

Such a record hardly befits Hemingway's portrayal of Golz's competence, and it is difficult to reconcile with Golz's silent accusations of Marty's war crimes.[80]

Hemingway also mentions Walter by name elsewhere in the novel[81]—a trivial oversight, or an irrelevant technicality, or evidence (according to Josephs) of Hemingway's refusal to fictionalize the "splendid" general,[82] or evidence that Golz is not Walter, or is at best part Walter, part invention. It's hard to believe that by the time of his writing the novel Hemingway had not learned something of Walter's blunders and violent discipline, especially with Gustav Regler, who openly criticized military incompetence and disciplinary abuses, as a house guest.

The historical context of the battle calls into question the function and meaning of Robert Jordan's death: "The action in the Guadarrama produced the first example of unrest in the ranks of the International Brigades as a result of being sacrificed for little benefit."[83] Jordan's death might strike us as futile because the battle was lost, the antifascist cause had been lost, and the general war in Europe had broken out despite the democratic nations' nonintervention in Spain, but also because the battle and its aftermath exemplified the callous wasting of volunteers' lives. The veterans who loudly condemned *For Whom the Bell Tolls* must not have considered the book Hemingway could have written. In light of the battle's reality and the book that could have been, they perhaps should have lauded Jordan's sacrifice.

During the battle's opening day, Robert Capa and Gerda Taro "took turns using an Eyemo movie camera to shoot footage for the Time, Inc. newsreel series *The March of Time*" and using a Leica to shoot still images.[84] Some of those images from the Republican side of the battlefield can be found in a 2007 collection of Gerda Taro's photographs, titled simply *Gerda Taro*,[85] and in a 1941 *Life* magazine spread in advance of the movie version of the film.[86] The interspersed Capa and Taro footage in the *March of Time* episode, showing troop and tank and armored vehicle movement through the pine forest, includes a moving version of Taro's photo of the Republican soldiers on field phones[87] and her image of the tank moving through dust[88]—so Capa filmed these—as well as staged footage of American officers at the War College in Washington, D.C., studying a map of the Republican's short-lived Guadarrama salient.[89] Richard Whelan credits their photographs and Capa's "eyewitness accounts" as a major source of Hemingway's descriptions[90]—though even if he missed the battle, Hemingway, like Robert Jordan, had traveled the area before and during the war.

The *Life* article published two photographs showing the countryside of the battle with buildings easily imagined as mills and perhaps taken from reverse angles. One "shows the almost precise spot" of the novel's action albeit without the bridge. The other, whose caption begins "This is the country," has a snow-capped ridge in the background with the bridge, we are told, just down the road out of sight[91]—and very nearly matches the novel's opening imagery and language (but for the gorge).[92] That the caption obviously followed the novel's language does not rule out the photos as a source for Hemingway's setting.[93] In other ways the *Life* photographs are a bit misleading. For one thing, Taro receives no credit for her two photos—only Robert Capa and "news pictures" are mentioned.[94] The warning that the new pictures "are necessarily suggestive rather than accurate"[95] doesn't fully address the representation problem. Some photo captions indicate a photo transplanted from another battle (Teruel and the Ebro), while other transplanted photographs have no such indication and thus imply accuracy.[96] And the photo claiming to be the novel's bridge is really a bridge near Barcelona.[97]

Allen Josephs's 1988 quest for the novel's actual setting yielded a bridge not fitting the novel's description spanning a gorge about five kilometers from the front line but within Republican territory, not behind the rebel lines. Indeed most of the area's high relief terrain sits in Republican territory.[98] We can adjust this map a little, as the front line is an approximation, and the two battle site photographs in the *Life* article reveal a landscape of softer contours than a word like "gorge" suggests, contours that very well might appear on the other side of the line. Yet as Josephs rightly concludes:

> Isn't it more enlightening . . . that for his setting, sometimes more Homeric than historic, he deepened a mountain stream into a gorge? That he saw in the suggestion of a cave's mouth a depth in the Spanish earth sufficient to hide his fugitive band? That he turned a stone bridge into "the steel of the bridge, straight and rigid across the gap" and at the same time something "spidery and fine in the mist that hung over the stream" (431), something that if blown properly could help stop the march of fascism forever?[99]

Or that he reimagined the mid March 1937 snows of the Guadalajara battle and the snow in the Capa photo, plus his own glimpses in late April of the snowy peaks of the Guadarrama,[100] into the novel's early June snowstorm?

Josephs's quest turned up no caves, either—there are no caves in this granite country.[101] Hemingway knew of other caves in use during the war, however. We see some in *The Spanish Earth*, as the soldiers carry munitions and armaments in and out of them, perhaps around Guadalajara, or perhaps the cave used by brigade staff during the Casa de Campo action that Hemingway helped film and mentioned in his short story "Under the Ridge."[102] There were the inhabited caves Josephine Herbst visited above Alcalá de Henares on the way to Guadalajara, and the caves she visited in walking distance of Fuentedueña, Julian's village in *The Spanish Earth*, where people lived during peacetime as well.[103] East of Madrid, toward Guadalajara and Brihuega and around Teruel, people took refuge in the caves.[104]

In September 1937, Hemingway crawled to a frontline position to observe the Teruel defenses with a Republican guide and a periscope, reminiscent of Robert Jordan's first inspection of the bridge with Anselmo, and he and Herbert Matthews spent three days "climb[ing] the steep mountain trails, [riding] over newly cut military roads through precipitous mountain country in trucks and staff cars, and visit[ing] the highest mountain positions on horseback with a cavalry escort."[105] The two correspondents then witnessed the December Republican siege and capture of mountainous Teruel. Though no International Brigade units participated in the initial action, three American volunteers, Alex Kunslich, William Aalto, and Irving Goff, led a small Spanish guerilla outfit behind enemy lines "to destroy the main supply bridge that spanned the Albarracin River." They encountered no resistance and planted explosives on the bridge set to detonate when a military vehicle drove over it:

> Later, from a distance, they heard an explosion and watched the small structure crumble into a ravine. Then they destroyed nearby telephone communications. But their noise attracted a fascist cavalry patrol, which started to pursue them. As the guerillas fled on foot, the deep snow stymied the fascists' horses, enabling the band to escape. The bridge remained down for a couple of days, preventing reinforcements from reaching the fascist defenders at Teruel.[106]

The Teruel snowstorm possibly provided Hemingway the imagery he utilized in *For Whom the Bell Tolls*, especially of the traffic jam up the mountain that Andrés sees. Hemingway's dispatch mentions three days of snow that "threatened to block the Government lines of communication" until "they were cleared by tractor-driven snowplows," and, once weather turned warm, watching armored cars head toward the attack.[107] "Troops and armored cars were stretched out ahead of us," wrote Matthews.[108] The assault caught the two up in their most intense infantry action of the war, over broken ground of gullies, ditches, gulches, and ridges, as they struggled for the little available cover from Nationalist small arms, machine guns, mortars, and aircraft. They watched the rebels' last stand on the fortified heights of the Mansueto peak. They saw men on both sides struck down.

If, unlike Guadarrama, this time the rebels were caught by surprise, they began planning their counterattack before Teruel's fall to the loyalists, finally recapturing it in February 1938. Even though the Republic claimed Teruel as a victory, the battle eventually became another costly and futile sacrifice of men for the Republic.

The Guadarrama offensive also occurred at a pivotal moment in the war's history, or at least in Hemingway's experience of the war. As discussed in chapter 1, within weeks Bilbao fell, and several of Hemingway's friends were severely wounded or killed. The Republic was still feeling Barcelona's civil war within the civil war, an event that probably influenced Hemingway's negative portrayal of the anarchists in *For Whom the Bell Tolls*, and also an event that ensured the centralization of government power and solidified the Spanish Communist Party's position within the Republic (partially by the scapegoating and delegitimizing of its rival internal communist group, the POUM). State repression and non-state actor repression by the communists and Comintern followed in the wake of the May Day riot.[109] The Barcelona violence turned the Republican idealism of one of its participants, George Orwell, into cynicism:

> No one in his senses supposed that there was any hope of democracy, even as we understand it in England or France, in a country so divided and exhausted as Spain would be when the war was over. It would have to be a dictatorship, and it was clear that the chance of a working-class dictatorship had passed. That meant the general movement would be in the direction of some kind of Fascism. . . . But it did not follow that the Government was not worth fighting for as against the more naked and developed Fascism of Franco and Hitler.[110]

As Meyers argues, the Republic's internecine conflicts became fodder for Hemingway's novel, which criticized its leaders "for their divisiveness and incompetence, which drove the pragmatists of the Left into the hands of the Communist disciplinarians."[111] Hemingway believed, with Robert Jordan, that the loyalist leaders couldn't be trusted with the Republic's welfare and would have to be replaced. Jordan worries that carrying out the doomed mission would "be a betrayal" of Pablo's people, yet "he was under Communist discipline for the duration of the war."[112] Hemingway was his own sort of pragmatist, as evidenced by his ambulance program, *The Spanish Earth*, and his pro-Republican dispatches and essays. He unenthusiastically conceded, with Robert Jordan, that the Republic needed the communists' discipline and military sense to win the war (not to mention material aid by way of the Soviet Union).

As we've seen, determining the extent of Hemingway's blind acceptance of the Republican and sometimes the Comintern line versus his deep insight and pragmatism has been the source of much debate. Stephen Koch, who in *The Breaking Point* finds that Hemingway initially bought utterly into the government's and the communists' positions, is at his best at the end of the book, as he watches Hemingway struggle through his loyalty to the Republic contrasted with the actualities of Republican politics on his way toward writing *For Whom the Bell Tolls*. "Hem had to square the Robles killing and the emergence in Valencia of what looked rather like a Stalinist state" with his own very public support of the Republic. Though Koch grossly exaggerates the degree to which the Republic was "clearly in service to Stalin,"[113] I appreciate his effort to record Hemingway's struggles with all that was going wrong with the Republic. He sees Hemingway's play *The Fifth Column* as a failure within this struggle, "an exceptionally nasty piece of work and the moral nadir of Hemingway's entire career" in its attempt to "dissolve the facts of the Spanish terror in a heroic antifascist glow" and in its acceptance of immoral executions as necessary and even "heroic" assassinations.[114]

While the play might in fact enact Hemingway's moral struggle, a kinder and I think more accurate analysis sees the play as purposefully raising the moral issue and leaving it unresolved rather than supporting and romanticizing the assassinations as if Hemingway were battling back his own conscience. Philip Rawlings has wearied of the killing and the lies, and by play's end asks to be shipped out as soon as possible.[115] Rawlings never earns our admiration in matters of love or war, and it's Robert Preston, the actual journalist with a wife and children and the man Dorothy Bridges ditches for Rawlings, who might be a closer self-portrait. "Let him go *back* to his wife and children now if he's so excited about them. I'll bet he won't. Those wife-and-children men at a war. They just use them as sort of an opening wedge to get into bed with someone and then immediately afterwards they club you with them. I mean positively *club* you."[116] If we ascribe Rawlings's profession as intelligence officer to Hemingway's attitude, do we also presume Hemingway approved of the outing as a fascist of an old acquaintance by the writer-narrator Emmunds in the story "The Denuncation,"[117] do we presume Hemingway actually outed or would have outed such a man? At the very least one should acknowledge the play's and the story's wartime acknowledgment of the political executions; Hemingway himself noted that some "fanatical defenders of the Spanish Republic . . . will criticize the play because it admits that Fifth Column members were shot."[118]

For Koch, with "Old Man at the Bridge," published in *Ken* on 19 May 1938, "The healing fountain was starting to flow." Koch quotes the old man's lines as evidence of Hemingway's emotional exhaustion and political recovery: "I am without politics. I am seventy-six years old. I have come twelve kilometers now and I think I can go no further."[119] Hemingway's war with himself wasn't quite over, and five weeks later Hemingway blasted Dos Passos in *Ken* by reasserting Robles's just execution, after a fair trial, as a spy.[120] Yet by *For Whom the Bell Tolls*, "Hem was not a little liberated" from the "lies," and "if the novel is not fully detoxified from Hemingway's trafficking in Popular Front propaganda—and it is far from that—it is nonetheless forthrightly defiant about his sometimes Stalinist friends, and the book left most of them gagging with outrage."[121] For Donaldson, it was the "disillusionment evident" in the four Spanish Civil War short stories written in late 1938 that "marked a midpoint in the process by which Hemingway transformed himself from a propagandizing journalist with a cause" into his true form as a great novelist.[122]

I don't believe Hemingway was ever as thoroughly duped as Koch does. Robert Jordan's evolving political thinking is, however, suggestive. He started fighting the summer of 1936, soon after the rebellion, and now, about ten months later, reflects on his political development. He characterizes himself during his initial visits to Gaylord's, the hotel occupied by the Russian and Comintern gang, with Karkov, the Soviet journalist who in the novel issues orders to generals, as rather too green. Back then he had accepted the malarkey about the modest backgrounds of military commanders like Enrique Lister the stonemason, the same peasant backgrounds presented in *The Spanish Earth*. Knowledge of their Russian training had been the first step of his enlightenment. What he perceived as the gang's "cynicism" he came to recognize as "truth," yet a truth he found "much better than the lies and legends."[123] Through it all he claims to have performed his duty while preserving his independent outlook.[124] How much Hemingway kept possession of his mind early in his involvement, when and to what extent he might have turned to a more truthful cynicism, where the concept of political assassinations in general and his knowledge and belief in the specific case of José Robles fall, and how much this possible self-portrait gets revisionist, presumably in good faith, are questions for the ages.[125]

Perhaps Hemingway gives us some indication of an attitudinal shift in his first dispatch after his return to Spain in the fall of 1937, shortly before beginning work on *The Fifth Column*, in potentially telling language about Republican troops: "Since I had seen them last spring they have become soldiers. The romantics have pulled out, the cowards have gone home along with the badly wounded. The dead of course weren't there. Those that were left were tough with blackened matter-of-fact faces and after seven months, they know their trade."[126] This passage really only redefines the romanticism, from inexperienced idealism to earned realism, cutting exactly the kind of romantic figure Hemingway gives us in Robert Jordan. It also happens to occur in Hemingway's only NANA dispatch with an appearance by Robert Merriman, the international brigader often identified as the model for Robert Jordan.[127]

Hemingway missed the battle of Belchite and had his account of Merriman secondhand: "Unshaven, his face smoke blackened, his men tell how he bombed his way forward, wounded six times slightly by hand-grenade splinters in the hands and face, but refusing to have his wounds dressed until the cathedral was taken."[128] The opening paragraph of this dispatch closes with a reference to Montana, where Robert Jordan taught at the university: The dust "blew in blinding clouds raised by the hoofs of pack animals and the wheels of motor transport, and in the gale the clouds of dust rolling over the bare hills of Aragon looked like a cesspool blizzard in Montana."[129]

Herbert Matthews, who knew Merriman as well as Hemingway did and knew Hemingway's wartime musings as well as anyone, never thought he transformed Merriman into Jordan.[130] Neither do Jeffrey Meyers or Allen Josephs.[131] Jordan and Merriman shared a first name, were both professors from the American west (of Spanish in Montana and economics in California, respectively) fighting in Spain, and they both disappeared in battle, presumed dead, while some of their cohort got away. I agree with Matthews and Meyers; other than these facts, and their quiet demeanor, Merriman and Jordan have little in common. Superficially, instead of Jordan's somewhat long blond hair, Merriman's brown hair was, by his twenty-eighth year, already receding, with what remained on top rather wispy.

Merriman was a regular brigader—as opposed to an irregular combatant—through and through. After an early appointment as the Lincoln Battalion's adjutant, the ambitious Merriman soon enough became its commander and was wounded at Jarama in February 1937. Merriman the college-boy proved able enough given his own and his soldiers' inexperience, their poor and motley equipment, and especially the horrendous leadership above them. Yet he had his detractors among his subordinates (as nearly all commanders do), some of whom considered him a "yes-m[a]n" and called him "Captain Murderman."[132] After his wounding he moved into training work for the internationals before becoming the XV International Brigade's chief of staff. His death occurred while serving in this job.

Politically, Bob Merriman stood slightly to the left of Robert Jordan. Neither belonged to a communist party, though many brigaders presumed Merriman a loyal communist and a Soviet sympathizer, as he had arrived in Spain from Moscow, where he had been studying the

Soviet's economic approach to depression-era agriculture. Cecil D. Eby speculates that his coming from Moscow may have precipitated his early rise in the brigade ranks:

> In the Soviet Union, the *Yezhovshchina*, purges that would eliminate three-quarters of the Central Committee, was under way, and it is likely that no one at Albacete [headquarters] was quite sure who or what stood behind Merriman. If he was a Kremlin spy, it would be better to treat him with kid gloves. The scuttlebutt in Albacete was that he had come straight from the Frunze Military Academy, until it was replaced by a rumor that he had come straight from the famous Lenin Institute.[133]

As for Jordan, in his study of Hemingway's relationship with his publisher Scribners, *The Lousy Racket*, Robert Trogdon reminds us that Hemingway revised Jordan's self-identification from "communist" to "anti-fascist" to appease the Book-of-the-Month Club.[134] Hemingway's "docile" attitude about the change suggests that Jordan's political affiliation with communism was a matter of little consequence.[135] In fact Jordan's politics as evidenced in the rest of the novel resist a communist label. He supports the Spanish communists only for the war effort, but otherwise thinks of himself as apolitical, knowing only enough Marxism not to be taken advantage of and to win the war for the sake of individual liberty and dignity.[136] Karkov considers him "of slight political development."[137] One must also keep in mind that the Spanish Communist Party of the Spanish Civil War, to the extent that we can characterize it as ideologically cohesive, was all in all a nonrevolutionary, bourgeois venture. Jordan believes in the Republic as Spain's best opportunity for its citizens to fully live their lives, and he believes in the war as the first great battle in the fight against fascism. As Josephs writes, because most American brigaders were communists, "Hemingway almost surely made [Jordan] a nominal communist only for the sake of realism. The removal of the word changed his putative affiliation, but it did not alter his critical nature one whit."[138]

Merriman was also passionately antifascist. And in graduate school at Berkeley in the 1930s, not far from California's suffering agricultural lands, he could not help being caught up in conversations about working conditions. According to his wife, "he increasingly sided with the weak, the have-nots," and his "curiosity led him to investigate everything on the campus, including the left-wing gatherings of the Social Problems club and the International Labor Defense Organization."[139] While in Moscow, he never became a communist devotee, but his academic interest in the effectiveness of the Soviet agricultural system, and his admiration for their cooperative efforts as opposed to the U.S.'s top-down, profit-driven model, sometimes led him to contemplate a more activist role in America.[140] He never got the chance.

The three American guerillas assigned to blow bridges at Teruel could have contributed to the creation of Robert Jordan, though like Merriman they differed greatly in background and personality from Hemingway's protagonist. According to Anthony Beevor, one Kh. U. Mamsourov, or "Colonel Xanthé," directed "all partisan activities" from August 1936 to October 1937 and claimed himself as the model for Robert Jordan.[141] Peter Wyden cites him as well, spelling his name a bit differently: "Santi" during the war, and later Mamsurov Haji-Umar. According to Wyden, he was a Soviet staff officer and a friend of Hemingway's friend Ilya Ehrenburg (a Soviet writer), "a fearless, swarthy guerilla specialist from the Causcasus. . . . [who] later briefed Ernest Hemingway on techniques of behind-the-lines warfare which the author incorporated in *For Whom the Bell Tolls*."[142] Josephs mentions a "Russian guerrilla named Starinov" who might be this same man.[143]

But the most intriguing guerilla-soldier candidate is Antoni "Antek" Chrost, a Polish volunteer who told his story to a note-taking Aleksander Szurek in 1967 in Warsaw. Chrost commanded a guerilla unit operating out of Alfambra on the Alfambra River in the Teruel province.[144] On an unspecified day, which William Braasch Watson dates as 20 September 1937, Chrost discovered in his modest headquarters barracks building "a well-known political commissar" sitting with a stranger, who "gaily" ribbed the commissar in Spanish: "I shit in the milk of the mother who bore you." Chrost had never heard of Hemingway before, but the newcomer's safe-conduct pass from Chrost's corps satisfied him. He answered Hemingway's questions about the unit's sabotage work and use of local guides.[145]

Three weeks later Hemingway returned, accompanied by two officers from the Corps and with a "permit to participate in an operation," and grateful to Chrost for trusting him. The objective of that mission was a train near enough to their base that the guerillas traveled lightly, "twenty kilos of dynamite and enough food for twenty-four hours. . . . Hemingway, as our guest and reporter, carried a lighter load: hand grenades, a revolver, and food but no dynamite." The group slipped through the fascist lines to hunker down and wait in a culvert beside a bridge.[146] A tempting target of opportunity presented itself on a road "jammed with trucks full of soldiers headed for the Front," but they resisted and moved to the tracks. The train's "smoke and sparks" were visible "a few kilometers away." They crawled to the tracks and set a mine.

> "Are you afraid?" Hemingway asked Antek.
>
> "There are no heroes here. We're all afraid. Maybe we won't even blow the train," he replied.
>
> The rumble of wheels was louder as the train came closer. The train blew up. Some cars were completely shattered. Hemingway took a picture by the light of the explosion; he was satisfied.

They withdrew.[147] That night, after feasting—per Szurek according to Chrost—Hemingway declared, "I'll write about you. . . . But in my book you'll be an American."[148]

Martha Gellhorn believed Herbert Matthews served at least partly as the model for Jordan.[149] She admired the "shy reserved" Matthews greatly, calling him an "angel" in a letter to Milton Wolff, and one of the few alive by 1977 to tell the story of the war straight.[150] Everyone who knew Matthews in Spain admired his great integrity.[151] George Seldes tells a story about Matthews which has the flavor of Robert Jordan and demonstrates his vigilance for facts. Once, when the *Times*'s man on the Nationalist side (William Carney) reported that Franco's troops had taken the Arganda Bridge and so had finally entirely encircled Madrid, cutting it off from outside support, Seldes and Matthews drove to the bridge where Seldes stayed safely with the parked car while Matthews, with sounds of shooting nearby and daring the distinct possibility of sniper fire, "walked across the bridge to the other side, and walked back." Soon enough they saw Republican supply trucks traveling the road as well.[152] Delmer liked Matthews for Jordan due to his "unsmiling and serious" demeanor and his outfit.[153]

Joel Hodson and Jeffrey Meyers have argued for T. E. Lawrence as an inspiration for Robert Jordan.[154] In addition to Merriman, Wolff mentions Phil Detro, who was also killed in action.[155] Six-foot-four-inches tall, Detro carried himself "like the hero of a Zane Grey novel" and "invariably wore a faded beret and a turtleneck sweater several sizes too large." He wanted to be a writer, and a flier, who rarely took things very seriously.[156] There's also Charles Sweeny, Hemingway's longtime soldier-of-fortune friend who didn't seek fortune:

> I didn't desire an orthodox military career in the United States Army, nor did I wish to be a pretty parade ground soldier. I did not then quite know what I wanted to do except be the kind of soldier who was not a common mercenary, but rather one who spent his life fighting in the cause of freedom and honour in any part of the world where those things were threatened. . . . A people's war, that's what I want.[157]

That vocation eventually took this self-described loner, after several other wars, to Spain, where he worked as a military advisor to the Republic in the spring of 1937 and again, a little later, until the end of the war.[158] With his "tidy" mind, "long hair," and preference for "casual clothes" and "unorthodox uniform,"[159] Sweeny bore some resemblance to Robert Jordan.

Hemingway might have known of Paul Patrick Rogers, the actual American professor of Spanish who spent August 1937 in Spain as part of a North American Committee to Aid Spanish Democracy observation delegation. He did know International Brigader Frank Ryan, whom Rogers described as unforgettable: "Big, tall, deep-chested; honest, brave & courageous face with a blue eye that will always remain in the memory—a man among men."[160] Rogers also met El Campesino, whom Hemingway certainly knew, and the story El Campesino liked to tell about himself would have doubtless stuck with Hemingway: "On July 19, immediately after the Fascist revolt, he went into the mountains with 20 men, 12 rifles, and 4 pistols. Completely defeated the first army sent against him within two days. By the end of four battles, he had an army of 400 and was within 4 miles of Mola."[161]

The other noteworthy personality was Werner Heilbrun, the German Jewish doctor to whose widow Hemingway assigned the earnings from Jasper Wood's *The Spanish Earth* book. Heilbrun, Hemingway wrote in an unpublished sketch, was a natural in war, as strong and flexible as a tree in a storm, a man who could have led a successful hasty attack to save Christ from the cross.[162] Heilbrun often worked through the night, "the work he did so well, so intelligently, so painstakingly so delicately and skillfully, and always with the languid air of doing nothing."[163] According to Regler, Heilbrun often left the safety of friendly lines, under fire, to tend to and bring back a wounded soldier from no man's land.[164] He was killed in a car the morning of 12 June 1937 by strafing from a Nationalist plane.[165]

In 1964 Carlos Baker received a letter naming the most bizarre candidate of all, a Spanish professor named Robert Jordan Carner, who taught at Radcliffe and Harvard in the early 1940s:

> The Cambridge legend was that he had fought in the Spanish Civil War with Hemingway & was the prototype for Robert Jordan in For Whom the Bell Tolls. Although Carner was my teacher and someone I occasionally talked to in local bars, I never heard him mention Hemingway. He was however sufficiently bitter & sufficiently drunk to uphold the legend. He had a badly fitted artificial foot which gave him a terrible limp, and we believed this came from the Civil War. He also looked somewhat like Hemingway—with black hair & eyes & a thick mustache. On no provocation at all, in class or on the street or in bars, he'd denounce Franco with what seemed genuine emotion and along with Franco the U.S. Govt. for its "hypocrisy" in recognizing him.[166]

Robert Jordan was a composite, with no small amount of his creator in him, but like the bridge he destroys, he is mostly invention. The *Life* magazine article about the film version of the novel, with photos from the war, includes head shots of representative Spaniards for Anselmo, Maria, and Pablo.[167] Its head shot for Robert Jordan?

Gary Cooper.

As for Pablo, El Sordo, and their bands, during that spring of 1937 Hemingway encountered a group in the Guadarrama that sounds a great deal like the novel's mountain partisans. Virginia Cowles was with him, and she has left a good account of this encounter with a group of "ragged soldiers" who continued clapping along to a love song while bullets struck the boulders around them. Their commander, "in boots and breeches and green turtle-necked sweater, had a forage cap pulled rakishly over one eye," and was called El Guerrero. "He had fought all winter in the mountain passes of Guadarrama and although his battalion had been wiped out on several occasions he had managed to get replacements, and, fighting desperate guerilla warfare, had prevented the enemy from moving their columns along the narrow roads." There was a nineteen-year-old peasant boy, "who had thrown a grenade among twelve sleeping men the night before" then "blushed" when presenting Cowles with wildflowers he had picked. And another, "who had held a machine-gun position single-handed for forty-eight hours, showed [her] a poem he had written extolling the beauties of nature." El Guerrero's wife had fought alongside him until her pregnancy, but he did produce another girl who had fought with them, with "plucked eyebrows and rouged lips and . . . wearing a man's uniform."[168]

Which brings us to Pilar and Maria.

SIX

Pilar and Maria

El Guerrero's wife may have inspired or otherwise contributed to that most original of Hemingway's characters, Pilar. Gertrude Stein is another possible model for Pilar, given the two women's burly figures, manly demeanors, forces of personality, homoeroticism, and power as storytellers.[1] Jacqueline Vaught Brogan, while declining to weigh in on the question of Pilar's historical model, sees the two extended lovemaking scenes between Jordan and Maria as deliberate imitations of Stein's prose, a fairly solid contention that oddly places Jordan, Maria, and Pilar all in bed together (and Stein and Hemingway to boot). For Jeffrey Meyers, there is "more than a touch" of Hemingway's mother in Pilar.[2] Edward F. Stanton and Allen Josephs have no doubt that "he based Pilar on Pastora Imparío," a famous flamenco dancer and singer.[3]

The other historical personage to consider is Dolores Ibárruri, more famously known as La Pasionaria. Lincoln Brigade veteran Alvah Bessie saw a great deal of Ibárruri in Pilar.[4] Paul Patrick Rogers, the professor of Spanish sent as an observer-delegate, met La Pasionaria on 9 August 1937 while visiting a home for orphaned refugee children run by Ibárruri:

> She is indeed a supremely dynamic personality—one of the most remarkable I've ever met, if, indeed, not the most remarkable. In her speech & actions, conviction of purpose & determination & human

> kindliness radiate. She dominates by grace & power of personality all with whom she comes in contact. She seems to lose herself in work for others—sacrifice might well be her middle name.[5]

The children adored her. It is just such a place where Jordan, shortly after meeting Maria, imagines her being taken care of while she cares for the displaced children.[6]

Stacey L. Guill has briefly remarked upon the "obvious parallels between Pilar and Ibárruri" in terms of their physical appearance, intelligence, oratorical skills, and revolutionary spirit.[7] A symbol of "revolutionary womanhood," during the initial days of the rebellion, La Pasionaria and Enrique Lister convinced the "rather reluctant" soldiers in barracks number 1 to fight for the Republic.[8]

While I view Pilar as a creative composite of several models enlivened with a great deal of invention, I propose that we extend Guill's observation into a political allegory whereby Pilar and Pablo reenact the power struggle between Spain's Communist Party and the Republican leadership. Interpretation of allegories can be pushed too far in the details of correspondences, in the exactness of equated terms. I agree with Josephs, for example, that Meyers pushes the political allegory too far in reading "Andrés's inability to convince his allies to call off the attack" as "represent[ing] the Loyalists' failure to persuade France and England to stop the German and Italian invasion."[9] But as we've already seen, Hemingway was playing with allegorical writing as early as May 1937, in his NANA dispatch on the chauffeurs of Madrid. With Pilar, Hemingway can dramatize La Pasionaria's leadership while elsewhere getting his digs in against the real Ibárruri, by accusing her of sending her son to safety in Russia and by making her (in Baker's words) "the occasion for a fine travesty on sentimental propagandists."[10] Furthermore, beyond her position in this relatively straightforward allegory of Republican political drama, Pilar functions within the more subtle and complex dynamics where gender roles, earth imagery, and wartime rhetoric intersect. Maria functions in these intersecting discourses as well and trumps Pilar in significance, as the rest of this chapter will explore.

La Pasionaria was not simply the "most famous woman in Spain," as Hemingway's narration introduces her in *The Spanish Earth*, not simply the voice and face of the "new nation" but also a leader and the chief rabble-rouser in the Communist Party. For three of Pablo's gang, "the bridge means nothing"; their duty lies with "the *mujer* of Pablo." For her, "the Republic is the bridge. Afterwards we will have time for other projects."[11] The vague reference to "other projects" speaks to the "revolution or Republic" question that so vexed the Republican wartime coalition of interests, its vagueness exactly matching the kind of deferring discourse employed by the antirevolutionary Spanish communists to keep the revolutionaries in the battle against Franco (while inflaming the right against the Republic). The deferment also matches La Pasionaria's advocacy for the unity of the Spanish left in the Popular Front: "The [communist] party believed that while a more acceptable program would have been a good thing, this common democratic front on a national scale was an even better thing. This would clear the way for the united action of the masses in the forthcoming crucial elections and for later political struggles."[12] Robert Jordan accepts Pilar for the same reason he and the Republic accepted the communists—for their discipline and ability to prosecute the war.[13] He later jokes about her taking on the morale-bolstering job of the commissariat.[14]

Yet as Agustín recognizes, Pilar is the inspiring spirit, Pablo the tactical brains.[15] Agustín also schools Jordan on Pablo's strategic intelligence: "It seems to me you do not understand politics, *Inglés*, nor guerrilla warfare. In politics and this other the first thing is to continue to exist."[16] And like Pablo, despite all odds the Republic (until the very end) continued to exist. Indeed it came to hope to win by merely continuing to exist until the general war broke out to force the allied democratic powers to come to its aid in their joint world war against fascism. Pablo distrusts presumptuous foreigners like the bossy Robert Jordan, pursuing their own interests,[17] but begrudgingly accepts him. He sees Pilar, too, for what she is, lumping her among the idealistically delusional.[18] In Pilar and in Jordan he resents the necessary intrusion of both the communists and the foreigners, resents and admirably resists, holding on to his core leadership, refusing to be vasalized or even particularly bothered, even as he lets them run this brief show.[19] By the end of the novel, Pablo has regained the reins.

Pablo wants to be left alone, like the Republicans, to continue his benevolent if slightly patriarchal and paternalistic leadership. No radical, he represents the middle-class bourgeois Republicans in power: "Until thou hadst horses thou wert with us," Anselmo charges. "Now thou art another capitalist more."[20] Hemingway most clearly signals the connection between Pablo and the Republican leadership when Jordan speculates about Pablo's political movement to the right, as Alejandro Lerroux and Indalecio Prieto had done, and compares the Republican politicians to "horse thieves," which is precisely what Pablo turns out to be.[21]

When Hemingway excluded Ralph Bates's "phony" story about women machine gunners killed at the battle of Brunete for his 1942 *Men at War* anthology,[22] he knew better. One wonders if he considered Bates a rival to his own legacy as heroic chronicler of the Spanish Civil War. Alfred Kazin's *Starting Out in the Thirties* describes a 1937 New York gathering in which Bates, "known as a novelist-adventurer . . . in the tradition of Malraux and Hemingway," held his audience in rapt attention as "he spoke with a D'Annunzian exaltation of the fiery breath of war, with a visible relish at being able to find words for the star-bursting shock with which the thud of a bomb reverberated in the brain."[23] And unlike Hemingway, Bates had lived in Spain for years with the working class, had fought for the government in 1936, and helped organize and eventually became a political commissar in the International Brigades.[24] (Malraux, who helped organize and served in a volunteer air force squadron for the Republic, and whose novel about the war, *L'Espoir,* appeared while the war was still being waged, also failed to make Hemingway's anthology, though Hemingway included two pieces of his own from this war.)

Hemingway knew better because the militiawomen of the Republic were famous and initially used as symbols of the inclusive, progressive, revolutionary nature of the forces fighting fascism. Beevor estimates just under one thousand women in the front lines but "several thousand under arms in the rear areas and a woman's battalion [that] took part in the defence of Madrid."[25] La Pasionaria herself wore a man's uniform to the Guadalajara trenches to visit the troops, "including two young women machine-gunners who . . . looked no more than sixteen or seventeen years old."[26] According to one account, the eighteen-year-old Antonia Protero was leading a company when she died in the battle; another woman successfully commanded a machine-gun company at Guadalajara.[27] Ibárruri appeared before the troops again the night before the Brunete offensive.[28] Orwell saw several militiawomen, though he notes that as early as the spring of 1937, and in anarchist Catalonia, "ideas were changing already," and women no longer fought "side by side with the men" and were "laughed at" by the men during drill, whereas "a few months earlier no one would have seen anything comic in a woman handling a gun."[29] The opening poem of Cary Nelson's anthology of American poems about the war, *The Wound and the Dream*, is Martha Millet's "Women of Spain," which ends: "Empty are the kitchens. / The women of Spain are on the barricades."[30] Women also worked in other new capacities to help with the war, and they served in the Cortes. Proponents of women's equality saw the war as a chance to fast-track their progressive, and sometimes radical, agendas.[31]

Still, Hemingway's objection to Bates's story was officially correct. In September 1936 the Republican government ordered the withdrawal of women from the front lines, though it took the gradual replacement of irregular militias by, or their incorporation into, the centralized army to end their significant combat contributions (which Thomas writes was fully completed by 1938).[32] Hemingway's decision to use a guerilla band allowed him female characters without violating his sense of the historical situation.

Just as women's suffrage under the Second Republic backfired, with more women voting against the leftist government and for the right in 1933, images of women's liberation in the wartime Republic brought negative consequences. Women in the Republic, whether or not they actively supported the war, became targets of insurgent aggression. Franco thought "all women captured in arms should be shot."[33] In July 1936, Juana Capdevielle San Martín, the wife of a Republican governor, was tossed in prison, where she miscarried when she heard of her husband's execution:

> She was released but some days later she was picked up by a Falangist paramilitary squad, raped and murdered. . . . [Women in captured territory] were dragged through the streets after having their heads shaved, being tarred and feathered or forced to ingest castor oil so they would soil themselves in public. In Nationalist prisons, they were beaten and tortured. Sexual humiliation ranged from being paraded naked through the streets, via sexual harassment to rape.[34]

Purportedly, Nationalist soldiers in September 1936 took "twenty pregnant women whom they found in a maternity wing and shot them against the walls of the cemetery."[35] Nationalist propaganda portrayed Republican women as whores due to the general idea of emancipation and revolutionary sponsorship of free love and calls for the abolishment of marriage from some Republican-affiliated political groups. General Queipo de Llano, the Nationalist commander over Andalusia, broadcast outrageous messages over the radio. On 23 July 1936, he declared that

> Our brave Legionaries and Regulares have shown the red cowards what it means to be a man. And, incidentally, the wives of the reds too. These Communist and Anarchist women, after all, have made themselves fair game by their doctrine of free love. And now they have at least made the acquaintance of real men, and not milksops of militiamen. Kicking their legs about and struggling won't save them.[36]

He later boasted, "Three militia girls to every Moor: what a time we're having!"[37] In Nationalist-held La Granja, Fernando reports to Robert Jordan, de Llano's broadcast was a topic of conversation.[38] (Unfortunately this reputed promiscuity perhaps, and their working proximity definitely, contributed to the occasional rape of Republican women by their male comrades. Like Robert Jordan's "wife" Maria, Robert Merriman's wife, Marion, was also raped, but by a Slav officer fighting for the Republic. She never reported it, nor told her husband.[39])

In the spring of 1938, Hemingway, Matthews, and Delmer visited international brigader Fred Keller at the hospital in Mataro, just north of Barcelona, where they met two nurse's aides. The pretty, "shy, serene" one was named Maria. Her communist father "had been executed in Andalusia when the war broke out. Maria had been imprisoned and, over the months, raped 24 times."[40]

Being not a militiawoman, a feminist, nor a proponent of free love, Hemingway's Maria denies her Falangist rapists any direct Nationalist rationalizations. Or, more accurately, she denies the reader a direct connection between her behavior and her sexual abuse—like the innocent bourgeois victims of the revolutionary Ronda massacre and the fascist soldiers who were really conscripted peasants. Maria was a Republican, and therefore a "Red," and therefore a whore. Her attackers call her "Bride of the Red Christ" and write the initials for the Union de Hermanos Proletarianos, a far leftist organization, on her forehead with iodine.[41] Early critics who regard her as jumping into bed with Jordan too quickly and unrealistically for a girl raised in Spain's cult of female virginity forget that she isn't a virgin and that the only way to undo losing her virginity to rapists is to pretend its loss to her one true love. Such criticism comes close to repeating the repressive attitude behind the Nationalist slander of Republican women and to sanctioning rape almost as preemptive retribution for some innate sexual wantonness.[42] In this vein, I suppose one could regard Maria's rape, in its echoing of actual rapes of Republican citizens, as a cautionary tale about potential revolutionary violations of proper womanhood, with Robert Jordan delivering her safely back to sentimental star-crossed heterosexual single-partner love till death do they part.[43]

Such ugly readings aside, less obvious than the historical basis for Maria's sexual victimization is the historical basis for his conservative treatment of her. Hemingway's, Jordan's, and Pilar's paternalistic attitude toward her matches the Republic's hasty retreat from the politics of emancipation and equality. *The Spanish Earth*, in its desperate bid to present a conventional, nonradical Republic to an international audience, understandably portrayed women only in traditional roles, as mothers, young wives, and girlfriends, never as soldiers or as field or industrial workers. By 1940 in the U.S., the only external pressure for a conventional heroine might have been the Second World War's incipient threat of women in uniforms, in factories, and in premarital and extramarital beds, though I seriously doubt Hemingway had any such considerations in mind. Nor do I think Hemingway drew Maria as he did to right history by correcting the propaganda against "Red" women. Nevertheless, Maria reveals a great deal about Robert Jordan's conventional support of a bourgeois Republic.[44]

Jordan's death and his instructing Maria to live a full life for both of them is echoed eerily in a 1950s Francoist catechism lesson on "Feminine Heroism":

> Do women also have opportunities for heroism?
> *Yes, though for them heroism consists more in doing well what they have to do every day than in dying heroically.*[45]

Despite the economic conflicts that led to the war, the novel eschews dialectic materialism for character as its motivating force, and in its longing for the transcendent and valorizing of heroic sacrifice it echoes, however faintly, Mussolini's definition of fascism: "Fascism, now and always, believes in holiness and in heroism; that is to say, in actions influenced by no economic motive, direct or indirect."[46] Jordan's death replays what Stephen F. Eisenman calls the Hellenistic pathos formula, a classical artistic tradition whereby the aesthetic treatment of pain and suffering and death signals their acceptance, even their welcoming, by the subject—and hence their justification by the culture that produced them through, for example, imperial conquest or slavery. Eisenman sees the formula's spirit in the revival of Hellenist classicism by Nazi Germany and the Soviet Union in the 1920s and 1930s and in the "underlying conception" of "the complete subordination of the body to doctrine, and the willing surrender of the autonomous, critical subject to the dictates of state authority and power." Against such imagery, argues Eisenman, stands Picasso's *Guernica*, one of the greatest works inspired by the Spanish Civil War, but one in which "no redeeming grace is visible," only a warrior reduced to "fragments" and the screams of "protest, terror and pain."[47] Jordan spends the novel resisting ideological subordination, yet he follows a fateful order anyway and dies a willing hero's death.

Jordan and Maria are hardly fascists, of course, and I certainly do not mean to relate all heroic deaths to fascism, but their relationship sends a rather nonprogressive conservative message. Or more kindly, in Jordan we see the very human struggle between the comfortable, the known, and the traditional on the one hand, and the need to shake things up on the other. Perhaps instead of reading the novel's human drama as a metaphor for the war, we are to read the war as an extension of basic internal conflicts with which we all struggle.

When important discussions or the possibility of a fight with Pablo arise, Jordan or Pilar send Maria away. For the bridge mission, he assigns her the least dangerous task of watching the horses, a task even more revealing than its simple act of gender-based relegation. Before he meets Maria, Robert Jordan admires Pablo's horses: "They are awfully good horses, though, he thought, beautiful horses. I wonder what could make me feel the way those horses made Pablo feel. The old man was right. The horses made him rich and as soon as he was rich he wanted to enjoy life."[48] As Anselmo tells us, and we come to believe, it's the horses that make Pablo a capitalist, a bourgeois property owner interested in clinging to what he has rather than working and sacrificing for any larger cause. Maria has this exact effect on Jordan, who more than once compares her to a colt.[49] Jordan and Pablo share an instinct and affection for horses, an ambiguous politics, and a possibly debilitating attraction to Maria.[50]

Once Jordan falls in love with her, he begins fantasizing about and romanticizing domestic life. His pining for "normal family life"[51] translates as a desire for a traditional middle-class marriage, and twice he insists upon marriage even when reminded that a postrevolutionary post-Church Republican Spain will have abolished the old-fashioned patriarchal institution.[52] Sleeping with her sharpens his mind against knee-jerk ideological clichés and turns it to his university job where he will smoke pipes with his students while he and his lovely Spanish wife will entertain them with his stories of the martyred and hers of being raped,[53] in a fantasy which patronizingly subordinates her to the traditional role and reenacts her victimization, the Falangist gang with barber sheers replaced by the collegiate crew with pipes. Her very name suggests an embrace and devotion to conservative principles. Pilar, the revolutionary, quips about her subservience.[54] The struggle between his military objective, of which Maria can play no part, and his marriage fantasy indicates a struggle between his loyalty to the progressive Republic and to his own comforting American, capitalist, conservative identity. His death conveniently spares him any more maddening turns; it relieves him of having to choose.

Marc Hewson argues that Jordan undergoes a transformation, as encapsulated in differences between the two extended lovemaking passags, from a fear of love in "the usual phallocentric equation of femininity with nothingness and the threat of male absorption," to a rejection of such "possessiveness and divisiveness" and an embracing of timelessness, "unity," "shared experience," and "the understanding of the importance of sexual union in the discovery of personal identity."[55] But that very divisiveness, by which Hewson means the lovers' possession of distinct points of view, recognizes Maria's subjectivity—whereas in the latter passage, the language of unity, timelessness, and integration belongs totally to Jordan's voice. His experience eclipses hers, excludes hers, silences her, as his articulation satisfies his own psychic needs. The experience may have even caused her physical pain, though she denies it and tells him it was good for her, too, yet there is no evidence the earth moved for either of them this time around (as before).[56] Through Pablo's mistaken presumption of his horse's feelings, and Jordan's mistaken presumption of Lieutenant Berrendo's arrogance, Hemingway has forewarned his reader to distrust Jordan's self-serving perspective, one that ultimately reaffirms the traditional gender hierarchy.

For Thomas Strychacz, the novel "disguises its fetish for militarism under the logic of moral necessity and, still more cleverly, inscribes it into a plot that results in noble failure."[57] This camouflaged fetish relates to what I'm calling the novel's conservativism insofar as Republican logic linked militarism with the fascist right. Fascism, militarism, technology, and sexism—this link relates to Maria insofar as the logic was decidedly gendered. "A notable phenomenon of the war was the spontaneous growth of a woman's movement after the 1936 elections," writes Anthony Beevor. "It was born, not of literature or theory from abroad . . . but of women's instinctive conviction that the overthrow of the class system should mean the end of the patriarchal system as well."[58] The war's rhetoric, verbal and visual, gendered the war, with Republicans fighting for the motherland and Nationalists fighting for the fatherland. A rebel leaflet encouraging Catalonian anarchists to switch sides, as but one example, pleads, "HELP US SAVE THE FATHERLAND."[59] Strychacz frames his analysis of the novel in terms of the "despotic gaze . . . of masculine vision and authority" against which the Republic's "glorious discipline of indiscipline" struggles.[60] In his poem "City of Anguish," the veteran Edwin Rolfe describes a rebel artillery bombardment of Madrid via "the masculine shriek of the shell descending."[61]

Early scholarship on *For Whom the Bell Tolls* that focused on the Nationalist technological advantage points in a gendered direction even as it lacks the theoretical language enabling more recent critics like Strychacz.[62] Allen Guttmann's argument for the novel as dramatization of "the conflict between the values associated with the natural landscape and the values associated with the tank and other machines," between "men close to the earth and the values of a primitive society against men who had turned to the machine and to the antithetical values of an aggressive and destructive mechanical order," for example, notes Maria's repeated "identifi[cation] with the Spanish earth" and calls Pilar "a kind of Iberian Earth-Mother."[63]

Guttmann also recognizes similar if ungendered terms of this conflict in *The Spanish Earth*, with fascist planes bombing rural Republican villages, as well as in writing by other Republican witnesses to the war. Republican propaganda, its posters especially, also tried to make hay with this dualist portrayal. The propaganda poster on the cover of Cary Nelson's poetry anthology *The Wound and the Dream*, for example, shows a Nationalist tank bearing down on Republican soldiers huddled against their earthen barricade. Soldiers have always had a rather intimate relationship with the land, and while this would have been no less true for the Nationalists, their technological superiority, in both quality and quantity of armament, and their offensive strategy drove the infantry-dominant, generally defensively oriented Republican army to become that much more dependent on natural fortifications and impediments. In his unpublished 10 May 1937 dispatch, Hemingway called geography "the government's other ally," and his dispatches from April 1938 emphasized the Republican infantry's digging into the hilly terrain, finding rocks for cover, and using the Ebro River to check the Nationalist advance:

> Yesterday in the steep grey hills above San Mateo I watched a mountain side spouting geysers of rockdust from an artillery barrage in which four shells were coming in almost on the second. . . . It seems hard to see how they can use more planes since the sky has sometimes seemed absolutely full of them, but so far no mechanical means have been able to blast a way through the Ebro defenses.[64]

(The dispatch was typically optimistic; the rebels broke through a few days later.)

Some of Hemingway's other writings support the gendering of the technology-versus-nature contest as well. An unpublished fragment characterizes the Italian intervention for Franco as a betrayal of the working-class, mostly rural Italian soldiery and a betrayal of their mother earth (as opposed to Mussolini's sons who fly planes).[65] In *For Whom the Bell Tolls,* the guerillas find safe harbor in mother earth's caves and El Sordo and his compatriots make their last stand huddled against boulders as the fascist planes deliver them to their deaths.

But an easy dualism of fascism, technology, professional militancy, aggression, and the masculine standing against democracy, agrarianism, citizen-soldiers, good-heartedness, and the feminine is problematic. Within the Republic the earth-versus-technology theme privileged the agrarian center and south and all but left out the industrialized north. Also, representations of such a dualism proved hard to maintain. In *The Spanish Earth,* for example, we see the Republic's tanks in action, we see a professionalizing army, we see that final fade as the Republican soldier's rifle becomes the new irrigation canal, shooting and flowing in the same direction and turning the notion of the Republican dead rejuvenating the land to a far more aggressive attitude; as Guttmann acknowledges, "the flow of water onto the hard, dry Spanish earth parallels the movement of *mechanized* equipment on the successfully defended Madrid-Valencia road" (emphasis added).[66] Hemingway's unpublished dispatch participates in this more aggressive rewriting of the martyrdom script as he pays respect to some brave Italian machine gunners and automatic riflemen fighting for the insurgency and killed at Brihuega: "The size of the pile of empty shells beside a dead machine gunner makes the only monument he will ever have except the six-foot spot where the grain will grow a little taller in a Spanish wheat field."[67] Robert Capa's photo-essay *Death in the Making* also struggles to maintain this populist, antimodern, antibellicose message as its pages go by and show an increasingly professional army. The Republican government in general struggled in its message to both its people and the international community—showing that the ragtag popular militias might garner support from the like-minded and the bleeding hearts, but such an army could not win the war, and such an army might not communicate any confidence that other nations' support would be money well spent. Images of a professional and equipped army, however, risk losing the support of the like-minded and the bleeding hearts, and the support of other nations who wonder what the army could possibly want. One should recall, too, that the government never fully trusted the popular militias, withholding arms from them entirely during Franco's first march on Madrid and providing less than adequate equipment to those militias not fully integrated into the centralized army.

In *For Whom the Bell Tolls*, the dualism does not hold firmly either. We see only fascist planes, but we hear about Republican planes, and we see long columns of Republican military vehicles. With the exception of the whippet-tank crew at the end of the novel, the Nationalist troops who appear on stage are, like the guerillas, cavalrymen who take cover behind large rocks. And as Strychacz writes, Robert Jordan's mastery of military arts, his "defense of killing as a means to an end, his cool competence, his fascination with efficient watching and killing at a distance, his acknowledgment that he enjoys killing, [and] his ability to separate emotional attachments from the demands of his task" share "affinities with a fascist masculinity."[68]

The novel's language also mixes natural and technological imagery: the train blown off its tracks by the guerillas topples over like an injured beast, the neck of Pablo's horse curves like a viaduct, and the fascists' planes look like sharks and bellow like lions.[69] Rod Romesburg points out a wonderful bit of ambiguity in Robert Jordan's emotional coming home to nature, as the novel's penultimate sentence "Jordan uses the physical beauty of the natural world as a sighting for one last killing" of Lieutenant Berrendo.[70] With a machine gun. And strangely paralleling the last image of *The Spanish Earth*, where the soldier aims his rifle in the direction of the flowing waters of the new irrigation ditch. Perhaps most significantly, Maria and Jordan's love-talk wish to take their happiness both "on a good horse" riding fast, and "in the sky like the little pursuit planes shining in the sun. . . . Rolling it in loops and in dives. *Qué bueno*!"[71] The earth also moves more than the one time the lovers make it move, in the bombing of El Sordo's gang before burying them and when the guerillas destroyed the train.[72]

For all the novel's romantically feminized depictions of the land, particularly in its many associations of Maria with the Spanish earth, it also expresses a subtle sense of betrayal by the feminine and the land. The land cannot save El Sordo's gang, and the chancre of a hill on which his men meet their end has the shape of "the breast of a young girl with no nipple"—a comparison El Sordo makes right after one of his partisans condemns the betrayal of La Pasionaria for sending her son to Russia for the war while exhorting the rest of Spain's sons to die on hilltops like this one, and after another man barks at his whining comrades to "Wipe the pap of your mother's breasts off thy lips and give me a hatful of that dirt. . . . No one of us will see the sun go down this night."[73] After Jordan's fatal wounding, Agustín calls the war "bitchery" and Jordan tells himself that he was "bitched."[74] Maria appears before him for the first time immediately after he commits to asking a comrade to kill him if he is too wounded to travel, their instant romantic bond precipitated by, predicated on, that primary commitment[75]—and it's Maria who later asks him to make a suicide pact.[76] Throughout the novel, his anxiousness, the very sort of anxiousness that spelled doom for his predecessor Kashkin, results largely from his relationship with Maria. Jordan and his "rabbit" Maria make love while Rafael kills two coupling rabbits and misses seeing the first rebel scout,[77] the first indication of the doom to come.

Two later essays expand on Guttmann's case for the novel's defense of the earthy and primitive Spanish soul by viewing this defense in mythic terms. Robert E. Gajdusek reads the initial revolutionary spirit, represented by Pilar's story, as a ritualistic feminine, Dionysian usurpation of the masculine, dictatorial Apollonian spirit, "in which the act of killing with sickle and scythe, or turning or tumbling with a wooden pitchfork, is part of a death process out of which comes renewed life."[78] I have a great deal of trouble, however, accepting the Ronda massacre as depicted by Hemingway (through Pilar) as a necessary, healthful, and sacred chafing process. Pilar rejects it while it happens, at the moment it achieves the peak of its Dionysian disorder; Pablo comes to reject it later. The effort to fit this moment into an earth-friendly literary scheme utterly distorts the horrible affair. It turns the Republican rhetoric of sacrifice for renewal on its head, into mindless murder for renewal.

Lisa Tyler, in acknowledging the confusion among the cults of Eleusis and Dionysus and implicitly observing the minor problem for Gajdusek that Dionysus is a male god, contends that "it is the matricentric myth of Demeter and Persephone which Hemingway contrasts to the patriarchal myth he associates with the Nationalist order, and that he explores this contrast throughout the novel, not simply in Pilar's tale," with Pilar as Demeter and Maria as Persephone, the abducted daughter rescued by the mother figure.[79] My general suspicion of mythic criticism applies to Tyler's essay as much as it does to Gajdusek's. More particularly, I wonder about the comparison of Maria with Demeter "the Grain-Mother"[80] when she is supposed to incarnate Persephone, I can't quite reconcile how "Hemingway emphasizes the fundamental contradiction between mothering and war" with his being "no essentialist,"[81] and I have more trouble than Tyler in locating Robert Jordan's place in this mythic cycle.[82]

The epic heft of *For Whom the Bell Tolls* might truly warrant a mythic approach. A more prosaic understanding of the novel as epic romance places it in the tradition of the Spanish romance, the short, epic narrative form followed by most Spanish Civil War poems.[83] Yet in the spirit of this chapter, I want to return the novel's gendered earth imagery to its wartime context, and in a manner that fully incorporates its central character. Appropriately, for a Westerner fighting for the homeland of a developing foreign country, two gendered political discourses converge on Robert Jordan in his regard for Maria.

The first involves the usual, traditional call to arms for men to protect women, children, and hearth, a call that inevitably conflates the woman with the homeland, with the land itself (such that *matria*'s love becomes the excuse for *patria*'s militancy). Noël Valis reminds us that the Spanish Republic symbolized itself "as *la niña bonita*, 'the pretty girl.'"[84] For Jay Allen, it was a woman killed in 1934 whose blood was the first "shed in the reconquest of Spain by the Old Spain and its allies."[85] Few students of the novel miss the determined linking of Maria with the Spanish earth, as no less than four times, including the first time Jordan sees her, he compares her to a grain or wheat field, and many more times to animal imagery, be it her short hair like a beaver pelt, her movement like a colt's, or his pet name for her, "rabbit." Alex Link connects Maria with Spain through that pet name, rabbit being the etymological source for the very word Spain,[86] and Anselmo talks about Republican soldiers picked off like rabbits by the fascists.[87] As Edward F. Stanton comments, she stands in for (Republican) Spain, for its innocence, beauty, victimization, and fertile promise: "Her parents have been murdered, her village sacked, she has been violated as Spain herself has been pillaged and raped by foreign and native soldiers for centuries"—the rape metaphor was commonly employed before, during, and after the war. Stanton, however, neglects to read this symbolism within a larger discourse and so celebrates the novel's unique vision of "Robert Jordan, in his double role as lover and soldier, recover[ing] the honor of both the violated woman and her country."[88] It makes sense that Pilar as La Pasionaria actively encourages the affair between Jordan and the girl who embodies Spain and its future. When Jordan worries that his Maria is more dream than reality, he compares her to the other objects of his sexual fantasies, summoned when he curled up on the floors and ground all over Spain.[89]

As surrogate for Spain, Maria's inspiration to protect and redeem primarily calls to her countrymen. Such a woman (and her citizen-bearing, state-regenerative womb) belongs as far from conflict as one can take her. Several of the guerillas admit a deep affection for her and concern for her welfare, including the manly, Pasionaria-like Pilar, whose erotic and paternal bond with Maria expresses Maria's political symbolism. El Sordo's passion for what Maria represents unconsciously echoes Robert Jordan's language. For Jordan, Maria has hair that ripples "as a grain field on a hillside"[90]; she feels like "all of life [that] was being taken from him"[91] and has "breasts like two small hills that rise out of the plain where there is a well, and the far country beyond the hills was the valley of her throat where her lips were."[92] For El Sordo, about to die on a hillside, Jordan's image of Maria as life becomes a general image of Spanish life:

> But living was a field of grain blowing in the wind on the side of a hill. Living was a hawk in the sky. Living was an earthen jar of water in the dust of the threshing with the grain flailed out and the chaff blowing. Living was a horse between your legs and a carbine on one leg and a hill and a valley and a stream with trees and the far side of the valley and the hills beyond.[93]

Lest we get too carried away with the nature imagery, we must keep in mind the war imagery El Sordo incorporated into his vision of the vital—Maria the colt perhaps transfigured into El Sordo's war-horse—as well as Robert Jordan's equating of his love for Maria with his love for the war, the Republic's ideals, his fallen brethren, and Madrid.[94] With its reference to both Madrid and the Guadarrama winds (as well as orphans, intimacy, and all that moaning), Rolfe's "Elegia" could have verily had Maria in mind:

> *Madrid Madrid Madrid Madrid*
> *I call your name endlessly, savor it like a lover.*
> *Ten irretrievable years have exploded like bombs*
> *since last I saw you, since last I slept*
> *in your arms of tenderness and wounded granite.*
> *Ten years since I touched your face in the sun,*
> *ten years since the homeless Guadarrama winds*
> *moaned like shivering orphans through your veins*
> *and I moaned with them—*

Under Franco, the poem continues, Madrid is "locked in the bordello of the Universal Pimp."[95]

Jordan couples with Spain when he makes love to Maria; both shudder beneath him. The difference between his sexualized Spain and El Sordo's mundane terrain is telling, and it points to the second gendered discourse operating on him, namely the West's erotic investment in and concomitant feminizing of non-Western lands and their nonwhite peoples. A helpful correlative might be found in the case of Vietnam. That country's own Maria debuted in *The Tale of Kieu,* a late-eighteenth-century poem frequently cited as a foundational and metaphorical national text. Kieu, a young woman bounced from man to man yet who manages to survive with her integrity (not her virginity) in tact, represents Vietnam's own history of centuries of ownership and exploitation by the Chinese and finally by the French, its beauty, and its indomitable spirit. In one of her twentieth-century manifestations Kieu becomes Phuong of Graham Greene's *The Quiet American,* the beautiful young Vietnamese woman who in the 1950s becomes the prize in a rivalry between two men, a tired old European and an arrogant young American, their personal war for her equating to the geopolitical struggle for Vietnam as the European colonial era passes and the U.S. neocolonial era flailingly emerges. Thomas Fowler, the European, admits he will die if he loses her; Alden Pyle, the not-so-quiet American, loves her because of his compulsion to save her.[96]

This erotic gendering occurs by way of Hemingway and his era's fetishizing of the primitive. Much of the reason Spain found itself at war followed from its attempt to catch up with the rest of Europe, to transform belatedly and hurriedly from an agrarian and somewhat feudal economy and social structure to modern, industrial ones. Thus Gertrude Stein, days away from death in 1946, could still recommend that Richard Wright visit Spain to experience the primitive past.[97] María DeGuzmán argues that U.S. expatriate modernists romanticized Spain because it still held "ties to the land, ties that, it was felt, had been lost in the United States through industrialization, mechanization, increasing urbanization, physical and psychological dislocation, and discontinuity."[98]

More than an underdeveloped European country, for many Anglo-American and European imaginations Spain was part of the Dark Continent. David Murad rightly argues that Hemingway counted on clichéd "images of Spain and gypsyness that he knew his Western readership would find charmingly familiar,"[99] and Noël Valis that with his deliberately clunky translations Hemingway "often falls into the trap of exoticizing the foreign."[100] But the matter goes deeper. Hemingway's line in *The Garden of Eden* that Africa begins at the Pyrenees[101] conveys a common conception based on Iberia's geographic proximity and arid similarity to northern Africa, their shared Moorish heritage, and the socioeconomic reality. Richard Wright repeats it in *Pagan Spain*,[102] as does Jay Allen in his preface to Capa's *Death in the Making*.[103] Allen elaborates:

> There is nothing new to be said about that land. It is indeed a tawny land and it is shaped like a bull's hide stretched to dry in the sun. And it really is African, for the straights of Gibraltar are an accident and Iberia runs from the Pyrenees to the Atlas. . . .
>
> There in the purple haze is not any more the Spain we used to go down to from Paris so joyously, crossing the Bidassoa, that rarest of frontiers that is a dividing line between worlds and centuries.[104]
>
> Spain was the last terra incognita on the map of the civilized world.

Coincidentally, in exact word choice, Maria's skin, eyes, and hair are described using Allen's color for the Spanish landscape: tawny.[105] As Havelock Ellis, whose work on human sexuality Hemingway studied, wrote in his 1908 *The Soul of Spain*: "Indeed, the Spanish character is fundamentally, it seems to me, not only African, but primitive, and—in the best and not in any depreciative sense of the word—savage."[106] Jordan pleasurably imagines Maria's already brown skin tanned even darker, as well as a certain "darkness underneath."[107]

Orwell discovered that this attitude held some sway within Spain, as his comrades from northern and more industrial Catalonia thought of Andalusians, in the southernmost part of Spain and the epicenter of Moorish Spain, "as a race of semi-savages. . . . They were gnarled, rustic-looking men, shepherds or labourers from the olive groves, perhaps, with faces deeply stained by the ferocious suns of farther south."[108] Genevieve Taggard's poem "Andalucía" sings of this "land of naked faces. / Country of silver and green sky; lonely country, country of throngs. / Arabia and Africa in gardens and in arid places. / Country of essential dances and the song of songs."[109] Pastora Imperio, the flamenco dancer and singer some believe to be the primary model for Pilar, was Andalusian: "The poet Ramón Díaz Mirete summed her up as '!Andalucía!'"[110]

The Spain of *For Whom the Bell Tolls* has a strong Andalusian cast.

Maria tells us she was captured, shaved, and raped in Valladolid, in central Spain, but the nurse who may have inspired her and the woman representing her in the *Life* spread were both Andalusian (recall Queipo de Llano's promising of Andalusian women as war booty).[111] The novel attends far more to Maria's coloring than to any other character's—and we never hear about skin color for anyone else. Rather astoundingly, the novel barely mentions the Moors fighting for the insurgency, even though they filled the Republican imagination and receive regular attention in Hemingway's dispatches, as if on some level Hemingway knew that these "savage, brutal soldiers" rumored to have castrated Republican prisoners would have spoiled the more intoxicating association of true (Republican) Spain with the idealized if condescending imagined aspects of African primitivism.[112] Yet Robert Jordan manages to go native all the way in his inhabiting of a Western stereotypical perspective of Orientalism, "that it is populated by men resigned to harsh chastisement of death who nevertheless seek every opportunity for erotic pleasure."[113]

When Richard Wright visited Spain in 1954, he sought a political, social, economic, and historical explanation for its troubled state. Yet the primitivism Stein had promised overtakes his imagination, and by the end of *Pagan Spain* Wright abandons such rational efforts. Instead, he chooses to define the Spanish character—the "Spanish animal," he says—as deeply, unshakably pagan, with a savage's mesmerism by (Catholic) ceremony, and constantly reminiscent of primitive Africa.[114] Hardly a chapter goes by that Wright doesn't bring sexuality to the fore, from imaging the rocky terrain around the Black Virgin as a "conglomeration of erect stone penises,"[115] to rhapsodizing for pages about the bursting and inviting sensuality of a new young friend's virgin fiancée,[116] to the "sexual animality" and "savage sexuality" of flamenco dancers.[117] In Seville for Holy Week, watching the precession of "white-hooded and masked penitents," he can't help himself: "The huge candles rested upon the hips of the penitents and the flickering flames danced above their heads, the molten wax streaming and sparkling in the bright sun, spattering in translucent spots on the dark cobblestones—flying white drops that were like semen spraying, jutting from the penises of sexually aroused bulls."[118]

Richard Bernstein's new history of erotic Orientalism, *The East, the West, and Sex*, includes northern and eastern Africa. He might as well have included Spain. As DeGuzmán writes, nineteenth-century Anglo-Americans projected onto Spain both a sense of their "racial origins" and the Spaniards' distinction "from 'Europeans' [due] to their 'Oriental' heritage."[119] If for Strychacz *For Whom the Bell Tolls* expresses its conservatism through its valuing of patriarchal militancy, for DeGuzmán it expresses its conservatism through its staging of a Western colonial enterprise by "transubstantiat[ing] the act of eating from colonialist consumption into the very act of communion with the country and its inhabitants. . . . *For Whom the Bell Tolls* actually conflates [Spaniards] with food" for Jordan's consumption.[120] DeGuzmán's book's larger project of establishing how "the construction of Anglo-American identity as 'American' has been dependent on figures of Spain" spins Pablo's suspicion of foreigners using the war for their own purposes a bit differently.[121] Related to Jordan's ideological conflict between the Republic's revolutionary potential and his bourgeois Anglo-Americanism, then, is his conflict between integral oneness and romanticized difference. It's the Western imagination's classic colonialist conundrum of going native while impossibly preserving itself. With Maria he has it both ways: Like the deeply tanned Catherine in Spain and on the French-Spanish (European-African) border in *The Garden of Eden*, Maria the Spaniard is and isn't African; like Catherine, Maria in Jordan's imagination has lighter hair as her body darkens in the sun.[122] Dark but no savage Moor, and gypsy-like only in the business of sexual ecstasy.[123]

Given Robert Jordan's participation in the Western fantasy of primitivism as being outside time and of the erotic animalism of the primitive Other, it fits that Hemingway characterizes his union with Maria by both mystical timelessness and animalistic urgency. To Agustín's question about what Jordan and Maria are doing, Pilar answers, "Nothing, . . . *Nada*. We are, after all, in the spring, animal."[124] Instead of indulging Jordan and the reader in the fantasy of the erotic, primitive Other, however, we are better served in sympathizing with the full complexity of Jordan's relationship with Spain and Maria. It is not enough to celebrate Jordan's "supreme symbolic union with Spain, the Spanish earth and people" through Maria's body.[125]

Like Frederic Henry, Robert Jordan is trapped by the sexual imperative, the resulting children, and the psychology of human mortality. Yet other forces are at work on Jordan, not only the idiocy of the war's management by the Republic and the complexity of its politics but also the difficulty of squaring these two gendered political discourses with the actual woman with whom he has fallen in love. What can he do with a woman whom he must emotionally separate from the gendered war rhetoric yet who tells him, "I want to go hold to the legs of the gun and while it speaks love thee all in the same moment"?[126] Hemingway twice puts Jordan in bed with Maria and his pistol, in one instance having her mistake the pistol for his penis.[127] What can he do with his own personification of the "brown shoulder of the mountain" at the bridge he must destroy, making the earth move with his dynamite, when the only brown-shouldered earth symbol around belongs to Maria?[128]

In death, as Guttmann and Stanton both suggest when they invoke Hemingway's elegy "The American Dead in Spain," Robert Jordan joins the other dead in nourishing the earth with their bodies and blood for the Republic's reflowering.[129] In dying for Spain, he dies for Maria; in dying for Maria, he dies for Spain. He sends her, and with her Spain's future in the form of her nubile and presumably fertile body,[130] off to survive, staying behind to tie up the enemy and give her and the others more time to escape. Yet inasmuch as he consistently predicated the depth of his love on its brevity from his imminent death, he must die to preserve the "truth" of his love. Potentially he must also die to prove the "truth" of his commitment to Spain, which is not always easy, simple, or certain. In both cases he uses some of the same logic he uses to justify obeying impossible orders: "because it is only in the performing of them that they can prove to be impossible."[131] Jordan's fantasy of absolute integration and the eternal moment with Maria during the second extended lovemaking passage, the last time they make love only hours before his death, prepares the way for his fantasy of integration with the Spanish earth.

Earlier I offered that, in dying, Robert Jordan escapes the troubling conflict between his loyalty to the progressive Republic and his more Pablo-like desire for a more conservative, comfortable, even isolationist bourgeois life. At this point I can offer a corollary, that in dying he escapes the troubling conflict between the two gendered discourses and the woman obliged to bear them. Or, more positively, that in dying he successfully divorces the discourses from the person in the only way he ever could, by killing that which could only always confuse them. He sends her away and thinks, "Now, finally and at last, there was no problem. However all of it had been and however all of it would ever be now, for him, no longer was there any problem."[132] For the last five pages of the novel, the last moments of his life, he does not think about her at all. From the first page of the book his primary relationship had always been with the Spanish earth, against whose pine-dressed body he repeatedly lay. In his death he restores Maria to her person and restores himself to the land which he had loved for twelve years. The suicide pact he made with Maria he now keeps with the Spanish Republic.

Are these two readings mutually exclusive? That in dying for Spain, Robert Jordan dies for Maria (and vice versa), or that in dying for Spain he frees the person from his ideological baggage? Yes and no. I see no reason to privilege one over the other. To paraphrase Jordan, it can all be true. Just as the novel refuses to simplify the war, it refuses to simplify him. What matters is that more than being simply a soldier's death for a noble cause, Jordan's death brings a personal resolution, and in that sense is welcome, even invited.

SEVEN

From Frederic Henry to Robert Jordan

For Whom the Bell Tolls turns *The Spanish Earth* on its head. It also turns Hemingway's antiheroic novel *A Farewell to Arms* on its head. Or so it would seem.

As often understood, the later novel revisits the earlier one politically. If ten years after the Great War's blood-drain *A Farewell to Arms* endorsed isolationism and antijingoism, on the eve of the next world war *For Whom the Bell Tolls* argued for commitment and war. Their very titles reflect the reversal. As do the romantic plots. The death of Frederic Henry's "wife" and baby leave him forlorn, without a country, without a family, without a future; the sacrifice of Robert Jordan for democracy and his "wife" grants his story dignity, purpose, and a future. Jordan's noble wartime self-sacrifice for another country's people casts Frederic Henry's abandonment of Italy in a relatively unfavorable light. The more scholars have scrutinized Henry's character, the more they question whether Hemingway ever esteemed his behavior as in any way heroic. Unlike his namesake Henry Fleming, from Stephen Crane's *The Red Badge of Courage,* Frederic Henry does not return to battle; he cannot declare, as Fleming does while marching out of the text, "I'm a man" (inasmuch as one trusts Fleming's self-opinion, anyway).

Despite the instant critical and commercial success of *For Whom the Bell Tolls,* it has since garnered far less attention by scholars, perhaps because of its apparently traditional attitude of soldierly martyrdom, perhaps because of its detailed engagement with the political situation of a war increasingly fading from American memory. For some readers, and not just the VALB crowd, the novel is not political enough. For others, the novel's politics are incidental to and stymie its study of characters. One of its chief experts, Allen Josephs, has weighed in on both sides. In an essay originally presented at a 1987 conference, he felt that in "inventing a world where politics were but a remembrance of nights past at Gaylord's" instead of "writing a political novel," Hemingway "crafted a powerful story with great moments, but he sacrificed giving us a great historical novel of the Spanish Civil War."[1] In his 1994 book-length study of the novel, he wrote: "Long after the politics and the particulars of the war itself are forgotten, readers will still be moved by the story of Robert Jordan and Maria and the band of guerillas who attempt to blow a bridge on which the future of the human race could turn."[2]

Chapter 6 moved from wartime gender roles and rhetoric to Robert Jordan, and this final chapter continues that momentum. Here this book performs its own kind of shift by examining *For Whom the Bell Tolls* as a character study and charting a path not from nonfiction works and historical documents to the novel but from Hemingway's first war novel to this one. For all of their differences, the two monumental war novels have their similarities. Politically, they reject the rhetoric of monarchy and nationalism in favor of that of people and place. Not king and country, but the people and the land. In terms of character, Hemingway's calling Robert Jordan a "chickenshit" in his 1940 letter to Gustavo Duran[3] aligns the image of this protagonist more closely with an interpretation of a less-than-magnanimous Frederic Henry.

The physical object of a pistol brings the novels together extratextually and intertextually. Scholars generally and correctly discuss the childbirth scene in *A Farewell to Arms* in relation to the caesarian birth of Hemingway's second son during the writing of the book. Of at least equal significance are his father's suicide by pistol during the writing of the book, which contributes to its elegiac mood,[4] and Hemingway's request to his mother for the pistol. It's hard not to think of this request in conjunction with Henry's purchase of a used pistol before heading back to the front, presumably the same pistol with which he later shoots an Italian sergeant. The woman who sells it tells Henry it belonged to a great shot and was recovered by his orderly, but we never learn the nature of the man's death.[5] Robert Jordan, meanwhile, has inherited the pistol his father used to kill himself, the pistol that Jordan's grandfather had carried in the American Civil War: "It had the softest, sweetest trigger pull you had ever felt."[6] If Hemingway indicates being haunted by his father's suicide subtly through the utter absence of attention to Henry's father, he indicates it forthrightly through Jordan's obsessive mulling over his father's suicide. Rafael's song about gypsy life strikes a chord with Jordan,[7] a song which Hemingway learned from a Republican soldier during the attack on Teruel in December 1937: "I had an inheritance from my father. It was the moon and the sun and I can move all over the world and the spending of it is never done." Henry and Jordan travel far from their fatherland only to end up in the same place: the *undiscovered country* of death, the phrase coming from Hamlet's soliloquy in which he contemplates suicide and used by Hemingway as a working title to *For Whom the Bell Tolls*. "'Where is your father now?' Hemingway asked the Republican soldier. 'Dead,' he said."[8]

Beyond simply reflecting Hemingway's preoccupation with suicide, *A Farewell to Arms* and *For Whom the Bell Tolls* dramatize suicidal acts, with Frederic Henry's fictional memoir and Robert Jordan's fateful mission expressing their desires to die. Hunting for suicide in Hemingway's fiction has always been a commonplace analytical exercise, one scholars don't always find justified. Investigating gender performance in the texts has become just as commonplace anymore, so it's with some chagrin that later in this chapter I pursue, among other explanations, a correlation between the protagonists' death wishes and certain textually manifested gender vulnerabilities.

"Rather than being a study in war, love or initiation," writes Michael Reynolds in *Hemingway's First War: The Making of* A Farewell to Arms, the novel "is more properly a study in isolation. Frederic's progression in the novel is from group participation to total isolation."[9] Henry has long since forgotten his own family. He only occasionally remembers to send them prewritten military postcards, and he assures Catherine that she'll never have to meet them. The movement to total isolation requires that he lose Catherine and the baby in some fashion, and one could argue that their deaths provide the only possible "romantic" ending to this self-imposed withdrawal. The only move left on this course of severing himself from the world is the absolute farewell.

The interpretation of *A Farewell to Arms* as a conscious or unconscious suicide note understands the novel as either a fictional memoir or a linear representation of how he tells this story to himself. As James Nagel originally and convincingly demonstrated, it is "a retrospective narrative told by Frederic Henry a decade after the action has taken place for the purpose of coming to terms emotionally with the events."[10] Whereas Nagel concludes that "through his love for [Catherine Barkley] he grew to be a better man, one who could love fully and assess himself truly,"[11] I conclude that Henry has failed to come to terms emotionally with his past, and from that failure emerges his desire to die. Gerry Brenner first proposed the idea that Henry commits suicide after he finishes narrating his story, though I agree with Nagel that Brenner fails to make his case.[12] But a stronger case can be made.

A death wish informs the autobiographical impulse. "Implicit in the search for totality in more traditional autobiographical criticism," claims Laura Marcus in *Auto/Biographical Discourses*, "is the paradox that autobiography *ex hypothesi* cannot be written from the standpoint beyond the grave which would secure this totalizing vision of the life. By extension, for the autobiographer to aim at this totalizing vision would itself be to aim for death."[13] In other words, to author a complete account of one's life implies a completed, finished life, as well as a desire to leave a piece of the self behind in an anticipation of death—perhaps not just a piece, but an ideal piece, faithful to the autobiographer's history and image of himself. It is to script one's life, one's idiosyncratic path to death. This is autobiography as thanatography; and if we quibble that Frederic Henry's book is a memoir rather than an autobiography, we would do well to remember Paul Fussell's line, "My war is synonymous with my life."[14]

Frederic Henry scatters throughout his memoir references to self-inflicted wounds and suicide. After Rinaldi mentions them when Henry returns from leave, Henry encounters the soldier who aggravated his own hernia and then on Henry's advice whacks himself on the head to escape the front lines. Henry himself is accused of trying to kill or otherwise injure himself by the doctor who tends to him at the field hospital, by Rinaldi when he visits him in the hospital, and by Miss Van Campen, the nurse, over his jaundice.[15] There are more subtle moments, such as the barber who nearly murders him while shaving him over confusion about his nationality,[16] followed toward the end of the novel by the only other shaving scene, when Henry shaves himself in a moment of misrecognition. Nurse Ferguson threatens to kill him if he gets Catherine pregnant, which is exactly what he proceeds to do.[17]

Catherine's own death can be viewed as her desired outcome. Her fiancé's wartime death has brought her to the brink; she saves herself by losing herself in Frederic Henry: "There isn't any me," she tells him. "I'm you. Don't make up a separate me."[18] She dies because she desires to relieve herself of her self, forevermore, in him. "I'm just gone all to pieces," the laboring mother tells her lover as she begs for more anesthesia: "*Give it to me!*" He turns it "all the way," to "three then to four" even though he fears taking it beyond two.[19] Still, we must account for the fact that we see and hear Catherine only through her lover's eyes as filtered through ten years of memory and emotion. So we can read her desire to dissipate into Frederic, and her visions of her death in the rain, as literal and self-fulfilling. Or we can read them as Frederic's explanation by way of projection—guilt-induced or not—to appease himself with the belief that she sought her final relief. Or we can read them as another form of projection, we can read them as his desire for dissipation and his visioning of his own final relief. His memory of her serves as a kind of role model.

Reading Catherine's death as a culmination of her own retreat from life's pains further insinuates Frederic's suicidal potential. *A Farewell to Arms* is his memoir; its language, including all of her language, comes to us from him. Critiques of Catherine as merely a reflection of his desires are in this sense dead on. Her words are his. If the language obtains self-abnegation adumbrating suicide, one needs to identify its proper source. Catherine's constant fear of dying in the rain foretells Frederic's death; she dies inside, out of the rain; it's Frederic Henry who walks away, alone and, in his memoir's last words, "in the rain."[20] Several times he actually practices being dead, practices speaking from beyond the grave, speaking as the dead, when he plays the part of Catherine's beloved dead fiancé and when he talks to the dead Catherine in the present tense. Ten years later, as he remembers calling on Catherine at the hospital, he drifts into a brief tangent about cemeteries he has visited.[21] This reverie Hemingway attaches to Henry's narrating moment, not the remembered one, and so indicates his present state of mind.

Frederic Henry likewise needs to relieve himself of his self. Just as Catherine could not endure the pain of her dead fiancé, neither can Frederic endure the pain of his dead beloved and other wartime traumas. Henry has earned his post-traumatic stress disorder from years of intimacy with the dead and dying, including the soldier bleeding to death on the stretcher above him in the ambulance whose blood drips onto him, his own nearly fatal wounding, his questionable value as soldier and officer, his murdering of an Italian soldier, and, of course, the deaths of Catherine and their child, for which he must feel no small amount of responsibility. The term *survivor's guilt* feels almost trite in his case. More romantically, Frederic Henry wants to die in order to be with Catherine. He can at once achieve total isolation and total, transcendent integration. She is his religion, after all. Her language of dissolving her identity into his belongs to him as he, in the memoir and in his death, becomes one with her.

The trauma of Catherine's and the baby's deaths only compounds the problem of his general war trauma and his malaise and self-disregard. He has no purpose, no reason for being in the Italian army nor, one suspects, for being at all. He confesses to the priest that he did not visit the Abruzzi even though he wanted to, failing to explain (even to himself) why he acted against his earnest desire for what he anticipated would be a salubrious trip. He returns to the front only to realize that his unit performed better without him. He admits to playing with Catherine's emotions selfishly. As an ambulance driver, he barely qualifies as a man according to the gender rhetoric of the day even as he is surrounded by real soldiers, a skillful surgeon, and a good priest. He receives his wound delivering meat and cheese. Unlike Hemingway, Henry did not manage any acts of heroism. "During the retreat Lieutenant Henry is given his one chance to command, and he makes a botch of it," writes Scott Donaldson, "los[ing] his ambulances and all his men but one."[22] Norris accuses him not only of murdering the Italian sergeant during the retreat[23] but also of doing nothing to prevent his soldiers from raping two young sisters.[24] His own identity never quite stabilizes. His name and nationality are frequently confused, the text not getting his full name right until a quarter of the way through and only after his wounding.[25] As Thomas Strychacz writes, "Even the most sanguine interpretations of Frederic Henry have had to observe at least some marks of war upon him: his multiple defeats, the atmosphere of loneliness and loss, his shell-shock, his occasional callousness."[26] Strychacz's discussion focuses on the various masquerades and pretenses Henry assumes as gestures of identity from an inauthentic core. Most harshly, Brian Way feels that at the end of the novel Henry is still "self-indulgent or self-pitying" and Frederic Svoboda finds him "babyish."[27] He not only fails to heed Fergy's warning by getting Catherine in trouble in the family way but also risks his lover's health and the baby's life by bringing them through a storm across the lake and away from the hospital care she knew. For Brenner, the novel demonstrates Henry's failure to find any source of meaning for his life.[28]

The unspoken suicide beneath the surface of *A Farewell to Arms* proves more than the mere application of the iceberg theory, Hemingway's early idea that the reader should sense the seven-eights of the story beneath the surface. It would have been out of character for Frederic Henry to kill himself on the spot. He is far too selfish and far too fearful of death. Moreover, killing himself on the spot, or even ten years later, if spelled out for the reader, would have risked turning the book into a tale of star-crossed love. Yet the circumstances of the horrors they've experienced, and their deep need for emotional escape and salvation, have flung these two broken and lost souls together. Catherine has lost the love of her young life, Henry has treated the affair as a game until after his nearly fatal wounding, and they consider one another each other's religion. The idea of star-crossed love is exactly that sort of dramatic romanticism about love and war that *A Farewell to Arms* teases its readers with only to dismiss.[29]

Both novels move toward the ultimate isolation. The different nature of Henry's and Jordan's suicides is suggested by an object associated with the pistol—a sword. In *A Farewell to Arms,* Henry declines to purchase a sword along with the pistol;[30] in *For Whom the Bell Tolls,* Jordan declines to toss away his grandfather's sword along with the pistol.[31] Such a romantic clinging is far from the despondency that afflicts Frederic Henry.

Indeed it is perhaps easier to read *A Farewell to Arms* as revealing a cosmic order through poetic justice. Just as *The Sun Also Rises* reveals a moral sense through the negative example of its characters and their lack of values, perhaps *A Farewell to Arms,* instead of celebrating Frederic Henry's disillusion, actually condemns him. He does not believe in country or God; he arguably believes in nothing but self-preservation (of which Catherine is an instrument); he arguably only loves her for what she provides him; he arguably commits murder. His fate could be his comeuppance (if not literal suicide, then self-exile to a life-in-death state).

We might also and more fruitfully link Henry's suicide to the book's title (and to Robert Jordan). As I've argued elsewhere, if "woman for the male psyche represents social integration, responsibility, and self-sacrifice for the community, then she also embodies that very social contract that got him to the battlefield."[32] Thus, "Catherine Barkley and the baby both must die . . . because for Frederic Henry to have a final farewell to arms, he must lose all obligatory social ties, must escape the social contract embodied in wife and child."[33]

The danger of or avoidance of family life for a male veteran's psyche has a precedent in Hemingway's first fictionalized self, in his first Great War book of fiction. *In Our Times* as a novel is a book of stories written by the fictional Nick Adams, a war veteran who in writing these stories retraces his journey from childhood, to the war and his wounding, and eventually to fatherhood. Some stories feature Nick, some feature a surrogate male protagonist. Some of the stories featuring Nick never actually happened to Nick. Nick Adams and his various avatars in *In Our Time* are dragged reluctantly into fatherhood, and this reluctance obeys the operative idea of the commitment to the social via the family that sends men to war, suffering, and death.

"On the Quai at Smyrna" associates war and death with childbirth in a story added in lieu of an introduction to the 1930 edition. Only a year after *A Farewell to Arms*, this new edition capitalized on the novel's success and linked the two books in the public's mind. Young Nick's surety at the end of "Indian Camp," the true inaugural story, "that he would never die"[34] can be understood as a desire never to become a father, as he has just witnessed a man commit a bloody suicide a bunk away from his wife giving birth. And if we (as I believe we should) accept what Nick tells us in the novel's excised manuscript pages from the final story, "Big Two-Hearted River," the incidents of "Indian Camp" never took place. Thus the full story is that of a war veteran who invents a foundational biographical story associating not just death but suicide with fatherhood, a story in which the suicidal father suffers from an accidentally self-inflicted leg wound written by a man, Nick Adams, wounded in the leg during a war for which he presumably volunteered (so accidentally self-inflicted) and by the end of the novel about to become a father—and both of these facts, the impaired leg and the impending fatherhood, we learn in a single story later in the book, "Cross-Country Snow."

Harold Krebs, in the novel's most intense study of a veteran's difficulty getting on in life, declines to date using the language of the very geopolitics that led to the Great War:

> But they lived in such a complicated world of already defined alliances and shifting feuds that Krebs did not feel the energy or the courage to break into it . . . he did not want to get into the intrigue and the politics. . . . He did not want any consequences ever again. . . . Besides he did not really need a girl. The army had taught him that.[35]

He watches the town girls walking on the sidewalk across the street from his porch, where he sits reading and finally understanding his war. Krebs's younger sister flirts with him, pledging to be his girl, such that Nick Adams's naming her "Helen" after his own wife and soon-to-be mother of his child suggests an effort to rewrite the terms of heterosexual romance from social consequences to innocent play. The young wife in "Cat in the Rain" wants a child while her husband does not, the story opening with no less than three references to the war monument outside their window. Such repetition in Hemingway is never accidental. It also happens to be raining outside, and the story's title peculiarly predicts, albeit in different terms, *A Farewell to Arms.* The next story, "Out of Season," connects pending childbirth with male suicide if we take into account Hemingway's extratextual comment that the young couple's fishing guide hangs himself after the story ends, after the couple have decided not to abort their child. The guide is himself a father and a veteran, and both "Cat in the Rain" and "Out of Season" are set in Italy, where Ernest Hemingway, Nick Adams, and Frederic Henry all served.

Perhaps Frederic Henry realizes how badly he needs his wife and child to die to complete his journey to isolation and his farewell to arms; perhaps this unconscious knowledge drives the book's suicide subtext. At the level of this necessity, Henry is responsible for their deaths, and on this level his guilt acquires a magnitude beyond survival.

The idea of social obligation—a man's to fight for his country and a woman's to bear children—we can extend in the context of Carolyn Marvin and David W. Ingle's *Blood Sacrifice and the Nation: Totem Rituals and the American Flag,* which among other things contends that the nation-state's fundamental sovereign power is the exclusive right to kill its own citizens, chiefly by sending its soldiers to war. Frederic Henry receives his wound at the moment the United States enters the war. His suicide amounts to a nullification, even a usurpation, of that power. His *anti-patria* position supports such a reading; the absence of his father in the text further reflects this *anti-patria* message. He and his wife and child are not simply biologically trapped but also politically trapped. In this light Catherine and the baby must die not just to consummate her self-effacing desire, nor just to release Frederic Henry from his symbolic social obligations, but also to deny the nation-state another citizen-soldier and the capacity to produce even more.

Among other ways, "Cat in the Rain" communicates the wife's desire to become a mother through her desire to grow her hair out into long, womanly tresses. References to Maria's possible pregnancy combine with her promise to Robert Jordan to grow her hair in a potentially threatening way to a man who will avoid following in his father's footsteps at any cost. Jordan avoids becoming a father, he avoids family life and all it might involve and symbolize, by ensuring that he does not survive. On the morning of his death, he ridicules the perfect romantic life with Maria that he has conjured. "There are always ways out," he tells himself.[36] And he finds his way out. In a stroke Robert Jordan refuses domestic entrapment, refuses betrayal of the high romanticism of his relationship with Maria, and refuses his father's inheritance.

But we must step back.

Earlier, in a flashback, Robert Jordan recalls ridding himself of the pistol his father used to commit suicide, but this act does not prove he has forever vanquished the temptation; rather, it reveals the degree to which he continues the struggle. Someone not worried about committing suicide would hardly bother with such an extravagant gesture. Chubb, the person who is with Jordan when he drops the pistol into the lake, and the only person in the book familiar enough with him to use a familiar name, recognizes that his friend's gesture signifies the ongoing psychomania: "I know why you did that with the old gun, Bob."[37] Indeed the next day Jordan acknowledges how much he remains his father the coward's son as he wishes himself a little courage.[38] In a different piece of writing, Hemingway might well have used the word *chickenshit.*

Irving Goff, the American volunteer from Brooklyn working as a guerilla behind Nationalist lines, was "amazed" when he read about the technique Robert Jordan used to blow the bridge:

> Goff found that the explosion techniques were practical only for mines and other industrial purposes, not for guerillas — unless they were bent on suicide. The getaway time allowed by Hemingway was much too short, and needlessly so. Did literary requirements conflict with authenticity? Goff preferred to believe that Hemingway was ignorant about guerilla warfare. "What he knew least he wrote a book about," Goff said in 1979.[39]

William Braasch Watson disagrees, and after studying the issue concludes that Hemingway knew exactly what he was doing in terms of Robert Jordan's guerilla tactics and technique. The grenade substitute for the lost blasting caps was a workable if risky solution.[40] And while I'd love to be able to use Jordan's demolition technique to prove he was "bent on suicide," I find it more reasonable to believe that he did not rig his death in this manner. He might have rigged it circumstantially, but he did not literally, technically, intentionally rig it.

Hemingway's hero evokes the "dynamitard" or "dinamitero" who had become a symbol of the Republican war effort. Kenneth Porter's poem "¡Salud!" from the fall of 1936 contrasts by verbal play the symbolic instrument of Nationalist Catholicism with this symbolic weapon of the Republic: "Futile the whip of cords — / only avails the scourge of dynamite!"[41] And Hemingway had written about a group of dynamiters assaulting Teruel in his "Fall of Teruel" dispatch. Perhaps on some level he wanted to differentiate between his hero and his hero's hero, the grandfather who served with distinction in the American Civil War, along the lines of this Nationalist sympathizer's description of the warrior symbol chosen by the "Marxists":

> Dynamite is not a weapon of war. It is rarely employed in military operations. Sometimes it is used in mines like those underneath the Alcazar, or to destroy bridges or works, but its use is necessarily ungallant and unlovely. It is not a hero's weapon, but rather the occasional tool of the technician. Nor is the dynamitard a war hero; he is the symbol of destruction, but of destruction at the rear of the fighting.[42]

Where has the grandfather's glorious sword gone?

Such a warrior is a far cry from the Spanish bullfighter whose art, grace, and courage Hemingway so greatly admired. Yet bullfighting too has its necessary ugliness. Does Hemingway paint his portrait of Pilar's first lover, the self-destructive bullfighter Finito, to compare or contrast the bullfighter's art with Robert Jordan's? Or is it the two men's passion for agency and self-actualization that ultimately matters? "How often have I heard Finito say that it is all knowledge and that the bull never gored the man," Pilar harangues, "rather the man gored himself on the horn of the bull."[43]

There is also some evidence that Hemingway had the subject of suicide on his mind. Donaldson writes that Hemingway had thought about "a novel based directly on his father's 'killing himself and why.'"[44] In a brief autobiographical sketch from the mid 1930s, Hemingway writes that if he had not spent so much time fishing, shooting, skiing, watching the bullfights, and boating, he might have produced more writing, or killed himself.[45] Less cheekily and closer in time and context, his fund-raising speech after the July 1937 Hollywood screenings of *The Spanish Earth* describes the pleas for death from the severely wounded who wanted their pain to end, something he knew firsthand and witnessed many times.[46] Less than two years later, in March 1939, he began writing *For Whom the Bell Tolls*. Four months into it, he wrote to his first wife Hadley, "Important thing for me to do is not get discouraged and take easy way out like your and my" fathers. "Because very bad example to children. Also have to finish this book."[47]

Philip Young was perhaps the first to recognize that the novel depicts "a subterranean struggle between [Robert Jordan's] wish to live and the old obsession with death. . . . This attraction toward death not only brackets the novel, as if to say that the whole book is to be read in the light of the inclination toward returning to earth which Jordan's posture indicates."[48] But he does not pursue the subject further. As I claimed earlier, Frederic Henry expresses his death wish through his memoir's recreation of Catherine Barkley. For Kenneth Lynn, Hemingway displaces Jordan's "death fantasies" onto Maria, who "has spent many hours thinking about suicide" and who shares those thoughts with her lover. By novel's end, according to Lynn, "the hero [is] permitted to debate the question that had been hounding Hemingway for years. If one is ready to die, is it not better to contrive to be killed than to commit suicide?" If suicide is the coward's solution, "the only respectable alternative is to remain conscious somehow until the Fascist cavalry appears; by engaging them with gunfire, [Jordan] can force them to kill him."[49] Lynn stops here, however, neglecting (as with Young) to document suicide's presence throughout the text and in effect hedging his interpretation. Most recently, Stephen Koch has asserted, without demonstrating it, that Robert Jordan's actions amount to an apolitical "*suicidal* choice." Koch's prose then falls prey to overwriting as he describes this choice as "not the 'separate peace' of old, but something closer to a separate war, a separate death, a solitary, tragic, purely individual heroism, a stand against his own defeat"—by which he means that Robert Jordan has discovered "his way of redeeming his own suicidal melancholia."[50] Thus Jordan succumbs to that melancholia for a noble cause.

As with *A Farewell to Arms*, Hemingway sprinkles references to suicide throughout *For Whom the Bell Tolls*. Knowing he is about to die, EI Sordo fakes suicide to draw Captain Mora up the hill in order to kill him,[51] obliquely setting up the end of the novel, when Jordan, knowing he is about to die, waits to kill Lieutenant Berrendo as he heads up the hill.[52] An officer kills himself rather than let Pablo's mob kill him;[53] Karkov, Jordan's Soviet mentor, carries poison for his own use;[54] Jordan thinks about the quality of Maria's parents' last words;[55] and as the group prepares to move toward the bridge, Pilar references Judas Iscariot's hanging himself.[56] Maria, after being rescued from the train and her imprisonment, hopes for death,[57] and she and Jordan make a pact to kill the other, if wounded, to prevent capture.[58] When she asks him if his father killed himself to avoid torture, he answers in the affirmative, deliberately mixing his father's emotional self-torture with the physical torture Maria meant. He was lucky, she says, he had a weapon—her father had no such luck. She then projects her clear desire to kill herself rather than endure further suffering and humiliation onto Jordan: "Then you and me we are the same."[59]

The lovers' suicide pact repeats the arrangement between Jordan and Kashkin, his Russian predecessor with Pablo's crew, and after Jordan promises to kill Maria if need be, his mind immediately goes to Kashkin, his Russian predecessor with Pablo's crew. The best evidence of Jordan's desire to die Hemingway communicates through Kashkin, the man on whom Pilar smelled death the way she reads it on Jordan's palm, and in many other ways Jordan's double.[60] It is on a mission led by Kashkin that this guerilla band rescues Maria,[61] the girl who will become Jordan's lover. It is Kashkin, according to Jordan, who worried himself to death on his last mission—according to the same Jordan whose worries dominate the three days of this nearly five hundred page narrative. "You have to be awfully occupied with yourself to do a thing like that," Jordan ironically thinks about his father's suicide as he wonders about his own susceptibility.[62] Among other things, Kashkin seemed to augur his own death; and among other things, Robert

Jordan (especially when with Maria) repeatedly feels his own death approaching.[63]

Kashkin and Jordan belong to the same *guerrilleros* group.[64] We are told at least twice that the two carry the same Russian cigarettes, with Pablo perhaps making a dig at Kashkin—and Jordan too?—when he describes them as "Much air and little tobacco."[65] Just as Pilar describes Kashkin's speech as "very rare and windy,"[66] Jordan, telling himself to "Stop worrying," calls himself a "windy bastard," with four-hundred-twenty-eight pages to go.[67] They look similar, with blond hair, and Maria likes them both, finding them attractive and brave.[68] (Had Kashkin also become fond of Maria? Had that been a part of his problem? Jordan permitted himself his relationship with Maria even though he had told Golz that a woman would be a dangerous distraction.[69]) For all the times the book tells us about Kashkin's shaky nerves, and for all the times Jordan evaluates Kashkin's state of mind, we witness Jordan's own worries, anxieties, and diffidence, and we hear him worry about worrying, from nearly the first page of the novel to the last. One can only imagine how much longer the book would be had Hemingway used his more usual first-person narration rather than the novel's third-person sometimes omniscient point-of-view.

When Jordan first tells the guerillas about the death of Kashkin, he reports that Kashkin killed himself to avoid being taken a prisoner.[70] Later, however, Jordan confesses that *he* killed Kashkin, who was severely wounded and would not be left for capture;[71] and still later, we learn not only that Jordan killed Kashkin at Kashkin's request,[72] but that Jordan now uses "old Kashkin's gun,"[73] the very submachine gun he likely used to kill Kashkin and the very gun in his hands at the end of the novel when he is willing to be left behind. So Jordan's double Kashkin shoots himself; Jordan shoots his double Kashkin; Jordan handles Kashkin's gun, perhaps at Kashkin's death and certainly at his own. It's a telling associative chain.

The most thorough earlier comparison of Jordan and Kashkin regarding suicide is Robert E. Fleming's article "Hemingway's Treatment of Suicide: 'Fathers and Sons' and *For Whom the Bell Tolls*." Fleming, after establishing Jordan's attraction to death, concludes that Jordan

> rejects the way of his father . . . By exchanging his life for the time his friends need to escape, Jordan shows that he has finally come to terms with his father's death. He does not refuse suicide simply to put himself in opposition to his father; instead, he makes a positive choice for a positive reason and allies himself with those who, like El Sordo, sell their lives dearly.[74]

Scott Donaldson agrees, averring that Jordan "manifestly repudiates that suicide."[75] I don't. "*Do it. Do it now,*" he tries to command himself at the end of the novel.[76] That he refuses to take his own life, all of a few sentences later, is moot—the deed is already done. Robert Jordan has done all he can, in Lynn's words, "to contrive to be killed."[77] Pilar's foretelling of Jordan's death in his palm speaks to a personal rather than a fated source for his death—it is literally in his own hands. As she once told Maria, in the context of the latter's desire to die: "nothing is done to oneself that one does not accept."[78] Just before the attack, and prefiguring his farewell to Maria and his death on the pine needle floor, he says good-bye to her, remembers his father, and then

> lay on the pine-needle floor of the forest and listened to the first stirring in the branches of the pines of the wind that would come with daylight. . . . Then he turned the gun, with the lock open and in the dark he put the muzzle to his lips and blew through the barrel, the metal tasting greasy and oily as his tongue touched the edge of the bore. . . . Now the clip was heavy again in his hand and he slid it back into the submachine gun and felt it click home.[79]

That would be Kashkin's gun clicking home, and to my ear the sensual language puts María here too. Then, after blowing the bridge but before his wounding, Jordan accepts "the ridding of the self that you had to do in war. Where there could be no self. Where yourself is only to be lost."[80] We might read Jordan's final moments even more cynically: Just like Kashkin, he lost the nerve to take his own life and left it to someone else. The label *chickenshit* here takes on a different cast.

The classical pathos formula whereby the victim dutifully accepts his suffering, as Stephen Eisenman observes, stoically flirts with or even depicts suicide.[81] Choosing death in battle gives Robert Jordan everything he wants. He fulfills the spirits of his cavalryman grandfather, his suicidal father, and his surrogate mother Pilar. And he gets the girl. He has told himself again and again that the intensity of his relationship with Maria is only possible because of his impending death, and such love is the only gift with which this world blesses us. By his own logic he must die to realize the truth of that love. Maria wants to die when loving him, and feels she dies each time; he feels he might, too.[82] They achieve an eternal now, their love simultaneously vital and annihilating—vital because annihilating, annihilating because vital. And when Jordan actually dies, because of his relationship with Maria, he again gets to have his death both ways. He dies in the forest, and, as he assures her, he lives on in her.[83] They have become one person, as they have told themselves over and over again. Because Robert Jordan wanted to die, when he does die at the end of the novel, we readers do not—this reader does not, anyway—feel particularly sad, or particularly ennobled.

Jordan's may ultimately be a romantic death, at once for love and for a noble and lost cause, a symbol of inspiration. In death he finds integration with the Spanish earth, and with Maria, in a merging of souls he knows would be impossible if he survived—this relationship will never fall prey to babies, nor to finances, nor the numbing effect of ordinary life. Perhaps he has not successfully divorced Maria the person from the Spanish earth; perhaps his sacrifice for her and it are one and the same, and even his hope that the wartime rhetoric of the dead providing the seed for the Republic's future translates literally into a child in her womb.

Or the joke is on him. When, on the night before the bridge mission, he refuses orgasm by manual stimulation from Maria, he figures he will need his unspent semen for the mission: "There are no pine needles that need that now as I will need it tomorrow."[84] His blood becomes the seed on that final pine needle floor, albeit ironically onanistic given the fruitless fate of the battle and the war. He wonders whatever happened to Onan. In fact, God killed Onan for his onanism.

When Robert Jordan declines Maria's offer for an alternative to straightforward coitus, presumably in the missionary position, he declines anything that two men could perform. Hemingway's description of Jordan's sexuality is stridently heterosexual. As we've seen, the novel presents a conservative exemplar of traditional gender roles more in keeping with *The Spanish Earth*'s propaganda for an apprehensive and conservative international audience than with the progressive agenda of many within the Republic. Yet there are fissures in this presentation. Two famously ecstatic lovemaking scenes between a long-haired nervous Nelly of an irregular soldier and a boyishly crop-haired young woman, the latter of whom holds a sexual bond of some kind with a manly matron, feed the possibility of a salient driven into the text by homoerotic forces—especially if in the very language of these scenes Hemingway mimics Gertrude Stein, the crop-haired, matronly lesbian who captivated his imagination.

Debra Moddelmog's quite recent essay, "We Live in a Country Where Nothing Makes Any Difference: The Queer Sensibility of *A Farewell to Arms*," is the latest of several scholarly efforts to expose the full complexity of Frederic Henry's sexual identity. Such suspicious criticism tends to target him rather than Jordan. Mark Spilka's 1990 *Hemingway's Quarrel with Androgyny*, the first thorough treatment of gender identity throughout Hemingway's work, is a great example. Spilka's book postulates the feminization of Lieutenant Henry through his experience of being wounded and hospitalized, and the creation of an Edenic androgynous union between Frederic and Catherine (which Hemingway then brutally takes away), but barely touches on Robert Jordan's gender vulnerabilities, instead focusing his discussion of that novel on Pilar, Jordan's mother, and Maria. Spilka concludes that the androgynous union in *A Farewell to Arms* "so absorbs male identity that [Catherine] is as threatening to it, finally, as any bitch heroine; and though she dies bravely, like a true Hemingway hero, it may be that she is sacrificed to male survival—so that this time the Indian in the upper bunk lives on!"[85] In early Hemingway, for Spilka, the blissful absorption of the self in the romantic other harbors the fear of self-destruction, an idea he does not then carry forward to *For Whom the Bell Tolls*.

Yet I suspect we can read Henry's and Jordan's gender vulnerabilities together, and in conjunction with the above analysis of a suicide impulse motivating their narratives. Specifically, the crude historical homophobic association of cowardice (including suicide), emasculation (such as battlefield unfitness), and homosexuality (between men) suggests that the presence of one of these leads to a paranoia for the others. It's quite possible, in other words, in *A Farewell to Arms* and *For Whom the Bell Tolls*, to read a homoerotic subtext not as part and parcel of the character and fate of each novel's male lead, but as imagined *textual* symptoms of, even subconscious worries about, their character and fate. Jordan is as strident to prove his bravery as the novel is his heterosexuality. Just as suicide sometimes becomes a term of Eisenman's pathos formula, so do gender ambiguity and homoeroticism.[86] Henry Carpenter, the suicidal character in Hemingway's prior novel, *To Have and Have Not*, was gay. Coincidentally, so was one of the three American guerillas assigned to blow the bridges at Teruel.[87]

For Moddelmog, "Catherine and Frederic's recognition that they both desire and wish to be each other collapses the strict boundary between male and female, between heterosexual and homosexual." She quotes Carl Eby that in other Hemingway works "the merger of lovers 'threatens to become a reversal of roles.'"[88] We've already seen a little of Henry's emasculating insecurities. His passive nature, his wartime duties more fit for "urnings" than men, and his leg wound, are also indicative. After accusing him of getting himself wounded, his buddy Rinaldi accuses him of being gay with the priest, and it's at this point he decides he loves Catherine in grand heterosexual fashion. When the couple meets up with a genuine war hero, she declares she finds him rather dull, expressing a preference for her nonheroic lover. Even his increasing attachment to her abjures totemic, autonomous manhood. Frederic Henry tries to wear a beard, but it just isn't him. Additionally, the memoir form is sometimes gendered feminine in its mirror-gazing introspection. One could even think of Henry's memoir as an elegiac biography of Catherine, effecting a gender reversal by casting himself as the wife writing the life of her great husband.

Robert Jordan has his share of insecurities, too. He knows most of the best soldiers are already dead, and most of them were high-spirited. Is he one of the precious few left? Either way, he knows he won't be around for long unless his attitude changes.[89] His life has been one of living up to his grandfather's example and living down his father's. The night before the attack, he still doesn't know which man's soul lives on in him.[90] He knows he can't write a story as well as Pilar can tell one;[91] he fears he will fail Karkov and the Republic because he won't be able to become the writer able enough to tell it truly.[92] Perhaps he dies because he can't write the war (but Hemingway's narrator can). Pablo accuses him of being a false professor for having no manly, authority-signifying beard, and it turns out he's right. Jordan is only an instructor, not a professor.[93] His fear of becoming his father he confuses with his identification with Kashkin, as Jordan sees himself dead, wishes he had confidence, and endlessly dithers. His telling Maria at the end of the novel that he exists in her now echoes Catherine Barkley's statements to Frederic Henry. Perhaps, if for different reasons, he also seeks to relieve himself of his self.

Jordan's insecurities yield slight textual expressions of gender insecurities, as when he berates himself as he wires the bridge for "shaking like a Goddamn woman"[94] and when Pablo accuses him of wearing a skirt[95] and having no *cojones* (testicles).[96] When Jordan and Pablo finally bond to accomplish the mission, Pilar—accuses them of being *maricones* (homosexuals).[97] One might easily dismiss these lines as inconsequential ribbing, though they are worth a little more contemplation. His long blonde hair also signals a potential gender ambiguity, for one thing by linking him with the similarly ill-fated George Armstrong Custer, a man the press of the day presented as "androgynous" and "on the border between masculine adulthood and the passionate nature of womanhood."[98] No wonder Jordan, at this moment in his life, remarks that his grandfather would have saved Custer from the massacre at Little Bighorn if he had been there[99]—if only grandfather's spirit were with Jordan this day, in Spain, instead of his father's. (Jordan does nothing to save El Sordo during his Custer-like last stand.) His bonding with Pablo is also suggestive in this context, as both Pablo's and Jordan's fathers let their women "bully" them.[100]

Still, the hypothesis that hints of Henry's and Jordan's gender and sexual anxiety as textual symptoms or unconscious correlations with their suicidal natures is only a hypothesis. One could just as easily see these hints as contributing to their internal struggles.

Or one could sever the suicides completely from the men's gender troubles. I suspect that *For Whom the Bell Tolls* exhibits as much a "queer sensibility" as Moddelmog finds in *A Farewell to Arms.* Spilka's biographical argument sees Maria and Jordan's "mystic exchange" of selves "as Hemingway's attempt to affirm and express his feminine feelings, his androgynous yearnings from infancy onward,"[101] though we don't need to import the biography to ask whether, as Moddelmog argues of Frederic and Catherine, Robert's and Maria's desire to become the other bespeaks a release from strict gender boundaries as well. Moddelmog's discussion of early-twentieth-century marriage manuals and their new promotion of sex within marriage notes that these publications came from "the more liberal sexual and marital reformers of the time."[102] Yet this promotion conveniently corroborates the widespread conservative buttressing of heterosexual union against the newly perceived homosexual threat. In terms of Hemingway, "the simultaneous orgasm" that such manuals advocated as "a form of shared bliss," both symbol of and means to "the complete union of two separate beings," uniting them forevermore,[103] sees its fullest realization not in *A Farewell to Arms* but in *For Whom the Bell Tolls*—when the earth moves as the lovers achieve the eternal now. The "cult of the mutual orgasm" for most imaginations of the day would have physically excluded male-male sex from this ecstatic union of souls. And, as already mentioned, Jordan declines any sexual act that two men could do, and he talks and fantasizes about marriage. In other words, the novel's cult of heterosexual mutual orgasm participates in or bears the historical influence of a cultural strategy to combat the emergent homophobia.

Furthermore, the novel's insistence on the transcendental nature of Jordan and Maria's heterosexual union operates within a separate but related cultural context. Ernest Becker's theory in *Denial of Death* that in a post-God modernist world romantic sexual love became the path to meaningful existence and spiritual attainment fits both novels. Frederic and Catherine explicitly replace traditional religion with the religion of each other. During the era's invention of homosexuality (and heterosexuality), heterosexual coupling also became spiritual as another way of defining, sanctioning, and sanctifying civilized heterosexuality against bestial homosexuality—it buttressed both threatened institutions, using religion to shore up heterosexuality and using the new spiritual investment in sex between husband and wife to shore up religion.

Hewson characterizes *For Whom the Bell Tolls* as a transitional text, citing Jordan's "conversion" from a selfish lover fearful of the loss of his male self in romantic union to someone at ease with "an alternate means of self-identification through openness, commitment, and love."[104] Yet whatever Cixousian feminization Jordan experiences or embraces, whatever openness the novel advances between gender and identity, it works in the limited service of heterosexual romance and on the level of socialized interpersonal roles, not broader alternative means to gender and sexual redefinition—Hewson's article tellingly ignores the erotic attraction between Pilar and Maria. After the second extended lovemaking passage, the one which Hewson interprets as enacting this conversion to openness, Jordan regrets that his impending death will prevent him from discovering even more about life.[105]

> If it can be suggested that Hemingway's interpretation of sexuality to this point in his career has been a stereotypically masculine one, we might view this passage as a veiled or unconscious admission of doubt as to the validity of patriarchal sexual identities and as an indication of the writer's desire to explore other avenues of sexual and gender self-expression than those he had previously walked.[106]

Thus the novel, for Hewson, advances Hemingway toward the explicit physical experimentation with gender and sexuality of *The Garden of Eden,* the next novel he would begin.

But, as already observed, Jordan's imagined absolute conjoining of selves through simultaneous orgasm excludes Maria's perspective. Whatever emotional openness Jordan experiences is inconsequential because predicated on his imminent death. If Hewson is correct about Jordan's postcoital regret, this regret, this fantasy, is similarly inconsequential. With hours to live, he has nothing to lose indulging even this extremely veiled articulation of alternative desires. His quite traditional understanding of gender roles leaves little room for emotional adventure. It's a long way from the barbershop scene of Maria's sheering and rape to that of Catherine Bourne's—and David Bourne's—tonsorial eroticism.[107]

Nevertheless, *For Whom the Bell Tolls* in some ways does anticipate *The Garden of Eden.* David Bourne's own conservative turn, from the adventurous Catherine to the conventional and safe Marita, and his turn from the risqué and uncharted honeymoon narrative to the old-school childhood Africa stories of hunting and paternal conflict, inherits something of Robert Jordan's spirit. Both novels also associate artistic power (specifically writing) with multidimensional gender and sexual identity. It's Pilar, not Jordan, who can tell a story; it's Catherine, not David, whose creative destruction instigates his most experimental work—the honeymoon narrative—and his best work—the Africa stories. I am intrigued that the sexual politics of *For Whom the Bell Tolls* do seem to provide a bridge, through Spain, from a work like *A Farewell to Arms* to one like *The Garden of Eden*, or for that matter from *The Sun Also Rises* to "The Africa Book," the work posthumously published first in digested form, as *True at First Light* and then, in complete form, as *Under Kilamanjaro.*

Another element *For Whom the Bell Tolls* and *The Garden of Eden* share is their evocation through Spain of Africa and the primitive.[108] Just as the gender play is inseparable from the racial play in the latter novel, the possibility of a queer sensibility in *For Whom the Bell Tolls* enters through the novel's primitive, might-as-well-be-Africa setting, given the West's centuries-long imaginative locating of homosexuality in the "uncivilized" regions of the world.[109] Catherine and David Bourne's gender-bending, race-mixing, and incest games take place in Spain and on the French border, but have their roots in the story David writes of his father, Juma, and their wives in Africa. In addition to Jordan's going native with Maria and the possibility of homoerotic anxiousness, we should not forget the mild hints of incest in *For Whom the Bell Tolls.* A reading as conservative as Stanton's nevertheless spies an "incestuous undercurrent in [Pilar's] relationship with her symbolic children," citing Pilar and her symbolic son Jordan though clearly alluding to her symbolic daughter Maria.[110] The observation that Maria and Jordan look so much alike they could be brother and sister points at once to this minor incestuous subtext and also to the modernist theorizing of homoeroticism as narcissistic.[111] All three of the novel's quietly titillating transgressions—racial, gender, and familial—link it to

The Garden of Eden and to the West's imaginings of primitive polysexuality. That this imagination includes cannibalism, often employed as a disguise for the others, neatly fits DeGuzmán's reading of *For Whom the Bell Tolls.* (In *The Garden of Eden* Juma's teeth are filed to sharp points, and the great sexual transgressors, Catherine and David, are always eating.)[112]

For Whom the Bell Tolls only flirts with the homoerotic, the miscegenous, and the incestuous, and in the process exploits its setting, Spain, where Europe flirts with Africa, where Robert Jordan goes native and stands above it all. His reference to himself as Tarzan, maneuvering through the bridge's trestles, is not so incidental after all.[113]

Tarzan?

Hemingway's Second War is not at present bearing witness to his bearing witness to the Spanish Civil War. But the novel never strictly bore witness to the war either. I expect this book's precipitate discussion in these final pages will have baffled those readers invested in this book's historical project and frustrated by its haste and deficiencies those interested in creative investigations of gender and culture. The success of Hemingway's ambitious novel rests on respecting the real story and on vitalizing it and going beyond it through fiction. *For Whom the Bell Tolls* combines documentary impulse, autobiographical investigation, and sheer invention in a way that encourages a multitude of approaches.

The analyzing of it is never done.

EPILOGUE

Two vignettes from *For Whom the Bell Tolls* that have received scant scholarly attention involve Spain's tradition of bullfighting. In one, Robert Jordan remembers taking command of a tank and directing it to a bullring for ammunition and to join with the infantry to repel the Nationalist assault into the Carabanchel suburbs of Madrid in November 1936. In the other, Pilar tells the story of her former lover, the bullfighter Finito de Palencia. After killing a bull in Valladolid, Finito and Pilar attend a party in his honor, where he spends the evening hacking up blood before shouting "No!" when the bull's mounted head is unveiled.[1]

Bullfighting held a complex relationship with the Spanish Civil War. Both sides used bullrings for marshalling, camping, and training their troops. Bullrings also proved convenient spaces for mass executions, most notoriously the fascists' slaughter of nearly two thousand loyalist defenders and noncombatants at Badajoz in November 1936, where Jay Allen reported the blood "palm deep."[2] Most matadors sided with the Nationalists, likely out of allegiance to their wealthy patrons. And whereas just before the war revolutionary leftists ploughed over fields of the aristocratic estates dedicated to bull breeding and planned "to slaughter the bulls for food,"[3] wartime Nationalist areas continued to enjoy the bullfights as part of normal bourgeois life.[4] On the other hand, like Finito most bullfighters came from the lower classes and suffered tremendously in one of the few available professional avenues to money and status in old Spain.[5] The sport also commanded a mass appeal—bullfighters of lesser rank earned their paltry keep performing in makeshift rings throughout the countryside. Joaquín of El Sordo's band turned to the Republic perhaps because of his failure in the ring.

Poems in Nelson's anthology *The Wound and the Dream* read the bull sometimes as symbol of the Republicans, sometimes as symbol of the Nationalists.[6] The enigmatic bull in Picasso's *Guernica* represents at once the brutality of Franco's methods and the primitivism of those who lived and worked the Spanish earth and their victimization at the hands of Franco.

Finito's sighting down his sword at the bull he is about to kill, Finito himself suffering internal injuries from other bulls and with but months to live, forespeaks the last scene of the novel—Robert Jordan sighting down his machine gun at Lieutenant Berrendo, Jordan himself suffering injuries with but minutes to live. Like a matador and a bull squaring off, the encounter between Jordan and Berrendo obtains a dignity absent from the massacre at Ronda, which Pablo organizes—as Pilar tells it anyway—as a *capea*, the type of bullfight in which everyone joins in,[7] as Hemingway describes in *Death in the Afternoon*:

> Sometimes the bull is killed if the town has the money to afford it, or if the populace gets out of control; everyone swarming on him at once with knives, daggers, butcher knives and rocks; . . . a swarm of choppers, thrusters and stabbers pushing into him, laying on him or cutting up at him until he sways and goes down. All amateur group killing is a very barbarous, messy, though exciting business and is a long way from the ritual of the formal bullfight.[8]

Primitivo fails to understand why Finito fought bulls when his short stature doomed him to internal injuries from the side of a horn when he went in for the kill, doomed him to an early grave; he fails to understand the inevitability of situation and character that marks men like Finito and Jordan: "Pilar looked at Robert Jordan and shook her head."[9]

Do we then interpret the unveiling of the dead bull's head, draped in the purple of Advent and Lent, as a sign of a resurrection of the people of the Spanish earth (and the Republic), bought with the martyred blood of Finito de Palencia and Robert Jordan, the bullfight itself suggesting the antagonistic yet dependent and respectful relationship of the people to the land? Or do we see in it the triumphant bull of fascism? Finito, after all, repeatedly cries *no* to the bull's head. Reading the novel in 1940, we know how the war ends. His bullfight occurred in Valladolid—the place where the Falangists raped Maria and from where Nationalist troops are rumored "to be sent to clear out these mountains"[10] (Lieutenant Berrendo and company?). Or perhaps Finito recognizes his own agonized complicity in the culture of Spanish aristocracy and its murdering of the earth and its true people. Or is it a mistake even to read the scene as a political allegory?

Finito's story has escaped much scholarly exegesis precisely because of its protean defiance of fixedness. The complexity of one's response mirrors the complexity of the bullfight itself, as an American bullfighter explained to Richard Wright: "There are two sets of identifications. . . . One is with the bull and the other is with the matador. It is only when the spectator can make the two identifications at once that the bullfight is really experienced."[11] *Guernica* similarly enriches the experience of it by confusing the allegiance-seeking gaze. So also does Hemingway challenge his reader to identify with Finito and the bull, with Jordan and Berrendo, and Pablo and Pilar, and all the rest. Pablo's horse, too.

But at least this much is clear: with the Ronda massacre and Finito's life and death, Hemingway starkly announces that the Spain of *For Whom the Bell Tolls* is not the Spain of *The Sun Also Rises*. Or—better—for Hemingway, with his Anglo modernist perspective, it is that Spain's dark side, perhaps the consequence of that gloriously tempestuous and ritualized country, the inevitability of the political situation and the Spanish character.

For Whom the Bell Tolls may have been the crowning achievement of Hemingway's Spanish Civil War witness, but hardly the only one. In June 2006, Hemingway scholars and fellow travelers gathered in Ronda, the birthplace of modern Spanish bullfighting, for the 12th International Hemingway Society Biennial Conference. James Meredith, the President of the Ernest Hemingway Society and Foundation, took the occasion to offer his thoughts on the profundity of that first spring of the Spanish Civil War for Hemingway's life:

> The year 1937 was not only the beginning of dramatic changes yet again in his immediate family, but also it was a time of emerging personal growth and, most certainly, literary regeneration and reconfiguration. It is almost too simple to say that it was a time of dramatic change in the life of Ernest Hemingway, because nothing was ever completely simple for him, but 1937 was, most significantly, a time when he started the year moving in one direction and ended it moving almost 180 degrees in the other, in terms of his various personal, public, and moral and literary lives.

Hemingway's experiences that spring "would shape and dominate his later literary achievements"—the best of the NANA dispatches, five short stories, his only play, and two novels: "a major revision of *To Have and Have Not*, which brought together the various moral fibers of the novel," and of course "the visionary core of *For Whom the Bell Tolls*."[12]

Yet of anything beyond the dispatches, the film, and the novel, the present study is woefully negligent. How fun and enlightening it would be to compare the Spanish Civil War stories of Hemingway with those of de Pereda (both have a story titled "The Denunciation"), or *The Fifth Column* with Gellhorn and Cowles's play about correspondents in the second World War, *Love Goes to Press*. This study does very little with the *Ken* essays and several other published nonfiction pieces from the war, such as "Fascism Is a Lie" and the foreword to Joseph North's *Men in the Ranks*.[13] The Hemingway Collection at the John F. Kennedy Presidential Library holds a number of unpublished notes, fragments, and other pieces from the war that this book does not tap. And much more has been written about *For Whom the Bell Tolls* than this study digests.

The brief biographical narrative could be significantly expanded. People like Evan Shipman do not receive their due, much less someone as prominent in these events as Martha Gellhorn. I considered, but declined, ferreting out and including as many correspondents, writers, combatants, and others as I could who crossed paths with Hemingway in Spain. There are known inconsistencies to be resolved. Milton Wolff, for example, writes that he first met Hemingway at the Café

Chicote in July 1937, that Hemingway and Capa attended his captaincy promotion ceremony[14] (which an obituary dates as January 1938[15]), and that he "saw Hemingway again around July 1938, just before the Lincoln's crossed the Ebro"[16]—only Hemingway was back in the United States all three dates. When exactly did they encounter one another, and in what circumstances? Whatever happened to Rollin Dart? Hemingway's postwar relationship with the war and the people he knew in it (much less with Spain itself, still under Franco's dictatorship when Hemingway died) would make a very long and interesting chapter by itself.[17] I have not completely sorted out the relationship among the CPUSA, the Comintern, the American Friends of Spanish Democracy, the Writers' Congress, and other leftist artist groups to my satisfaction. I would love a more complete list of the films shown in Madrid theaters that strange spring of 1937. Parts of this book could also use a more thorough understanding of the verbal and visual rhetoric of wartime politics and propaganda.

The analysis of it is never done. A book like this one does not measure its success on the conclusions it presumes to draw but on the inquiries it hopes to open.

NOTES

INTRODUCTION

1. Photographs EH5384P and EH5381P, Ernest Hemingway Collection, John F. Kennedy Presidential Library and Museum, Boston, hereafter JFK.
2. Dispatch of 22 December 1937 (Box 3, Folder 1), Herbert Matthews Collection, Harry Ransom Humanities Research Center, University of Texas–Austin (hereafter HRC).
3. William Braasch Watson, "Dispatches," 67. Quotations from the NANA dispatches follow the Diplomatic Text established by William Braasch Watson's "Hemingway's Spanish Civil War Dispatches" (hereafter "Dispatches"). Instead of the titles assigned by Watson for his article, I will use titles originally assigned by NANA, as these are the ones by which the dispatches are cataloged and most frequently referred to. Additional information or quotations from Watson's commentary will be cited "in 'Dispatches.'"
4. "In front of Teruel," Photograph EH4705P, (JFK). Matthews probably took this photo, because the copy at JFK bears a *New York Times*/Wide World Photos credit and another copy, from Matthews's own collection, has been entrusted to Peter Davis of Villon Films.
5. Dispatch of 22 December 1937, THIRD LAST ADD (HRC: Herbert Matthews Collection, Box 3, Folder 1).

6. Dispatch of 22 December 1937 (HRC: Herbert Matthews Collection, Box 3, Folder 1).
7. "Miscellaneous Fragments [Spanish Civil War]" (JFK: Item 716).
8. A cropped version of the photo without Hemingway appeared as part of *Life*'s photo-essay, "The War in Spain Makes a Movie" (12 July 1937), 21. The image with Hemingway, and several of Ferno's more graphic shots, can be seen online at Nederlands Fotomuseum. The cameraman's name was actually spelled Fernhout. It was "Americanized" to Ferno for the film credits, and that is the spelling I have chosen to use.
9. Unless otherwise noted, all quotations from *The Spanish Earth* are my transcriptions.
10. George Seldes, unpublished interview with Peter Davis, 11 October 1981.
11. Sontag, 75–77.
12. Matthews to Edwin James, 22 March 1937 (HRC: Herbert Matthews Collection, Box 1, Folder 2).
13. Stott, 191.
14. Beevor, 276.
15. Excerpt of Hemingway letter to Duran "circa late August or early Sept. 1940" per Carlos Baker's notes (Princeton University, Carlos Baker Collection of Ernest Hemingway, Firestone Library [hereafter PU]: Folder 35, "Gustavo Duran"). Duran participated in a postwar 1940 interview with Hemingway and *New York Times* reporter Robert Van Gelder (see Trogdon, *Reference*, 220–224). During the second World War, Duran helped Hemingway operate his "Crook Factory" counterespionage operations in Cuba. One can see an image of Duran riding a motorcycle in Robert Capa's *Death in the Making*, on the unpaginated fourth page from the end, and reprinted blurrily in Schaber et al. (122, plate 63).

1. Hemingway's War

1. See, for example, Thomas, 209; Preston, *Spanish*, 109.
2. Thomas, 216.
3. Hemingway, "Preface," vii.
4. Schoots, 99–100.

5. Thomas, 367.
6. Hemingway, "King Business in Europe," *By-Line*, 80–81.
7. Luis Quintanilla quoted in Paul Quintanilla, 101. Luis writes that he directed the mounting of the flag and Alfonso departed on 13 April; these events actually took place on 14 April.
8. Brochure introduction to Quintanilla exhibit of 20 November to 4 December 1934, at the Pierre Matisse Gallery (PU: Box 11, Folder 18, "Quintanilla").
9. 10 May according to Thomas (56) and Lannon (19); 11 May according to Beevor (23) and Preston, *Spanish*, (46). It may be that the incident of 10 May inspired an outbreak on 11 May.
10. P. Quintanilla, 105.
11. P. Quintanilla, 106.
12. Carlos Baker, ed., *Ernest Hemingway: Selected Letters, 1917–1961* [hereafter *SL*], 341–342, 26 June 1931.
13. See Beevor, 8; Thomas, 13.
14. Graham, 26, 77.
15. Beevor, 24. On these several months of violence, see Beevor, 21–26; Preston, *Spanish*, 40–56; Thomas, 55–56; and Reynolds, 69–75.
16. Hemingway, "The Friend of Spain: A Spanish Letter," *By-Line*, 144–152.
17. Graham, 29.
18. Thomas, 73.
19. P. Quintanilla, 119, 121.
20. P. Quintanilla, 121–122.
21. "The Arts," *Newsweek* (1 December 1934), 30; also Bruccoli, 31, "Introduction to *Quintanilla*."
22. Ziffren to Hemingway, 13 November 1934 (PU: Box 17, Folder 8, "1934").
23. Allen to Hemingway, 13 November 1934 (PU: Box 17, Folder 8, "1934").
24. "The Arts," *Newsweek* (1 December 1934), 30.
25. Luis Quintanilla did not believe the consul's telegram boasting "that on the first day more than two hundred picketers appeared, on the second more than six hundred, and on the third there were more than a thousand" (P. Quintanilla, 122).

26. Pierre Matisse to Hemingway, 22 November 1934 (PU: Box 17, Folder 8, "1934").
27. For a full list see the duplicated document in Bruccoli, 35.
28. The copy with Matisse's signature can be viewed online at "The Art and World of Luis Quintanilla," maintained by Paul Quintanilla (www.lqart.org/textfold/excerpts.html#matisse). See also P. Quintanilla, 135–136. A photocopy is housed in the Carlos Baker Collection (PU: Box 11, Folder 18, "Quintanilla").
29. P. Quintanilla, 134.
30. Beevor, 37.
31. Ibárruri, 161.
32. Lannon, 25.
33. See P. Quintanilla, 147–152.
34. Marshall to Carlos Baker, 23 March 1936 (PU: Box 17, Folder 11, "1936").
35. De Pereda to Carlos Baker, 2 June 1936 (PU: Box 2, Folder 25, "De Pereda").
36. Hemingway to de Pereda, 23 July 1936 (PU: Box 2, Folder 25, "De Pereda").
37. 26 September 1936 (*SL* 454).
38. Marshall to Carlos Baker, 23 March 1936 (PU: Box 17, Folder 11, "1936").
39. 5 February 1937 (*SL* 456).
40. 9 February 1937 (*SL* 458).
41. Dos Passos to Hemingway, undated (late October 1936?) (PU: Box 2, Folder 32, "Dos Passos").
42. *Billings Gazette* (November 8, 1936), 3.
43. Baker, "Notes on John N. Wheeler, (Gen'l Mgr. NANA) and his letters to EH Nov. 25, 1936–June 1, 1939" (PU: Box 17, Folder 11).
44. Hemingway to de Pereda, 9 December 1936 (PU: Box 2, Folder 25, "De Pereda").
45. Hemingway to Maxwell Perkins, 15 December 1936 (*SL* 455).
46. Baker's note beginning "Hemingway declared himself . . ." (PU: Box 18, Folder 1, "1937").
47. "Ernest Hemingway to Aid Sending Spain Ambulances," *Chicago Daily Tribune* (12 January 1937), 5. See also "Writer to Aid Loyalists,"

New York Times (12 January 1937), 4; and "Footnotes and Headliners," *New York Times* (17 January 1937), 60.

48. Leonard Lyons, "The Post's New Yorker," *Washington Post* (15 January 1937), 12.
49. "Hospital Group Sails for Spain," *New York Times* (17 January 1937), 32.
50. Consul General at Barcelona (Perkins) to the Secretary of State, 4 February 1937, *Foreign Relations of the United States* (Department of State) (hereafter *FRUS)* 1937 v.1, 478.
51. Signed by John N. Wheeler and Hemingway (HRC: Hemingway Collection, letters, Box 3, Folder 14).
52. Hemingway to Chase, 11 February 1937 (PU: Box 18, Folder 1, "1937").
53. MacLeish letter to "Jerry," 28 January 1937 (Archibald MacLeish Papers, Manuscript Division, *Library of Congress* [hereafter LoC]: Box 8, Folder "Fortune"). MacLeish wrote in hand on the right margin: "Probably 'Jerry' is Jerome who was a communist in NY charged with what the comrades called, in their pompous lingo, 'Agit-Prop.'"
54. "Hemingway Off to Spain," *New York Times* (28 February 1937), 30; "Central Madrid Again Bombed After Respite," *Washington Post* (28 February 1937), 1–2. Neither article mentions Shipman. See Baker's notes, "Hemingway at Spanish Civil War, 1937–1938," and his notes for his interview with Franklin (PU: Box 18, Folder 1, "1937").
55. Note from George Seldes to Carlos Baker, 2 December 1961 (PU: Box 18, Folder 1, "1937").
56. Rexford G. Tugwell, Center for the Study of Democratic Institutions, letter to Carlos Baker, 19 July 1967 (PU: Box 17, Folder 11, "1936").
57. Herbst, 150.
58. Regler, *Owl*, 283.
59. "British Actor Vanishes from Party on Liner," *Washington Post* (7 March 1937), 2.
60. Thomas, 357.
61. *Chicago Tribune* (30 August 1936). See Knightley, 218.
62. Thomas, 362.
63. Luis Quintanilla was there, finding a Republican priest willing to minister to the defending Nationalists and participating in an assault with dynamiters (P. Quintanilla, 171–177).

64. De Echeverria, 34–35.
65. Preston, *Spanish*, 132.
66. Beevor, 180.
67. Lannon, 49.
68. "Dispatches," 17.
69. "Dispatches," 22.
70. 12 April 1937 (*FRUS* 1937 v.1, 278). The Republic could hardly have found a more faithful proponent inside the U.S. government than Bowers (see for example Bowers to President Roosevelt, 11 August 1937, *FRUS* 1937 v.1, 372).
71. Beevor, 208.
72. 88,000 Italians and "between 16,000 and 20,000" Germans ("Dispatches," 14–15).
73. The U.S. had begun stamping "not valid for travel in Spain" on all passports of passengers disembarking in France at Havre as of 20 January 1937 (Consul at Havre [Wiley] to the Secretary of State, 20 January 1937, *FRUS* 1937 v.1, 473).
74. Secretary of State Hull to the Ambassador in Spain (Bowers), 9 March 1937 (*FRUS* 1937 v.1, 489); Consul General at Barcelona (Perkins) to the Secretary of State, 20 April 1937 (*FRUS* 1937 v.1, 284). It's not certain whether Hemingway knew about the new passport policy. He presumably would have learned about the refused passports discussed by Hull on 9 March, but Perkins's memo mentions a Department of State press release of 13 March, which appears to announce the new policy (285).

    On first notice of the medical unit Hemingway had inspected, the Department of State wrestled with what Perkins called the "somewhat perplexing practical question" of its handling of these volunteers (to Secretary of State, 22 January 1937, *FRUS* 1937 v.1, 474). Hull initially replied by instructing Perkins to distinguish between ambulance units incorporated into military forces versus those merely attached for humanitarian services (Secretary of State to the Consul General at Barcelona [Perkins], 27 February 1937, *FRUS* 1937 v.1, 483–484). The unfeasibility of this position, combined with the U.S.'s aggressive care to avoid any appearance of non-neutrality, led to the later passport policy.

The U.S.'s position toward individual citizens in Spain who were against U.S. policy became far more complicated in short order: when France arrested volunteers trying to get into Spain, when some in Spain tried to desert the Republican military and sought U.S. assistance, when the Republic jailed deserters, and especially when Nationalist forces captured U.S. citizens. Generally the Department of State declined any support whatsoever, though it made exceptions in the event of impending execution or prolonged imprisonment by Franco (see the cases of Harold Dahl and Antonio Fernandez Villa in *FRUS* 1937 v.1, 511–562 passim).

75. P. Quintanilla, 199. At a rate of "$500 for each cabled dispatch and $1000 for mailed articles of up to 1200 words," Hemingway was "the world's highest paid war correspondent" (Donaldson, 380).
76. "Dispatches," 19.
77. Franklin's memoir notes that Hemingway "was to meet someone and fly over the war area along the frontier in an observation plane" (219), though it never names Ivens nor mentions the film at all. Franklin himself, after a couple of weeks of almost comically secretive arrangements, traveled to the border by train and crossed by foot with a contingent of international volunteers (218–224).
78. Ivens's chronology notes "Madrid" on 20 March and "Guadalajara Brihuega" on 21 March (Joris Ivens Archives [hereafter JIA] 215). A draft of an Ivens telegram to MacLeish says, "Left Paris March seventeenth arrived Madrid twenty-first with Hemingway" (JIA 228). The chronology lists "French Delegation" on 22 March and "Garibaldi" battalion on 23 March. Paul Quintanilla writes that "through my father Hemingway received the necessary intelligence he needed to study the rout of the Italians at Guadalajara" (200).
79. Though it is generally and probably correctly supposed that Ivens introduced Hemingway to Regler, Regler's memoir has Hemingway appearing alone one day and bringing Ivens along with him the next day (*Owl*, 290–291).
80. JFK: "Hemingway Sees Dead Strewing Battlefield," NANA release version, Item 465.
81. "Dispatches," 19.
82. "Dispatches," 20.

83. Cowles, 20.
84. JIA 215.
85. "Dispatches," 24. Hemingway, on 9 April, writes about that day's action and the action witnessed four days earlier. Ivens's chronology notes confirm "Morata" on 5 April and "Casa de Campo" on 9 April.
86. "Dispatches," 25.
87. JIA 215.
88. "Dispatches," 27.
89. "Dispatches," 28.
90. "Dispatches," 28–29.
91. Cowles, 33.
92. Cowles, 33. Baker lists several others at the homestead that day (308). Pastoras might be the "Pastora" from *For Whom the Bell Tolls*, who dances at the banquet for Pilar's first lover, the bullfighter Finito (*FWTBT*, 185). Josephs identifies the "Pastora" of the novel with Pastora Imperio, the woman he believes to be the model for Pilar (114). The "Pastoras" Cowles, Gellhorn, and Hemingway saw might have been Imperio.
93. Cowles, 31–32.
94. Cowles, 26, 17. For another portrait of the local woman called Kasja, see Dorothy Parker, "Soldiers of the Republic," in Hemingway, *Men at War* (989–992; reprinted from the *New Yorker*). See Cecil D. Eby's description of the local "girls at the Florida" (*Comrades* 121–122). See Delmer on the Moorish sisters and prostitutes, Farida and Fatima (315–319).
95. Cowles, 20.
96. Note from George Seldes to Carlos Baker, 2 December 1961 (PU: Box 18, Folder 1, "1937").
97. Cowles, 17.
98. In Ira Wolfert, "Hemingway Sailing Sees Crisis at Hand in Spain," dateline 14 August 1937 (HRC: Ernest Hemingway Collection, Box 15, Folder 11).
99. Cowles, 22.
100. Cowles, 21.
101. Cowles, 22.
102. Herbst, 140.
103. Herbst, 161–162.

104. Baker note on Gustavo Duran dated 26 February 1962 (PU: Box 18, Folder 1, "1937"). Duran also lists Lillian Hellman, though she was not in Madrid that spring. Did he mean Gellhorn? Or Gerda Taro?
105. "Dispatches," 31.
106. "Dispatches," 32.
107. "Dispatches," 33.
108. Watson writes that "there is no date for this dispatch, but since he was being limited to one story a week and his last piece had been written on the 11th, this one was probably written around the 18th or 19th" ("Dispatches," 29). Except that in the NANA promotion box this piece carries a date of 14 April 1937 (JFK), and the once-a-week rule logic falters given that he wrote the next dispatch on 20 April.
109. JIA 215.
110. Schaber et al., 18. Schaber's evidence is a Taro photo captioned "Cast: Spanish Earth," though according to the Robert Capa Archives at the International Center of Photography, it was taken at Valsequillo, near Cordoba, and "the caption was probably put on later by some agent or editor making an erroneous connection" (email from archivist Cynthia Young, 16 September 2010).
111. "Dispatches," 34. The NANA dateline is 22 April 1937. The radiogram, stamped "1937 APR 21," reads "Wednesday" and it indicates it was written "today," but "Wednesday" is crossed over in pencil by an editor and replaced with "April 22" (HRC: Ernest Hemingway Collection, Box 1, Folder 25). Wednesday was in fact 21 April. Watson dates it 20 April ("Dispatches," 33).
112. Cowles, 27.
113. Cowles, 28.
114. Matthews, *Half*, 120–121. For a photo of Vidali, see Schaber et al., 62.
115. Beevor, 173; Preston, *Spanish*, 182–183; Thomas, 463.
116. Graham, 191.
117. Note from George Seldes, 2 December 1961 (PU: Box 18, Folder 1, "1937").
118. Regler, *Owl*, 279.
119. Regler, *Owl*, 292.
120. Beevor, 161.
121. Merriman and Lerude, 133.

122. Merriman and Lerude, 134.

123. "Banquet Will Honor D.C. Fighters in Spain," *Washington Post* (23 April 1937), 1. The group met "at the Chapin Grill, 1219 G Street Northwest, under the auspices of the Communist Party." In addition to the broadcast, they watched "Spanish playlets." The *Post* article does not mention Hemingway. An ad in the *New Republic* for a similar gathering to listen to the broadcast at the Mecca Temple in New York lists a slightly different cast of speakers: Commander of the Brigade, Political Leader of the Brigade, Dos Passos, Herbst, Ivens, Franklin, Father Leocadio Lobo, "*and others speaking from Spain*" (27 April 1937, 31).

124. Franklin, 216; 234–235. Seldes 2 December 1961 note to Baker confirms Franklin's ignorance of the political situation (PU: Box 18, Folder 1, "1937").

125. JIA 215. See also Koch, 163.

126. Matthews telegram to Edwin L. James, 17 April 1937 (HRC: Herbert Matthews Collection, Box 1, Folder 3).

127. Matthews, *Education*, 95.

128. Cowles, 30. Only Herbst's diary dates it, 28 April (Yale Collection of American Literature, Beinecke Rare Book and Manuscript Library [hereafter YU]: "Spanish Journal," Elinor Langer Collection of Josephine Herbst [hereafter "Journal"] 126).

129. Wolff, 116–117. Wolff's nonfiction account softens his accusation of untruth, from outright denial to "Gee, I don't know a thing about this stuff," and offers no retort by Hemingway (in Nelson, *Remembering*, 10).

130. Herbst, 167.

131. "Dispatches," 38. The radiogram stamp impossibly dates its receipt in New York as "37 APR 31," and the message's dateline reads "FRIDAY"—which would have been 30 April. Someone in New York penciled in a date of "May 2" (HRC: Hemingway, Box 1, Folder 25), the date carried on the released dispatch (titled "Writer Says Rebels Seek to Force Foes to Attack") and the date often cited.

132. Cowles, 38. See Hemingway's report of the armored car being fired upon ("Dispatches," 38). Cowles simply might not have mentioned Gellhorn. Herbst's diary places Gellhorn in Madrid at the Florida the night of 26 April, as the entry of 27 April says Gellhorn, Cowles, and a

third person were "sitting on the stairs last night during shelling, too upset to compose for sleep" (YU: "Journal," 41).

133. "Dispatches," 37.
134. "Dispatches," 38.
135. Herbst, 1 May, (YU: "Journal," 60).
136. Thomas, 641.
137. Plans to leave on 3 May per cable from [Percy J.] Philip to [Edwin] James, both of the *New York Times*, 8 April 1937 (HRC: Herbert Matthews Collection, Box 1, Folder 3).
138. "Dispatches," 41, 42. The typescript is dated 10 May (JFK: Item 853), though Watson has compelling evidence for dating it 9 May ("Dispatches," 39–40).
139. Beevor, 276.
140. Regler, *Owl*, 311–312.
141. Hemingway, "Preface," ix.
142. On Brunete see Beevor, 277–286; Thomas, 689–696; Preston, *Spanish*, 275–277; Cecil D. Eby, *Comrades*, 176–202.
143. For a first-person account of the congress, see Malcolm Cowley's "To Madrid" series in the *New Republic*. Cowley lists other attendees: "from France, Malraux and [Julien] Benda, and Chamson; from England, Stephen Spender and Sylvia Townsend Warner; from the Soviet Union, [Alexis] Tolstoy, Fadayev, and Ehrenbourg; from Denmark, Hans Anderson Nexö. They were joined by a Spanish delegation that included [José] Bergamin, . . . Alvarez del Vayo . . . and Machado and [Rafael] Alberti. . . . They were also joined by writers from the International Brigades: Ludwig Renn, Gustav Regler, Ralph Bates" ("To Madrid III," 153). Elsewhere he names American Dick Mowrer and Dutchman Jef Last (152), "Vishnievski and Stavski, the roaring boys from Moscow" (154), Anna Louise Strong (155), and "a Cuban Negro poet" (154) he identifies in a later article as Nicolas Guillén ("To Madrid IV," 179). See also the *Ce Soir* article of 11 July 1937, with photographs by Capa and Taro, which adds to this list Claude Aveline and Tristan Tzara (France), Anna Seghers and Erich Weinert (Germany), and Mikhail Koltsov and Roman Karmen (U.S.S.R) — Karmen was one of the filmmakers behind *Madrid in Flames*, an early propagandistic documentary (see Schaber et al., 29). Dolores "La Pasionaria" Ibárruri's memoir

provides a longer list with a good deal of overlap, but her inclusion of Dos Passos and Hemingway, both returned to the United States over a month, renders it less reliable (267).

144. "Hemingway Off to Spain," *New York Times* (15 August 1937), 31; Ira Wolfert, "Hemingway Sailing Sees Crisis at Hand in Spain" (HRC: Ernest Hemingway Collection, Box 15, Folder 11). On Boucher see Leonard Lyons, "The Post's New Yorker," *Washington Post* (1 September 1937), 12.
145. Telephone interruption according to Herbert Matthews's cable to Raymond McCaw, 16 September 1937. Matthews's own dispatch of 15 September (filed 14 September) mentions Hemingway and Gellhorn (HRC: Herbert Matthews Collection, Box 1, Folder 4).
146. "Dispatches," 49.
147. "Dispatches," 50.
148. Beevor, 299.
149. Orwell, 68. On the terrain and the lack of artillery, weapons, and soldiers, see Orwell 17, 19, 24, 33, 35.
150. See Beevor, 294–300; Preston, *Spanish*, 276–277; Thomas, 701–707.
151. Thomas, 712.
152. "Dispatches," 58.
153. "Dispatches," 53, 54.
154. Donaldson, 408.
155. "Dispatches," 54–59.
156. See Watson, "Story," or Josephs's summary of Watson, *Undiscovered*, 145.
157. Paul Patrick Rogers, diary entry of 12 August (HRC: Paul Patrick Rogers Collection, Box 1, Folder 5).
158. Beevor, 318. In addition to its strategic goals, the offensive may have had the goal of boosting morale, as the "lull in major military operations is further affecting the impaired morale of Loyalist Spain and many rumors are in circulation, the most persistent of which concerns an impending armistice" (Counselor of Embassy in Spain [Thurston] to the Secretary of State, 17 November 1937, *FRUS* 1937 v.1, 449).
159. "Dispatches," 62.
160. Matthews, *Education*, 96. Beevor writes that Hemingway, Matthews, and Capa came up with Prieto and Rojo on 19 December (317).

161. Matthews, *Education*, 98.
162. "Dispatches," 63.
163. Matthews, *Education*, 99.
164. Matthews, *Education*, 106. They might have had to fix the car—it was "broken-down" when they found it; they might also have only used it to get to their own, nine kilometers back. Hemingway's radiogram bears a dateline of 21 December, the day Watson also dates it. Matthews tells us he sent his dispatch to Madrid by courier, as did Hemingway according to his dateline ("Dispatches," 64). A version of Matthews's dispatch forms part of *Education*'s narrative (99–106).
165. Matthews, *Education*, 107.
166. Letter to Hadley Mowrer, 31 January 1938 (*SL* 462). On Hemingway's sometimes fraught relationship with NANA, see Donaldson (411) and Watson, "Dispatches."
167. Matthews dateline 24 December 1937 from Teruel by courier to Barcelona (HRC: Herbert Matthews Collection, Box 3, Folder 1). A condensed version of this dispatch appears in *Education*, 107.
168. P. Quintanilla, 210. Luis Companys and Juan Negrin attended. See also Jay Allen's account in L. Quintanilla (14), in which one can also see several of Quintanilla's stark sketches from the battle.
169. Matthews in *Education* names Delmer and Capa, and cites 28 December for that part of its narrative (108), though his dispatch is dated 27 December. The dispatch names Allen; Allen names Quintanilla and says they left the day after Christmas (in L. Quintanilla, 16).
170. "Hemingway Sees Victory for Government in Spain," *Washington Post* (28 January 1938), 30.
171. Rollin Dart to Hemingway, 1 Feb 1938, 5 Feb 1938, 6 Feb 1938 (JFK: "Incoming Correspondence, from Rollin Dart").
172. Regler, *Owl*, 314–315.
173. "First-Hand Picture of Conflict in Spain Given by Volunteer Here," *Washington Post* (18 March 1938), X17.
174. Titled "Luis Quintanilla: An Exhibition of Drawings of the War in Spain," MoMA Exhibition #74 ran from 15 March to 18 April 1938 (Museum of Modern Art Exhibition History List, http://www.moma.org/research/archives/exhibhistory.html#1929). Paul Quintanilla credits Hemingway for bringing the show to the museum's attention;

the show later traveled the country for eighteen months (P. Quintanilla, 211, 218). A copy of the brochure is at Princeton (PU: Box 11, Folder 18, "Quintanilla") and is quoted in P. Quintanilla's book (216) as well as online (www.lqart.org/textfold/excerpts.html#moma). Hemingway's text was reprinted as the introductory section to his "Three Prefaces" for *All the Brave* (7); the frontispiece is a Quintanilla drawing of himself and the book's other contributors: Jay Allen, Elliot Paul, and Ernest Hemingway. ("Three Prefaces" is also in Trogdon, *Reference*, 209.)

175. "Hemingway Off to Spain," *New York Times* (19 March 1938), 3.
176. "Guns and Castanets" announced in April 1938 for June release ("Book Notes," *New York Times* [7 April 1938], 21) and listed as a June forthcoming book in "Books and Authors," *New York Times* (8 May 1938), 106. None of the contributors liked the title. The editor, Louis P. Birk, let Ralph Bates decide. Bates sided with the contributors. A September 1938 article noted that the book had been scheduled for October publication ("Books and Authors," *New York Times* [4 September 1938], 65). According to the first announcement in the *Times*, ten percent of the as-yet-untitled book's proceeds "will go to the Abraham Lincoln Brigade, to which the volume is dedicated" ("Books and Authors," *New York Times* [3 April 1938], 98). The published book bears no dedication, though it came out much later than planned—in 1939, after the disbanding of all the International Brigades—too late for proceeds to help.
177. 29 March 1938, *FRUS* 1938 v.1, 169.
178. Hemingway to Jack Wheeler, 2 June 1938 (JFK: "Outgoing Correspondence, to Jack Wheeler").
179. Counselor of Embassy in Spain (Thurston) to the Secretary of State, 29 March 1938, *FRUS* 1938 v.1, 275.
180. Ambassador in Spain (Bowers), then in France, to the Secretary of State, 30 March 1938, *FRUS* 1938 v.1, 277.
181. Ambassador in Spain (Bowers), then in France, to the Secretary of State, 2 April 1938, *FRUS* 1938 v.1, 279.
182. The Counselor of Embassy in Spain reported on 16 April having lost contact with Hemingway and company (Counselor of Embassy in Spain [Thurston] to the Secretary of State, 16 April 1938, *FRUS* 1938 v.1, 283). Whitaker reappeared on 25 May, a few days after "a committee representing the Abraham Lincoln Brigade" had taken up the

matter with the ambassador, because as long as the war continued, organization funds could only be used to transport volunteers to Spain, not bring anyone out (Ambassador in France [Bullitt] to the Secretary of State, 26 May 1938, *FRUS* 1938 v.1, 286–287). In June the State Department was still pressing the Friends of the Abraham Lincoln Brigade and the Medical Bureau of the North American Committee to Aid Spanish Democracy for both repatriation and French medical care funding (Ambassador in France [Bullitt] to the Secretary of State, 10 June 1938, *FRUS* 1938 v.1, 294). Bullitt later wrote that these organizations sought to help from the fear of losing face "in the circles from which these volunteers have been drawn," from "belief that the morale of the volunteers now fighting in the international brigades is adversely affected," and due to, "of course, a sense of responsibility for having brought these men to Spain" (Ambassador in France [Bullitt] to the Secretary of State, 27 June 1938, *FRUS* 1938 v.1, 304). Eventually Louis Fischer, a reporter for the *Nation* who had once fought in the International Brigade, agreed to contribute $21,500 to the cause (Ambassador in Spain [Bowers], then in France, to the Secretary of State, 8 August 1938, *FRUS* 1938 v.1, 316). Fischer claimed to be the first American to join the brigade (in Matthews, *Half*, 206).

183. Arrived the night before his dispatch of 3 April ("Dispatches," 69). P. Quintanilla cites 1 April (220), though his dates are not always reliable.
184. Hemingway to Jack Wheeler, 2 June 1938 (JFK: "Outgoing Correspondence, to Jack Wheeler").
185. In Thomas, 781.
186. "Dispatches," 69–70.
187. "Dispatches," 71.
188. Carroll, 174. Cecil Eby doubts this version of Merriman's heroic death, believing instead that Merriman and his comrade in arms David Doran were huddled for cover in a vineyard and "gunned down like terrified animals without firing a shot in return" (*Comrades*, 353). For Eby's full account, including Hemingway's dispatch, see 331–336 and 353–356. Hemingway could only have known the heroic version.
189. "Dispatches," 70.
190. Carroll, 174–175.

191. Carroll, 175. Carroll quotes Alvah Bessie's *Men in Battle* on the collapsed bridge (108), omitting the fact that it had been bombed.
192. "Dispatches," 72.
193. "Dispatches," 73.
194. "Dispatches," 74.
195. "Dispatches," 75.
196. In "Dispatches," 73.
197. "Dispatches," 77.
198. "Dispatches," 76. The unnamed division commander is Enrique Lister.
199. "Dispatches," 79–80.
200. "Dispatches," 80–82.
201. Baker, *Story*, 327; Gellhorn, 59.
202. "Dispatches," 83–84.
203. In L. Quintanilla, 8–9; also in Trogdon, *Reference*, 210–211.
204. "Air Raid Siren Halts Showing of War Film," dateline 24 April, *New York Times* (25 April 1938), 6.
205. "Dispatches," 86–87.
206. "Dispatches," 89–90.
207. "Dispatches," 92.
208. "Dispatches," 91.
209. "Dispatches," 92.
210. "The Time Now, the Place Spain," *Ken* (7 April 1938), 36–37.
211. "Dying, Well or Badly," *Ken* (21 April 1938), 68.
212. "A Program for U.S. Realism," *Ken* (11 August 1938), 38. Also in *By-Line*, 292.
213. Gellhorn, 62.
214. "Hemingway Returns, Tired of War in Spain," *New York Times* (31 May 1938), 12.
215. Carroll, 181–183.
216. "18 Wounded Back from War in Spain," *New York Times* (3 July 1938), 11.
217. In Stephen J. Monchak, "Aged by Two Years at Front, Matthews Tells of Spain War" (4 March 1939). Publication unknown (HRC: Herbert Matthews Collection, Box 3, Folder 2). Matthews dates it in *Education*, 138–139.
218. Moorehead, 153. Among those troops marching by was Randolfo Pac-

ciardi, an Italian officer who had fallen for Gellhorn: "Hemingway was crying for Pacciardi, for what Spain had done to him, and what would now become of him. At that moment, said Martha, she really loved him" (Moorehead, 153).

219. Reynolds, *1930s*, 299.

2. STYLE, POLITICS, AND THE NANA DISPATCHES

1. See "Dispatches," 4.
2. Baker, *Story*, 329.
3. Knightley, 231–232. In my view, Knightly does not sufficiently acknowledge his paraphrasing of Baker.
4. Donaldson, 426.
5. See Donaldson, 411, 420.
6. McCaw's note accompanying the list is dated 23 September 1937 (HRC: Herbert Matthews Collection, Box 1, Folder 4).
7. Letter from James to Matthews, 21 October 1937 (HRC: Herbert Matthews Collection, Box 1, Folder 4).
8. Dispatch included in Raymond McCaw's note of 20 May 1937 to Mr. [Edwin] James. McCaw had underlined these (and other) lines. (HRC: Herbert Matthews Collection, Box 1, Folder 3.) Though days of tension preceded the violence, the precipitating event was the attempt "to seize control of Barcelona's central telephone exchange" from the CNT by "a detachment of police," perhaps on its own initiative (Graham, 266). As Graham reminds us, "it is important to make the distinction here between the underlying causes of the May days, and the 'high political' opportunities and consequences which *then* emerged from the evolution of the conflict in both street and cabinet office" (267). Suspicion of anarchist-Nationalist collusion had been around for some time (e.g., Ambassador in Spain [Bowers], then in France, to the Secretary of State, 16 March 1937, *FRUS* 1937 v.1, 255), so the accusation should be understood in that context as well as the political opportunism seized by the Republic and the communists. As soon as the violence broke out, the government accused the radicals of being in league with the rebels (see Ambassador in Spain [Bowers], then in France, to the Secretary of State, 5 May 1937, *FRUS 1937* v.1, 292).

9. Edwin James to Bertrand Weaver, 20 November 1937 (HRC: Herbert Matthews Collection, Box 1, Folder 4).
10. Edwin James to M. B. Tenney, 25 April 1939 (HRC: Herbert Matthews Collection, Box 1, Folder 10).
11. McCaw to James [20?] December 1937 (HRC: Herbert Matthews Collection, Box 1, Folder 5).
12. Matthews's originally submitted "attack on Teruel" piece, if it still exists, is not included in the HRC materials.
13. Matthews to James, 11 April 1937. James supported McCaw on these changes, though later acknowledged that altering quoted sources was perhaps unwarranted (29 April 1937). Both letters are in HRC: Herbert Matthews Collection, Box 1, Folder 3.
14. Matthews to James, 6 July 1937 (HRC: Herbert Matthews Collection, Box 1, Folder 3).
15. Undated [July] 1937 (HRC: Herbert Matthews Collection, Box 1, Folder 4).
16. James to Arthur Hays Sulzberger, 23 April 1937 (HRC: Herbert Matthews Collection, Box 1, Folder 3).
17. Ivens, *Camera*, 112.
18. Franklin reports that each morning he and Hemingway visited different parts of the front and came back together about noon: "Then he would write his report [by hand], combining his stuff and mine." Franklin typed it up, passed it by the censors, and sent the cable (232).
19. Matthews to Sulzberger, 22 March 1939 (HRC: Herbert Matthews Collection, Box 1, Folder 9).
20. "Promotion Box: Hemingway, For Immediate Release, February 5, 1937," 2 (JFK: Box 15, Folder 3, HRC).
21. Matthews to Edwin James, 9 April 1937 (HRC: Herbert Matthews Collection, Box 1, Folder 3).
22. Baker, *Story*, 329. Baker's notes (PU: Box 18, Folder 8, "1938") date the *Times* request to NANA as 8 April 1938, and NANA's to Hemingway as 15 April 1938, the date of "The Bombing of Tortosa" dispatch.
23. John H. Wheeler/NANA to Hemingway, 31 August 1938 (HRC: Ernest Hemingway Collection, Box 3, Folder 14).
24. Hemingway to Wilson [c. 10 December 1938] (JFK: "Outgoing Correspondence, to Wilson").

25. "Fascism Is a Lie," in Trogdon, *Reference*, 193.
26. Reynolds, *Paris*, 45.
27. *By-Line*, 340 (emphasis mine).
28. Moreira, 99.
29. Although in the fragment "Gustav had a fever," the narrator leaves the *Times* reporter behind. It's not clear if the piece was intended as fiction or nonfiction (JFK: Item 442).
30. Advertisement, "Best Sellers of the Week Here and Elsewhere," *New York Times* (24 January 1938), 21.
31. Hemingway to Hadley Mowrer, 31 January 1938 (*SL* 462).
32. "we" in typescript and radiogram (HRC: Ernest Hemingway Collection, Box 1, Folder 1 and Folder 25) and "this correspondent" in NANA promotion box version (JFK: Item 243) for "American Veterans Tell of Escaping Insurgents" of 4 April 1938.
33. The original NANA dispatch includes John Gates, Joseph Hecht, George Watt, and—wrongly—Waters (JFK: "American Veterans Tell of Escaping Insurgents," NANA Release version, Item 243). Watson's diplomatic text corrects the name (to Copic) and adds four more (Merriman, Doran, Keller, and Ivan) ("Dispatches," 71–72) but still leaves out Alvah Bessie, Simon Lenof, Felix Kusman, Leonard Lamb, Milton Wolff, Ely Biegelman, and Alvin Cohen (HRC: Ernest Hemingway Collection, radiogram 4 April 1938, Box 1. Folder 26).
34. Stott, 178–179. He specifically includes Hemingway and others (180).
35. Stott, 27–28.
36. "Dispatches," 29.
37. "Dispatches," 30.
38. "Dispatches," 30.
39. "Dispatches," 30.
40. "Dispatches," 31.
41. "Dispatches," 31, 32.
42. Thomas, 591. "Not only did Raven get well, he also became one of the best fund-raisers the Lincoln Battalion ever had. Crowds in Madison Square Garden wildly shouted, 'No pasarán!' as Raven (with the fraudulent rank of 'lieutenant' bestowed by Party propagandists) rose eyeless to address them. Who but a stone-heart could say no to a man who had given not only his blood but also his eyes to the Spanish

Republic? . . . The VALB arranged what became a tumultuous marriage for Raven and set him up in a New York florist business" (Cecil D. Eby, *Comrades*, 96–97).

43. In addition to the poems in Nelson's anthology, see the excerpt from Boris Todrin's "Spanish Sowing" in Guttmann (179–180). See Nelson on the active role of poetry on the Loyalist side (10). The poets of the war assumed an international identity, creating an "echolalic" body of work that "adopted forms, themes, and metaphors from their frontline Spanish compatriots" (24), with "poet after poet deploying some of the same images and phrases" creating a "chain of verbal correspondences that connect poem to poem and poet to poet and poet to soldier across the world" (27) and amounting to "one vast poem, a huge intertext," a "metapoem" that "is not Spanish alone" but also "American, British, Canadian, French, German, Italian, and Russian" (28).
44. "On the American Dead in Spain," *New Masses* (14 February 1939), reprinted in Bruccoli, 76, and Nelson, *Remembering*, 37. (The drafts at the JFK [Items 357 to 359] are titled "The Dead on the Jarama.")
45. "Dispatches," 84.
46. "Dispatches," 71–72.
47. "Dispatches," 58.
48. Hemingway to Wilson [c. 10 December 1938] (JFK: "Outgoing Correspondence, to Wilson").
49. Donaldson, 394.
50. Matthews to James, 8 May 1937 (HRC: Herbert Matthews Collection, Box 1, Folder 3).
51. Matthews to James, 6 July 1937, and undated [July] 1937 (HRC: Herbert Matthews Collection, Box 1, Folder 4).
52. Cowles, 20.
53. 20 August 1938 (in Davison, 128).
54. Ambassador in Spain (Bowers), then in France, to the Secretary of State, 5 May 1937, *FRUS* 1937 v.1, 292.
55. "Dispatches," 34.
56. Moreira, 77.
57. See Hemingway, "Treachery in Aragon," *Ken* (30 June 1938), 26. Hemingway's criticism in a cable and letter around this time to Dos Passos for getting General Walter's nationality incorrect splits hairs.

Dos Passos had referred to Walter as Russian, and Hemingway seized upon this as evidence of Dos Passos's ignorance, citing the general's Polish origins—he was no Russian general (c. 26 March 1938 [*SL* 463]). Yet though Walter, whose real name was Karol Świerczewski, was born in Warsaw, Poland, he "spent his youth in Russia, . . . fought in the Red Army" in the revolution, and spent his career as a Soviet military officer (Krzyżanowski, 6). He was in Spain with the Soviet army. Hemingway may have based his character General Golz on him: "I am *Général Sovietique*," Golz tells Robert Jordan as he sends him on his mission to blow the bridge (*FWTBT*, 8). For discussion of Walter as Golz, see chapter 5.

58. Knightley, 232; Baker, *Story*, 402. Hemingway's casual comment to colleagues calling dibs on Pepe Quintanilla, the executioner of Madrid, is not sufficient evidence.
59. Moorehead, 125.
60. Knightley, 234–235.
61. Stott, 11.
62. "Dispatches," 46–47.
63. Donaldson, 433.
64. In Donaldson, 436.
65. It at least sounds almost exactly like Dolores Ibárruri in her memoir. To the anarchists' complaint that they had no arms, she retorts "that they had more arms than did many other fronts. . . . What they didn't have and what they were constantly demanding were airplanes and tanks. And they didn't have them because the Republic government didn't have them either, except for those it received as aid from the Soviet Union" (283–284). Yet the various Catalonian militia were not as well equipped with small arms as the more regular Popular Army units, and because of the terrain, tanks and planes were in fact necessary.
66. Hemingway's comments in "Hemingway, en Route Home Expects Loyalists to Win," NANA staff correspondent dispatch dateline 10 May 1937 Paris (HRC: Box 15, Folder 2). Though arguably he was propagandizing by hiding the communist influence—to mention the communists to an American audience would not gain sympathy for the cause.
67. An article on the communists' limited role appeared in late November 1937, as discussed in a missive from the Ambassador in Spain

(Bowers), then in France, to the Secretary of State, 2 December 1937, *FRUS* 1937 v.1, 461. His "Anarchism: Spain's Enigma" appeared in the *New York Times* (22 August 1937, pp. 6, 14).

68. "The Home Front" (JFK: Item 477.5).
69. Graham, 144–145.
70. Graham, 75, 181.
71. Thomas, 628.
72. Graham, 184.
73. *FWTBT*, 207.
74. Nelson, *Wound*, 7.
75. Thomas, 643.
76. Graham, 197–198.
77. Graham, 174–175.
78. Though many held the impression that the Soviet advisers often acted as if they were in command. Delmer certainly felt this way (300, 313).
79. Nelson, *Wound*, 8.
80. See for example the following U.S. Department of State correspondence: 26 October 1937 (No. X-250, *FRUS* 1937 v.1, 436–439); 2 December 1937 (No. 1380, *FRUS* 1937 v.1, 459–462); and 25 January 1938 (*FRUS* 1938 v.1, 152–153).
81. And at the Fifth Regiment headquarters before the regiment was parceled out to regular army units after the formation of the unified command (*FWTBT*, 234–235).
82. Regler, *Owl*, 275, 277. He calls Gellhorn "the most devoted of all" the reporters to the left (283).
83. Donaldson, 443.
84. To Bernard Berenson, 14 October 1952 (*SL*, 789).
85. Karkov only bothers with Jordan because he respects his writing (*FWTBT* 248).
86. *FWTBT*, 246.
87. *FWTBT*, 238–239.
88. Ivens to Hemingway, 26 April 1937 (JFK: "Incoming Correspondence, from Ivens").
89. Watson, 52.
90. Ivens to Hemingway, 26 April 1937 (JFK: "Incoming Correspondence, from Ivens").

91. Graham believes in the commissariat's "objective importance" even as "it never ceased to be vehemently denounced" by officers and politicians (146–147), not to mention the rank and file. Cecil Eby is more cynical in defining the commissar's role: "Commissars outranked military commanders, who were only 'technocrats.' While their avowed purpose was to inculcate liberal values, their real purpose was political indoctrination" (8). The Lincoln brigaders called their least favorite commissars "comic-stars" (*Comrades*, 103).
92. Hemingway to Jack Wheeler, 2 June 1938 (JFK: "Outgoing Correspondence, to Wheeler").
93. "Dispatches," 88.
94. In Capa, *Death*, iii.
95. Schoots, 121.
96. Franklin, 235.
97. Letter to Carlos Baker, 1 April 1951, in Baker, *Artist*, 228.
98. *Soviet Literature* 11 (November 1962), 159–163 (PU: Box 6, Folder 11); see also *SL* 419.
99. Hemingway wrote his most propagandistic piece for *Pravda*. See Hemingway, "Humanity"; the draft at the JFK ("During the last fifteen months . . ." undated [JFK: Item 370]); or Donaldson's summary (438).

3. MAKING THE FILM

1. Schoots, 117. The cable is in the Nederlands Foto Archief, John Fernhout Archief, Rotterdam.
2. "Budget for Production 'The Spanish Earth' in Spain" (JIA 216). The report goes through 26 February 1937 and so includes Ivens and Ferno's expenses prior to Hemingway's arrival in Spain.
3. Ivens to Ferno, 16 December 1936, quoted in Schoots (117); several copies of the letter (in Dutch) are in the Ivens archives (JIA 217). Several people the letter lists in conjunction with his plans: Malraux, Ehrenburg, Aragon, Regler, and Buñuel.
4. "Future Picture Spain" (JIA 216).
5. To Carlos Baker, 13 January 1965 (PU: Box 18, Folder 1, "1937").
6. Van Dongen gives sole credit to Dos Passos in two separate interviews (Achtenberg, 54; unpublished with Peter Davis, 25 September 1981).

7. Thomas J. Brandon of Brandon Films, Inc., to Carlos Baker, 13 January 1965 (PU: Box 18, Folder 1 "1937"). Brandon thinks MacLeish might have helped Dos Passos, though in an interview Van Dongen does not mention him (Achtenberg).
8. Frank S. Nugent, "The Screen," *New York Times* (30 January 1937), 21.
9. "News of the Screen," *New York Times* (28 January 1937), 23.
10. Frank S. Nugent, "The Screen," *New York Times* (30 January 1937), 21; Mae Tinée, "Official Movie Tells Story of Spanish War," *Chicago Daily Tribune* (25 March 1937), 15. See also the Cameo's advertisement in Bruccoli (53).
11. Thomas J. Brandon of Brandon Films, Inc., to Carlos Baker, 13 January 1965 (PU: Box 18, Folder 1, "1937").
12. Alexander, 37.
13. For information on the content, see Frank S. Nugent, "The Screen," *New York Times* (30 January 1937), 21; and Brandon to Baker, 13 January 1965 (PU: Box 18, Folder 1, "1937"). The Cameo's advertisement's left side lists the following: "The Abdication of Alfonso. The Rise of the Republic. Suppression of the Asturian Miners. The Victory of the 'Popular Front.' The Invasion by Franco's Moorish Troops. Hitler's & Mussolini's Planes over Spain. The Siege of the Alcazar. The Recruiting of the Loyalist Army. The Defense of the Guadarrama Sector. The Evacuation of Children from Madrid. The Incendiary Bombing and Bombardment of the City. The Firing and Shattering of Homes. 'La Pasionaria,' (Bruccoli, 53).
14. Ivens, *Camera*, 103.
15. De Pereda to Hemingway, 9 February 1937 (JFK: "Incoming Correspondence, from de Pereda"). Hemingway declined de Pereda's request to take him along to Spain; he was also critical of de Pereda's writing.
16. "Madrid in Flames," (JFK: Item 563). Amkino was the Soviet film industry's U.S. distribution company; Soyuzkino the Soviet film industry's controlling body.
17. Watson, "Joris Ivens," 44 (also 42).
18. De Pereda to Baker, dated "August" (HRC: Prudencio de Pereda Collection, Box 1, Folder 4).

19. Thomas J. Brandon of Brandon Films, Inc., to Carlos Baker, 13 January 1965 (PU: Box 18, Folder 1, "1937").
20. MacLeish to "Jerry," 28 January 1937 (LoC: Box 8, Folder "Fortune"). On "Jerry" see chapter 1, note 53.
21. Mae Tinée, "Official Movie Tells Story of Spanish War," *Chicago Daily Tribune* (25 March 1937), 15.
22. De Pereda to Baker, dated "August" (HRC: Prudencio de Pereda Collection, Box 1, Folder 4).
23. Western Union Telegram, 1937 January 27 AM 11 46 (JFK: "Incoming Correspondence, telegram from MacLeish"). See the Cameo advertisement (Bruccoli, 53).
24. MacLeish to Hemingway, 8 February 1937 (JFK: "Incoming Correspondence, telegram from MacLeish").
25. "News of the Screen," *New York Times* (28 January 1937), 23.
26. "Screen Notes," *New York Times* (20 March 1937), 23.
27. "News of the Screen," *New York Times* (8 May 1937), 23.
28. "Bergner Returns in 'Dreaming Lips,'" *New York Times* (19 May 1937), 26.
29. It opened on Friday, 19 March 1937 (per "Display Ad 17," *Chicago Daily Tribune* [16 March 1937], 18), and the *Tribune* has one more ad for it on 23 March 1937 ("Display Ad 15," 16).
30. Frank S. Nugent, "Off with the Gun," *New York Times* (7 February 1937), 165. Nugent still thought the film "worthy of the designation" of one of the best documentaries thus far that year ("The Annual 'Semi-Annual Report,'" *New York Times* [4 July 1937], 99).
31. Mae Tinée, "Official Movie Tells Story of Spanish War," *Chicago Daily Tribune* (25 March 1937), 15.
32. "Film on Spain Banned," *New York Times* (25 March 1937), 27.
33. Eugene Pharo, "Pennsylvania Peace," *Washington Post* (10 April 1937), 7.
34. "Waterbury Bars 'Spain in Flames,'" *New York Times* (21 July 1937), 12.
35. "Labor Advances Hailed in Survey," *New York Times* (12 July 1937), 5.
36. By Judge Louis E. Levinthal, Common Pleas Court No. 6, Philadelphia (Eugene Pharo, "Pennsylvania Liberty," *Washington Post* [7 December 1937], 13).
37. "Gags on Movies," *Washington Post* (29 November 1937), 9.

38. MacLeish to "Jerry," 28 January 1937 (LoC: Box 8, Folder "Fortune").
39. "News-Names," *Chicago Daily Tribune* (17 January 1937), 24; "Hospital Group Sails for Spain," *New York Times* (17 January 1937), 32.
40. Dos Passos to Hemingway, 1 February [1937] (PU: Box 2, Folder 32, "Dos Passos"). Dos Passos arrived in Spain after Hemingway, not before, as Ivens's memoir wrongly reports.
41. MacLeish to Hemingway, 8 February 1937 (JFK: "Incoming Correspondence, from MacLeish").
42. MacLeish to Hellman, 24 December 1936 (HRC: Lillian Hellman Papers, Box 87, Folder 7).
43. Ivens, *Camera*, 104. Ivens does not name MacLeish; he says that the scenario was "prepared by one of our committee in New York" (104).
44. Ivens, *Camera*, 105.
45. Ivens, *Camera*, 105–106.
46. MacLeish to Hellman, 24 December 1936 (HRC: Lillian Hellman Papers, Box 87, Folder 7).
47. MacLeish to Hellman, 24 December 1936 (HRC: Lillian Hellman Papers, Box 87, Folder 7).
48. See Cecil D. Eby, *Comrades*, 13. Eby does not mention Ivens or Hellman, nor does Ivens's biographer Schoots mention Hellman or the volunteers; but Schoots tells us Ivens boarded the *Normandie* at the end of December and landed on New Year's Eve (117–118), the same ship and landing date as this group (per Eby), and a 28 December 1936 letter from Hellman's secretary confirms that she shipped out on that Saturday as well. The *Normandie* sailed at one o'clock p.m. with 672 passengers ("Normandie Sails with 672," *New York Times* [27 December 1937], 31).
49. In the letter of 24 December 1936, MacLeish tells Hellman that "I have sketched an outline of the scenario which Ivens will have with him on the boat and which you will be able to tear into at your leisure" (HRC: Lillian Hellman Papers, Box 87, Folder 7). Hellman's secretary's letter of 28 December 1936, to Mr. M. H. Behram asking for his support (borrowing heavily from MacLeish's letter) begins: "Just before Miss Hellman left for Europe on Saturday, she asked me to write you this letter" (HRC: Lillian Hellman Papers, Box 87, Folder 7).
50. Cecil D. Eby, 9.

51. Cecil D. Eby, 13–14. The group "held a clandestine bon voyage celebration (sans alcohol) in the Second Yiddish Theater near CP headquarters a few hours before they embarked" (12)—a number of the volunteers were Jewish (15). See also the chapter "Tough Jews in the Spanish Civil War" in Wald (16–45). Hemingway's great wartime friend, Dr. Werner Heilbrun, was a German Jew in Spain fighting the anti-Semitic fascists.
52. Cecil D. Eby, 15.
53. Cecil D. Eby, 15.
54. Cecil D. Eby, 17.
55. 14 January 1937 (JIA 216). See also Schoots, 85, 118; and Stott, 18–19, 27.
56. Madrid-Film receipts from February 1937 bear the U.G.T. stamp (JIA 216).
57. Wire draft JIA 228.
58. Hellman, *Unfinished*, 66. She made it to Spain in the fall of 1937; see *Unfinished* (83–115) and "Day in Spain."
59. Ivens, *Camera*, 106–107.
60. Gellhorn unpublished interview with Peter Davis, 12 October 1981.
61. Ivens's chronological table of shot footage, 21 January to 17 February 1937 (JIA 215).
62. Ivens, *Camera*, 114–115.
63. Names listed in Ivens's chronological table of shot footage, 21 January to 17 February 1937 (JIA 215).
64. Soviet source "written by Gobuliev" in *The Book of the XV Brigade*, 37.
65. Regler, *Owl*, 287, 289. Peter Wyden's account of the battle tries to recast Regler's, but misreads it, wrongly turning the Moor and Nationalist advance across the Manzaneres into their taking of the Arganda Bridge across the Jarama (278–279).
66. See Thomas, 572; and Beevor, 209–210.
67. Ivens (JIA 215).
68. "Het Volk," 6 March 1937, as apparently typed and translated for Ivens (JIA 214).
69. JIA 215. Regler's memoir cites Nenni's presence as well as the commander's wound, which he remembers as a leg wound (*Owl*, 289, 290)—perhaps a slight leg wound during the first engagement that

drove the Moors back across the Manzaneres, and the face wound in the battle to stop the Nationalists after they took the Pindoque railway bridge?

70. See Moorehead, 136. The Gellhorn figure in an unpublished Hemingway vignette needles the narrator with Pacciardi's interest (JFK: Item 824).
71. Hemingway landed at Plymouth, U.K., on 6 March en route to France. "British Actor Vanishes from Party on Liner," *Washington Post* (7 March 1937), 2.
72. There is no evidence that he was deliberately excluded, per Stephen Koch's accusation (62). Exactly who attended is unclear. Koch says Ivens's "Comintern superiors" and "a number of the most important Soviet propagandists in Europe" (62) were there, though he cites no specific source, and one can only assume his source is Schoots. Schoots claims "about one hundred invited guests, including Vladimir Pozner and the director Jean Renoir" (120), though he appears to rely on a 1977 interview with Ivens, and in general Ivens is a fairly unreliable source. The "Het Volk" article published shortly after the event, and presumably either written by an attendee or after an interview with Ivens, reports his showing the "rough material" to "a few people in Paris, among which the German Director Erwin Piscator" (6 March 1937 [JIA 214]). In his memoir, Ivens says he showed it to "a few film people and writers in Paris" (*Camera*, 111); but also says he met Hemingway in Madrid two weeks after meeting him in Paris, when in fact they flew to Valencia from France together, or at the very least met up in Valencia prior to driving together to Madrid. Some draft pages from the memoir's section on Spain are dated 1951; the memoir's prefatory "history" says that he wrote it during the Second World War, so only a few years later. Donaldson says Willi Münzenberg, the Comintern propaganda chief in Europe, was there, but does not provide his source (389).
73. Ivens to MacLeish, 26 February 1937 (JIA 228). *Queen Mary* shipping schedule provided by Will Kayne, an official historian for the *Queen Mary* (www.queenmary.com). Ivens uses the word "negatives" in this wire, in a separate wire draft to MacLeish (JIA 228), and in an undated letter from late March or early April (JIA 228). But it's likely he sent

developed material, as MacLeish viewed it as soon as customs released it (MacLeish to Hemingway and Ivens, 7 April 1937 [JFK: "Incoming Correspondence, from MacLeish"]). A second copy of the developed material should have been made by the Spanish embassy in Paris.

74. An undated cable draft from Ivens to Wenceslau Roces in the Ministry of Public Instruction and Fine Arts in Valencia suggests Ivens sent Ferno ahead to Spain, possibly to film for two weeks in "excellent village . . . near Madrid" on "second important picture" (JIA 228)—though none of Ivens's film schedules indicate that Ferno ever filmed in Fuentedueña alone. This note was written before MacLeish quashed Ivens's proposal for two films.

75. Regler, *Owl*, 291.

76. Regler, *Owl*, 292–293.

77. Hemingway, "The Heat and the Cold" (in Trogdon, *Reference*, 188).

78. Ivens to MacLeish undated, but references to filming "these few days" at Guadalajara and Dos Passos's not having appeared provide a timeframe (JIA 228). Are the "Italian casualties" the film's dead Nationalist troops, or the wounded Republican Volunteers?

79. MacLeish to Hemingway and Ivens, 7 April 1937 (JFK: "Incoming Correspondence, from MacLeish"). See note 74.

80. Ivens, *Camera*, 113.

81. Hemingway, "The Heat and the Cold" (in Trogdon, *Reference*, 190).

82. Hemingway, "The Heat and the Cold" (in Trogdon, *Reference*, 190).

83. Of the fundraising remarks, there are two typescript versions with a few minor and one major difference: the Hemingway version is in first person as Hemingway, with Ivens in third person (JFK: Item 717b); the Ivens version is in first person as Ivens, with Hemingway in third person (JIA 218; printed in Bakker, 247–249). That Hemingway wrote it for both of them to use, depending on which one attended a particular fundraiser, seems assured. Both versions' style sounds like Hemingway, asking (in second person) "have you ever been wounded;" and describing the experience, including riding in the back of ambulance trucks. The Hemingway version contrasts the post-shock pain and the desire to die with ordinary suicide wishes. The Ivens version has a handwritten title at top, "Speech Hemingway," and what appear to be Ivens's alterations for his time to read it. Some present the speech as

Ivens's without crediting Hemingway at the very least as a collaborator (e.g., Bakker). Schoots does not acknowledge Hemingway's authorship, but calls it "unadulterated Hemingway" (131). For an additional portrait of Heilbrun by Hemingway, see the unpublished fragment "Gustav had a fever . . ." (JFK: Item 442).

84. John T. McManus, "Down to Earth in Spain," *New York Times* (25 July 1937), 134.
85. Note by Seldes for Baker dated 2 December 1961 (PU: Box 18, Folder 1, "1937").
86. Gellhorn unpublished interview with Peter Davis, 12 October 1981.
87. John T. McManus, "Down to Earth in Spain," *New York Times* (25 July 1937), 134.
88. Ivens, *Camera*, 109.
89. Ivens, *Camera*, 110.
90. Ivens, *Camera*, 124–125.
91. Ivens, *Camera*, 124 (for placing this plan chronologically as I have, see the discussion later in this chapter). MacLeish cable to Hemingway and Ivens also uses the word "continuity" (7 April 1937 [JFK: "Incoming Correspondence, from Ivens"]).
92. Ivens to Hemingway, 26 April 1937 (JFK: "Incoming Correspondence, from Ivens").
93. Ivens to Hemingway cable, 28 April 1937 (JFK: "Incoming Correspondence, from Ivens").
94. Ivens to Hemingway telegram, 5 May 1937 (JFK: "Incoming Correspondence, from Ivens").
95. Ferno filmed in Madrid as late as 24 May 1937 (Ivens to Hemingway, 24 May 1937 [JFK "Incoming Correspondence, from Ivens"]).
96. "Creators' Congress," *Time* (21 June 1937), 79–80.
97. Koch—and Donaldson after him—misread a June 1937 letter from Gellhorn to Hemingway, which they believe shows that Ivens picked Hemingway for the speech, MacLeish for the Writers' Congress chair, and excluded Dos Passos (Koch, 222; Donaldson, 395). The letter, which appears to be Koch's (and Donaldson's) sole source, is actually about the new composition of the Contemporary Historians, Inc. board.

    The "letter" is a transcription from tapes by Bernice Kert, held in the Baker collection at Princeton (PU: Box 4, Folder 11, "Hemingway, Martha Gellhorn"). Koch reads the "he" who became president (not *chair*) as referencing MacLeish, whereas I believe "he" refers to Ivens. The letter does not mention Hemingway or the congress at all; the context for the misread line is the film—setting up a July screening in Hollywood, and wooing NBC. The context alone suggests a post-Carnegie composition. Furthermore, the letter carries the general date of June, though all the notes are in chronological order and this one follows one from 10 June and precedes one from 17 June (Koch cites it as "undated" and "summer" [304 notes 3 and 4]). This is probably the letter Gellhorn says is on the way to Hemingway in her 11 June telegram to him right after informing him of Ivens's promotion to the presidency of the Contemporary Historians, Inc. (JFK: "Incoming Correspondence, from Gellhorn"). MacLeish first wrote to Hemingway of an impending meeting on the night of his writing, 10 June 1937, with the goal of restructuring the committee and naming Ivens president (JFK: "Incoming Correspondence, from MacLeish"); he wrote again on 16 June, confirming Ivens as the new president and not naming Dos Passos at all (JFK: "Incoming Correspondence, from MacLeish"). Ivens also cabled Hemingway about the committee composition on 15 June (JFK: "Incoming Correspondence, from Ivens"), and mentions his presidency in a letter postmarked 17 or 19 June (JFK: "Incoming Correspondence, from Ivens").

Bernice Kert's use of the letter is ambiguous, simply stating that while Gellhorn admired Ivens greatly, she did not trust others and "watched with some skepticism their maneuvering to infiltrate all situations and committees" (302). But again, it seems clear to me that Gellhorn's comment about sinister communists specifically refers to Ivens's move to become president of Contemporary Historians, Inc. On the same page Kert writes that in a "rapid succession" of telegrams "Ivens was reminding Hemingway that he had promised to write the narration for the film and also to address the coming Writer's Congress in New York," though I have nowhere found such a series of telegrams, and Kert provides no citation. Correspondence in May from Ivens to Hemingway talks about the narration in process and does not remind him of his promise. In a cable of 24 May 1937, Ivens says they must be in New York the morning of 4 June (JFK: "Incoming Correspondence, from Ivens"), in clear reference to the congress.

98. Gellhorn, 53.
99. "Creators' Congress," *Time* (21 June 1937), 79–80.
100. Paul Romaine to Carlos Baker, 4 February 1963 (PU: Box 18, Folder 3, "1937 Writers' Congress").
101. De Pereda to Carlos Baker, 2 June 1967 (PU: Box 2, Folder 25, "De Pereda").
102. Hemingway, "Fascism Is a Lie" (in Trogdon, *Reference*, 194).
103. "Creators' Congress," *Time* (21 June 1937), 79–80.
104. De Pereda to Hemingway, 5 June 1937 (JFK: "Incoming Correspondence, from de Pereda").
105. 16 June 1937 (JFK: "Incoming Correspondence, from Ivens").
106. Ivens to Hemingway, 17 or 19 June 1937 (JFK "Incoming Correspondence, from Ivens").
107. De Pereda draft of *The Spanish Earth* with introductory notes (HRC: Prudencio de Pereda Collection, Box 5, Folder 9, "Commentary, *The Spanish Earth*" [1937]).
108. Per introductory notes attached to the de Pereda draft of *The Spanish Earth* with introductory notes (HRC: Prudencio de Pereda Collection, Box 5, Folder 9, "Commentary, *The Spanish Earth*" [1937]).
109. Ivens to Hemingway, 17 or 19 June 1937 (JFK "Incoming Correspondence, from Ivens"). If he ever wrote those promised comments, that letter has not survived. Jeffrey Meyers writes of an encounter in New York when Ivens advised Hemingway on revisions to the narration, in particular to let the images speak for themselves. Hemingway initially took minor offense, though then realized Ivens was right. Meyers provides no source documenting this encounter (*Biography*, 312).
110. Gellhorn to Hemingway, 18 June 1937 (JFK: "Incoming Correspondence, from Gellhorn").
111. Ivens to Hemingway, 19 June 1937 (JFK: "Incoming Correspondence, from Ivens").
112. Hemingway to Gellhorn, undated (JFK: "Outgoing Correspondence, to Gellhorn").
113. MacLeish to Hemingway, 16 June 1937 (JFK: "Incoming Correspondence, from MacLeish").
114. Per two separate Ivens schedules, one written in English, the other typed in Dutch (JIA 215).

115. Denning, 389–390. Denning devotes an entire chapter to Welles's antifascist agenda.
116. According to de Pereda, Blitzstein was later murdered as a random hate crime for his homosexuality (letter to Carlos Baker, 22 June 1967 [PU: Box 2, Folder 25, "De Pereda"]).
117. *Cahiers du Cinema* in English 5 (November 1966), 42 (in PU: Box 2, Folder 25, "De Pereda").
118. De Pereda to Carlos Baker, 22 June 1967 (PU: Box 2, Folder 25, "De Pereda").
119. Ivens to Hemingway at Cat Cay (Bimini, FL), 29 June 1937 (JFK: "Incoming Correspondence, from Ivens").
120. "Needed spanish voices" (JIA 215).
121. Ivens's chronological table of shot footage, 21 January to 17 February 1937 (JIA 215).
122. "Statement of mechanical expenses" (JIA 214).
123. Gellhorn, 52.
124. Ivens, *Camera*, 129.
125. Gellhorn letters to Hemingway, transcribed by Bernice Kert (Princeton), dated 6 June 1937, 17 June 1937, 2 July 1937, and 24 July 1937. The date for the White House event moved around a little, but by 29 June had settled on 8 July (Ivens to Hemingway, 29 June 1937 [JFK: "Incoming Correspondence, from Ivens"]).
126. Gellhorn and Ivens unpublished interviews with Peter Davis, 12 October and 4 June 1981.
127. Around 1938, President Roosevelt told Gellhorn: "Spain's a vicarious sacrifice for us all" (Davis interview).
128. Ivens, *Camera*, 130–131.
129. Gellhorn, 55.
130. Ivens, *Camera*, 131–132.
131. Ivens, *Camera*, 132.
132. It's possible that *The Spanish Earth* also played in the Spanish Pavilion at the Paris World's Fair, which opened 12 July. Stacey Guill makes this case based on three slight references related to Picasso's *Guernica*, which was at the fair (103n). Yet there are no mentions in any Hemingway, Ivens, or other Contemporary Historians material that I've seen. Guill quotes Jordana Mendelson's *Documenting Spain:*

Arts, Exhibition Culture, and the Modern Nation, 1929–1939 as stating that Luis Buñuel chose the films for the pavilion, though Mendelson does not name *The Spanish Earth* (Mendelson, 162). Buñuel was the Republic's Minister of Propaganda serving in Paris with whom Ivens worked and to whom Ivens promised a copy of the initial rushes. He was certainly in a position to provide footage from *The Spanish Earth* or possibly the completed film—if a copy were ready and able to be shipped to Spain in time (a big *if*). On 28 January 1938, Ivens wrote to Hemingway complaining that Buñuel's distribution of the film throughout Europe ruined any chance for financial gain (JFK: "Incoming Correspondence, from Ivens"). Regardless, Guill's chapter on the Spanish Pavilion's representation of the war and its resonances with *The Spanish Earth* and *For Whom the Bell Tolls* is illuminating.

133. John T. McManus, "Down to Earth in Spain," *New York Times* (25 July 1937), 134. The paper also reported that Mrs. Hemingway accompanied her husband; in a letter to Ralph Ingersoll, Hemingway writes that he paid for her ticket himself (27 July 1938 [JFK: "Outgoing Correspondence, to Ralph 'Mac' Ingersoll"]).
134. Per Ivens's typescript memoir draft (JIA 215), though Nichols is not included in Schoots's list of seventeen (130–131). See Hellman, *Unfinished*, 69.
135. Gellhorn, 56.
136. Reynolds, *1930s*, 273.
137. In Viertel, 46.
138. Gellhorn, 56.
139. Ivens, *Camera*, 128.
140. De Pereda to Carlos Baker, 29 August 1964 (PU: Box 2, Folder 25, "De Pereda").
141. In Achtenberg, 52.
142. Ivens, *Camera*, 129. Meyers and Donaldson credit Hellman and Frederic March (Meyers, *Biography*, 313; Donaldson, 397).
143. In Ivens's memoir draft dated 2 April 1951 (JIA 214). Other letters confirm the sound work in Hollywood (e.g., Hemingway to Ralph Ingersoll, 27 July 1938 [JFK: "Outgoing Correspondence, to Ralph 'Mac' Ingersoll" LoC: Container 10]).
144. Another version of the story: "'Orson Welles did the narration for

Hemingway's film, "The Spanish Earth,"' an agent attests at the Onyx. 'But Welles, who worked without pay, wanted single-billing. Hemingway refused, threw out the complete narration—and did it all himself" (Leonard Lyons, "The Post's New Yorker," *Washington Post* [25 August 1937], 12).

145. Leaving on 14 August. Gellhorn left three days later (and so also missed the premier) on the *Normandie* with Dorothy Parker, Alan Campbell, and Lillian Hellman (Moorehead, 133).

146. See also Stacey Guill's argument on the collaborative nature of the film (57–78).

147. MacLeish to Hemingway, 10 June 1937 (JFK: "Incoming Correspondence, from MacLeish"). The board meeting was held that very night, and Ivens did indeed become the president, with MacLeish his vice president to handle administrative scut work. Louise Eaton replaced Anita Marburg as secretary and treasurer. The board hoped that the William Morris Agency, which Ivens hoped would distribute the film, would provide an assistant secretary and treasurer (MacLeish to Hemingway, 16 June 1937 [JFK: "Incoming Correspondence, from MacLeish"]). For more correspondence on the new board composition, see note 97 above.

148. Wood's restatement of Hemingway's objections that appears on the rear lining of the book's second issue is taken from a telegram Hemingway sent him on 19 July 1938.

149. Ivens to Hemingway, 26 April 1937 (JFK: "Incoming Correspondence, from Ivens").

150. De Pereda to Carlos Baker dated only "August" (HRC: Prudencio de Pereda Collection, Box 1, Folder 4).

151. De Pereda to Hemingway, 14 August 1943 (JFK: "Incoming Correspondence, from de Pereda").

152. Helen Van Dongen unpublished interview with Peter Davis, 25 September 1981.

153. Richard Griffith quoted in Achtenberg, 46.

154. Van Dongen in Delmar, 35.

155. Helen Van Dongen unpublished interview with Peter Davis, 25 September 1981.

156. Unknown author to Ivens, 2 July 1937 (JIA 215).

157. Dos Passos, *The Theme Is Freedom*, 136–137.
158. Koch, 127.
159. Ivens, *Camera*, 131.
160. John T. McManus, "Realism Invades Gotham," *New York Times* (22 August 1937), X3.
161. "Hemingway Film Seen," *New York Times* (9 November 1937), 27.
162. Ivens, *Camera*, 103.
163. Hellman, *Unfinished*, 66.
164. Hemingway to Waldo Pierce, 27 July 1937 (*SL* 458).
165. Schoots, 46.
166. Thomas, 438.
167. Schoots, 111.
168. Schoots, 116.
169. Koch, 54–55, 61.
170. Watson, "Joris Ivens," 40–41.
171. Herbst, 155.
172. Koch, 146.
173. Such as Stanley Weintraub (273), who also draws on Herbst's memoir.
174. Koch, 153–154.
175. Herbst, (YU: "Journal"), entry for Thursday, 22 April 1937, manuscript pages 12 and 16.
176. Paul Preston, who similarly interrogates Koch, adds that Dos Passos's nonfictional telling of the luncheon says not a word in complaint about Hemingway's behavior (*We Saw Spain Die*, 80). Koch acknowledges that in the diary "at some point that morning, Dos Passos told Herbst that *he* thought Robles was dead—a detail she does not mention in the memoir, though it is clear that she wrote the memoir (in 1960) with the 'Diary' in front of her. Dos Passos making this statement must have been a matter of suspicion becoming conviction rather than new information" (296). This summary does not do justice to the diary, which challenges the Herbst-Hemingway tête-à-tête. Either Herbst did not have the diary in front of her when she wrote the memoir, or she deliberately rewrote history, perhaps fitting the diary to her twenty-year-old memory, perhaps for other motives.
177. See Ivens's 15 July 1937 letter to the directors of the Contemporary Historians (JFK: "Incoming Correspondence, from Ivens") as well as

the undated draft cable to "Roces" (JIA 228), who would be Wenceslau Roces, the Republic's Deputy Minister of Public Instruction and Fine Arts, and a member of the PCE and Unión de Escritores y Artistas Proletarios (Union of Writers and Artists Workers). This letter also expresses his desire to have gone back to Spain: "I could have done great work in Madrid."

178. The Ivens to Hemingway letter of 21 January 1938 was enclosed in a letter of Van Dongen to Hemingway (11 February 1938 [JFK: "Incoming Correspondence, from Ivens"]).

179. Schoots, 136. It's possible that Ivens's word choice of "assignment" is inaccurate, and this nonnative English speaker intended a word like "project" or even "job" (which can be self-initiated). Other phrasing in the letter, such as a reference to "a long talk with my people," would appear to validate Schoots's reading.

180. See Baker, *Story*, 307; Watson in Sanderson, 50; and all of Koch.

181. Schoots, 119.

182. Ivens, *Camera*, 123.

183. Ivens, *Camera*, 124.

184. Ivens, *Camera*, 123.

185. Ivens, *Camera*, 123.

186. Here again Koch either exaggerates Schoots or neglects to provide additional specific source information. See the differences in note 72 above.

187. Schoots, 70.

188. Schoots, 96.

189. Schoots, 102.

190. Schoots, 108.

191. Schoots, 108–109.

192. Schoots, 114.

193. Schoots, 107.

194. Schoots, 137.

195. Koch, 51.

196. Guill, 70–71. In a note Guill acknowledges the controversy over Ivens's politics, and it is possible to see his disavowal of communism in *The Spanish Earth* as a necessary *wartime* tactic.

197. "Does one get into the making of documentary films because one is

aware of economics, politics, and humanity, or vice-versa? I do not know. I think it goes both ways." Van Dongen in Achtenberg, 49.

198. Schoots, 74.
199. Ivens, "Notes on the Avant-garde Documentary Film," in Bakker, 225.
200. Schoots, 133.
201. Schoots, 109.
202. Schoots, 169.
203. Ivens, *Camera*, 111.
204. Manuscript draft dated 2 April 1951 (JIA 214).
205. Ivens unpublished interview with Peter Davis, 4 June 1981.
206. Donaldson, 390.
207. Watson, "Joris Ivens," 44.
208. Ivens unpublished interview with Peter Davis, 4 June 1981.
209. Watson, "Joris Ivens," 50.
210. Bernice Kert's transcription (PU: Box 4, Folder 11, "Hemingway, Martha Gellhorn").
211. Hemingway to MacLeish, undated [10 or 11 June 1937] (JFK: "Outgoing Correspondence, to MacLeish"). The insistence here suggests a concern perhaps deeper than lack of business and legal experience—on which others in the group would have provided advice or more likely continued handling themselves—or deeper than mere foreign citizenship.
212. Unpublished Gellhorn interview with Peter Davis, 12 October 1981.
213. In Schoots, 136.
214. Ivens to Hemingway, 28 January 1938, enclosed in a letter of Van Dongen to Hemingway (11 February 1938 [JFK: "Incoming Correspondence, from Ivens"]).
215. Watson, "Joris Ivens," 53.
216. Schoots, 139; Koch, 250; Donaldson, 401.
217. Schoots, 139. Schoots accurately summarizes the letter as telling about a talk between Ivens and "M.,"—who Schoots believes "can scarcely have been anyone other than Willi Münzenberg" (137), a talk about China which Koch turns into the ordering of Ivens to China: "I cannot tell you how I had to work. Went to M., times are tough—good to talk things over before going to China" (JFK: "Incoming Correspondence, from Ivens").

The paragraph about the "rendez-vous" to be set up by Van Dongen appears in a postscript. The prior paragraph warns Hemingway about letting Hollywood get its hands on *The Fifth Column*, and the following paragraph bemoans the lack of support for Spain in America, and specifically the lack of "leading people in North American Committee. Louis Fischer is trying to give the movement for Spain a new push." Ivens asks Hemingway for help motivating the Friends of the Lincoln Battalion, the Raven Fund, the Medical Aid Bureau, and the Motion Picture Artist Committee. These were all supported by the communists, to be sure. Given the surrounding paragraphs, we should not necessarily see the "rendez-vous" paragraph as an open invitation into the American Comintern inner sanctum, but rather in the context of continuing to support the Spanish Republic. And if Louis Fischer is an example of a leading person, we should perhaps relax our suspicions.

218. Moreira, 190; see also 121, 144–145, 186. In Spain Hemingway had learned to be "suspicious of Communist propaganda" (131). See also Yanagisawa.
219. De Pereda to Baker, 2 June 1967 (PU: Box 2, Folder 25, "De Pereda").
220. See letters of [November 1937?], 28 January 1938, 11 February [1938] (JFK: "Incoming Correspondence, from Ivens").
221. Ivens to Hemingway, 30 March 1938 (JFK: "Incoming Correspondence, from Ivens").

4. THE FILM AND THE BOOK

1. Throughout this chapter, otherwise unattributed quotes are from the narrative of *The Spanish Earth*, as is this one. Transcriptions are my own.
2. Ivens's notes indicate a "Hans" on a white building. This would refer to Hans Kahle. Regler writes that Hemingway loved him so much that he once "proposed to write a whole book about him" (*Owl*, 297). In the film, the officer clearly in charge on the rooftop is undoubtedly Kahle.
3. Cowles, 34.
4. Quote from Regler (*Owl*, 291). Regler's discussion would place it around the time of the fight for the Arganda Bridge, though it is a bit confused, as he places Hemingway on the scene when Hemingway was weeks away from arriving in country.

5. Ivens, *Camera*, 127.
6. Helen Van Dongen, unpublished interview with Peter Davis, 25 September 1981.
7. Hemingway, *Fifth Column*, 111.
8. Ivens, "Documentary: Subjectivity and Montage" (1939), in Bakker, 254, 256.
9. John C. Mosher, "The Current Cinema," *New Yorker* (21 August 1937), 59.
10. "The Screen," *New York Times* (21 August 1937), 7.
11. "The Screen," *New York Times* (6 December 1937), 19.
12. Ivens, *Camera*, 133–135.
13. "'Night Must Fall' Called Best Film," *New York Times* (18 December 1937), 18.
14. Geoffrey B. Pingree, "The Documentary Dilemma and the Spanish Civil War," in Valis (307).
15. Waugh, "Water," 22.
16. Costa, "Joris Ivens and the Documentary Project," in Bakker, 21.
17. In Bakker, 20–21.
18. Ivens to MacLeish, 26 February 1937 (JIA 228).
19. André Stufkens in Bakker, 61.
20. Ivens, "Notes on the Avant-garde Documentary Film" (1931), in Bakker, 225.
21. Ivens, "Documentary: Subjectivity and Montage" (1939), in Bakker, 250.
22. Ivens, "On the Method of the Documentary Film" (1932), in Bakker, 232.
23. Ivens, "On the Method of the Documentary Film" (1932), in Bakker, 231.
24. Bill Nichols, "The Documentary and the Turn from Modernism," in Bakker, 155.
25. Frank S. Nugent, "Dragging 'The River,'" *New York Times* (6 February 1938), 157.
26. A. O. Scott, "Quasi-Reality Bites Back," *New York Times* (26 September 2008). See also Iris Barry, "Challenge of the Documentary Film," *New York Times* (6 January 1946), SM9.
27. See Ivens, "Documentary: Subjectivity and Montage" (1939) and

"Repeated and Organized Scenes in Documentary Film" (Bakker, 252, 269); and Van Dongen in Achtenberg (51, 55).

28. Van Dongen in Achtenberg, 54.
29. Waugh, "Men Cannot Act," 143–146.
30. Waugh, "Men Cannot Act," 143.
31. Ivens, "Repeated and Organized Scenes in Documentary Film" (1953) in Bakker, 265–266.
32. Brian Winston, "'Honest, Straightforward Re-enactment': The Stating of Reality," in Bakker, 163. Winston's entire spectrum: "non-intervention—permissions—delays & repetitions—re-enactment of witnessed action—re-enactment of history—re-enactment of the typical—re-enactment of the possible—acting." To this spectrum we should add the use of actual footage representing a moment but not actually of that moment.
33. Ivens, "Repeated and Organized Scenes in Documentary Film," in Bakker, 270.
34. "The Screen," *New York Times* (21 August 1937), 7.
35. In Ferguson, 103.
36. In Achtenberg, 52.
37. Waugh, "Men Cannot Act," 148.
38. Waugh, "Water," 21.
39. In Achtenberg, 52.
40. Waugh, "Water," 18.
41. Ivens, "Documentary: Subjectivity and Montage" (1939), in Bakker, 256. See Waugh's discussion in "Water," 18.
42. Ivens, "Documentary: Subjectivity and Montage" (1939), in Bakker, 256–257.
43. Waugh, "Men Cannot Act," 150l.
44. Preston, *Spanish*, 20.
45. Thomas, 536.
46. Alpert, 18.
47. See Keeley.
48. Fraser, 470.
49. Thomas, 733.
50. Beevor, 108.
51. Unpublished Gellhorn interview with Peter Davis, 12 October 1981.

52. Herbst, YU: "Journal," 40.
53. Entry for 15 August 1937 (HRC: Paul Patrick Rogers Collection, Box 1, Folder 5, "Diary").
54. Graham, 36.
55. Waugh, "Men Cannot Act," 151.
56. Orwell, 9–10.
57. Orwell, 19. See also Beevor, 127.
58. Cecil D. Eby, *Comrades*, 108.
59. Orwell, 41–42. For a sampling of (mostly Republican) language from the loudspeaker and leaflet war, see Beals.
60. Some fascist propaganda directly targeted the International Brigades. Herbst's diary includes the text for a leaflet dropped over the Jarama lines, telling the "foreigners of the International Brigades" that they "have been cheated by shameless recruiting agents" and promising to return them to their homes if they "come over to Nationalist Spain." It claims that several "comrades who came over voluntarily have already been expatriated" (Herbst, YU: "Journal," manuscript page 7).
61. Orwell, 112–113.
62. Orwell, 28–29.
63. Coleman, 67.
64. Waugh, "Water," 20.
65. Thomas, 534–535.
66. JFK: Item 717b.
67. 28 August 1937 (JFK: "Incoming Correspondence, from Ivens").
68. 31 August 1937 (JFK: "Incoming Correspondence, from Ivens").
69. Douglas W. Churchill, "Caught on the Wing in Hollywood," *New York Times* (24 April 1938), 149.
70. Gerald G. Gross, "Shakespeare and Howard, Fontanne and Barrymore Are Lined Up for New Season at the National," *Washington Post* (26 August 1937), 12.
71. "News of the Screen," *New York Times* (16 September 1937), 29.
72. "Providence Bans 'Spanish Earth,'" *New York Times* (11 December 1937), 22.
73. "Hemingway Film Banned by Censor in London," *New York Times* (24 October 1937), 32.
74. "Hemingway Film Seen," *New York Times* (9 November 1937), 27.

75. 14 November 1937 (JIA 214).
76. *Daily Telegraph* (9 November 1937 and 15 November 1937); *Evening News* (12 November 1937) (JIA 214).
77. *World Film News* 2.9 (December 1937).
78. *Spectator* (12 November 1937) (JIA 214).
79. *Liverpool Post* (10 November 1937).
80. *Manchester Guardian* (9 November 1937).
81. London *Times* (9 November 1937).
82. *New Statesman* (13 November 1937).
83. *Birmingham Post* (25 November 1937); *Today's Cinema* (9 November 1937) (JIA 214).
84. *London Mercury* (December 1937) (JIA 214).
85. A letter from Rollin Dart to Hemingway, 25 January 1938, confirms the film's showing in France and the Cuban ban (JFK: "Incoming Correspondence, from Dart"), though Dart might have his information from Ivens, as the two had just met prior to Ivens's departure for China.
86. Ivens to Hemingway, 28 January 1938; attached to letter from Van Dongen of 11 February 1938 (JFK: "Incoming Correspondence, from Ivens").
87. According to Schoots, "After World War II the GDR authorities erased Gustav Regler from history because the once-so-valued writer had turned dissident around 1939. While living in Eastern Europe, Ivens accepted the removal of a shot showing Gustav Regler and the accompanying text" (133).
88. Papers dated 26 July 1937, all according to letters of David C. Mearns, Chief, Manuscript Division, Library of Congress, to Carlos Baker, 1 March 1965 and 8 March 1965 (PU: Box 18, Folder 1, "1937").
89. MacLeish to Shumlin, 2 November 1937 and 12 October 1937 (LoC: Container 51, Folder "Contemporary Historians, Inc."). The folder also contains a proposal by Contemporary Historians to finance the Chinese picture, dated 13 Octber 1937; and an undated appeal for support that MacLeish probably wrote around this time, as it names Contemporary Historians (rather than History Today, Inc.), mentions the recent release of *The Spanish Earth*, and names the same directors as the 2 November letter.

90. Dart to Hemingway, "25th Tuesday" [25 January 1938] (JFK: "Incoming Correspondence, from Dart"); see also Ivens to Hemingway, 28 January 1938 (JFK: "Incoming Correspondence, from Ivens").
91. "News of the Screen," *New York Times* (28 February 1938), 19.
92. Undated letter written "Monday night" from Rollin Dart to Hemingway (PU: Box 18, Folder 5, "1937–1938: Spanish Civil War"). Probably written Monday, 14 March 1938, because Dart writes that he "hope[s] Gustav got off all right" and mentions that Luis Quintanilla's Museum of Modern Art show opens "tomorrow." Regler left the Hemingway's in Florida to be in D.C. by the 17 March; Quintanilla's show opened on 15 March.
93. Ivens to Hemingway, 28 January 1938, 30 March 1938, and 8 June 1938 (JFK: "Incoming Correspondence, from Ivens").
94. Shumlin to Archie [MacLeish], 28 July 1938 (LoC: Folder "Contemporary Historians, Inc." Container 51), lists the officers of History Today, Inc., as Shumlin, MacLeish, Bloomgarden, and Ivens; and the directors as Shumlin, Hellman, and Julia Dorr.
95. Ivens to Hemingway, 28 January 1938 (JFK "Incoming Correspondence, from Ivens"); Leonard Lyons reports hearing that Hellman wrote the treatment ("Clubs, Orchestras and Celebrities Catch the Alert Eye of Mr. Lyons," *Washington Post* [20 March 1938], TS2). A young man from a village organizes his fellows to build a road to a Chinese textile mill to avoid sending the village's cotton to the Japanese mills: "This struggle culminates in the building of the road, but the building of the road coincides with the actual invasion of China by Japanese armies. The great blows of the war are of course at some distance on the coast, but in the village there is always the sense of the approaching armies, and eventually there is an actual air raid upon the village in which the bridges of the road are bombed. Here, of course, the bombing of the bridges symbolizes the destruction by Japanese imperialism of the creative work of the new Chinese society. This event galvanizes the life of the village and enables the young man to mobilize the village for action, and the picture ends with the heroic defense of the road by the villagers and the Chinese troops which support them" (General Outline of Proposed Picture [LoC: Container 51, Folder "Contemporary Historians"]).

96. Hemingway to de Pereda, 3 September 1943 (HRC: Prudencio de Pereda Collection, Box 1, Folder 10).
97. Ivens, *China*, 29.
98. Ivens, *China*, 69.
99. Alexander, 190. Schoots states that "Maddow had to drastically rewrite it" and cites Alexander as his source without acknowledging Maddow's uncertain recollection (149).
100. Hemingway to MacLeish, undated (PU: Box 18, Folder 10, "1938: The Spanish Earth").
101. Shumlin to Hemingway, 28 January 1939 (PU: Box 18, Folder 12, "1939"). Shumlin does not specify exactly which North American Committee—to Aid Spanish Democracy? for Spain? They might in fact be the same organization.
102. Shumlin to MacLeish, 4 March 1962, attached to a letter from Shumlin to Hellman, 21 May 1971 (HRC: Lillian Hellman Collection, Box 87, Folder 7).
103. Hellman to MacLeish, 25 March 1971 (HRC: Lillian Hellman Collection, Box 87, Folder 7).
104. MacLeish to Hellman, 15 January 1971 (HRC: Lillian Hellman Collection, Box 87, Folder 7).
105. MacLeish to Hellman, 12 May 1971 (HRC: Lillian Hellman Collection, Box 87, Folder 7).
106. Brandon to Hellman, 19 July 1971; Hellman to Brandon Films, Inc., 27 October 1971 (HRC: Lillian Hellman Collection, Box 87, Folder 7).
107. Hellman to André Romus, producer for Radiodiffusion-Télévision Belge, Institut des Emissions Française, Centre de Production de Liège, 15 January 1974 (HRC: Lillian Hellman Collection, Box 87, Folder 7).
108. Hellman to Ivens, 15 December 1975 (HRC: Lillian Hellman Collection, Box 87, Folder 7).
109. Rita Wade to Elsie Velasquez, Royalty Department, Films Incorporated, 17 December 1984 (HRC: Lillian Hellman Collection, Box 87, Folder 7).
110. Dart to Hemingway, undated (PU: Box 18, Folder 5, "1937–1938: Spanish Civil War"). On dating this letter 14 March 1938, see note 92 above.

111. *The Book of the XV Brigade*, 197, 291.
112. See Ingersoll to MacLeish, 8 July 1938 (LoC: Container 10, "Correspondence, Hemingway, Ernest 1927–1936"), and Pauline to Ernest, 29 April 1938 (JFK: "Incoming Correspondence, from Pauline Hemingway"). Dart once claimed to have saved the first draft of *The Fifth Column* from the Hotel Florida during a bombardment (Leonard Lyons, "The Post's New Yorker," *Washington Post*, 5 March 1938, X10).
113. Dart's letters to Hemingway, from 13 January to 14 April 1938, suggest the three-month stint (JFK: "Incoming Correspondence, from Dart").
114. Hemingway to Ingersoll, 27 July 1938: "Dart is back with the Fifteenth Brigade. It was the only thing for him to do and I hope he does it well" (LoC: Container 10, "Correspondence, Hemingway, Ernest 1927–1936").
115. Delmer, 332.
116. The book acknowledges Garrison Films, Inc. "For their help in securing the manuscript." Decades later Wood recalled that Dart handled the contracts and Garrison transcribed the film from the sound track. Tom Brandon told him "that he had done it himself" (Jasper Wood letter to Richard Allen Davison [23 October 1987], in Davison, 127). Not true: the book's formatting of the commentary follows a typescript version, and there are significant differences between this version and the final film's sound track narration. The most significant difference is sequencing of reels 3 and 4. Elsewhere the book omits sound track words or lines, includes script words or lines not on the sound track, and slightly modifies the sound track's language. It should also be noted that Welles's sound track does not exactly match the Hemingway sound track either, though they are very similar.
117. Wood to Hemingway, undated (JFK: "Incoming Correspondence, from Wood"). Contains references to *FWTBT* and Hemingway's recent marriage to Gellhorn of 21 November 1940, which Wood probably learned about from Robert Capa's photo-essay "The Novelist Takes a Wife" in *Life*, 6 January 1941. The film of *FWTBT* was not yet made (1943), and Wood's address indicates he was living with his parents. The letter's bracketed speculative penciled date of "[after 21 Nov 1941]" presumably erred on the wedding year.
118. W. Ward Marsh, 9B.

119. Hemingway to Jasper Wood, 19 July 1938 (HRC: Ernest Hemingway Collection, Box 3, Folder 4, "Letters").
120. Birk to MacLeish, 26 May 1937 (JFK: "Incoming Correspondence, from MacLeish").
121. MacLeish to Birk, 28 May 1937 (JFK: "Incoming Correspondence, from MacLeish").
122. An argument he had already made with the fifty-thousand-word minimum length. Birk to MacLeish, 29 May 1937 (JFK: "Incoming Correspondence, from MacLeish").
123. Birk to Hemingway, 9 June 1937 (JFK: "Incoming Correspondence, from Birk").
124. MacLeish to Hemingway, 27 May 1937 (JFK: "Incoming Correspondence, from MacLeish").
125. Either the Modern Age Books or the *Life* project might be to what MacLeish refers in a letter to Hemingway of 16 June 1937: "The other arrangement for the purchase of stills from the big picture stands so far as I know, although I have been very careful since our previous communications on this subject to keep my hands off entirely" (JFK: "Incoming Correspondence, from MacLeish"). One typescript and one manuscript, both untitled but for a *Life* magazine address, are probably early drafts for the spread (JFK: Items 717 and 717a).
126. "Dying, Well or Badly" (21 April 1938), 68; "The Cardinal Picks a Winner" (5 May 1938), 38–39.
127. Sigmund Aaron Lavine and Malcolm Cowley quoted in Stott, 211.
128. Stott, 213.
129. Reynolds, *Hemingway's Reading*, 186, Appendix VI, item 1984.
130. Quoted in Reynolds, *1930s*, 101.
131. Reynolds, *1930s*, 89.
132. Jasper Wood letter to Richard Allen Davison (23 October 1987), in Davison, 127.
133. Hemingway to Jasper Wood, 19 July 1938 (HRC: Ernest Hemingway Collection, Box 3, Folder 4, "Letters").
134. Wood, 9.
135. Wood, 11.
136. Wood, 10.
137. Wood, 12.

138. Quoted in Ivens, *Camera*, 135.
139. Wood, 13–14.
140. Wood, 14.
141. Publication date according to Hanneman (45), as well as "Book Notes," *New York Times* (27 May 1938), 15.
142. Telegram of 19 July 1938 and letter of 20 August 1938 (both HRC: Ernest Hemingway Collection, Box 3, Folder 4, "Letters"); undated manuscript telegram draft ("extremely grave business" [JFK: "Outgoing Correspondence, to Wood"]).
143. Jasper Wood letter to Richard Allen Davison (23 October 1987), in Davison, 127.
144. Hemingway to Wood, 19 July 1938 (JFK: "Outgoing Correspondence, to Wood").
145. Hanneman, 45.
146. "Rare Edition, His First, Is Selling Fast," *Washington Post* (6 November 1938), PY3.
147. Wood, 9.

5. THE WAR, THE FILM, AND THE NOVEL

1. Quoted in Nelson, *Remembering*, 31.
2. Nelson, *Remembering*, 13.
3. Nelson, *Remembering*, 8–9.
4. See "The Counselor of Embassy in Spain (Thurston) to the Secretary of State," 6 November 1938, *FRUS* 1938 v.1, 335.
5. *FWTBT*, 30.
6. *FWTBT*, 317. Paul Patrick Rogers's diary documents the testimony of Moors who had fought for Franco sitting in Republican prisons, who claimed they were forced by machine guns at their backs to lead the attacks and be "those who first ran into death. This they were bitterly resentful of. Back on the other side, they said, their fellow Moors felt very keenly about this (some of the recent reports of Moors rebelling & mutinying along with Spaniards would seem to bear this out)" (HRC: Paul Patrick Rogers Collection, Box 1, Folder 5, "Diary," entry for 10 August 1937).
7. *FWTBT*, 105.

8. *FWTBT*, 151.
9. *FWTBT*, 193.
10. *FWTBT*, 195.
11. *FWTBT*, 304.
12. *FWTBT*, 117–119.
13. *FWTBT*, 302–304.
14. *FWTBT*, 138.
15. *FWTBT*, 367.
16. *FWTBT*, 275.
17. *FWTBT*, 40.
18. The Consul General at Marseille (Hurley) to the Secretary of State, 22 June 1937 (*FRUS* 1937 v.1, 520).
19. Nelson, *Remembering*, 23.
20. *FWTBT*, 165.
21. To the Counselor of Embassy in Spain (Thurston), *FRUS* 1937 v.1, 495.
22. Vice Consul at Valencia (Wells) to the Secretary of State, 15 July 1937, *FRUS* 1937 v.1, 526.
23. Vice Consul at Valencia (Worley) to the Secretary of State, 22 November 1937, *FRUS* 1937 v.1, 557.
24. Delmer, 334.
25. Cecil D. Eby's thoroughly documented *Comrades and Commissars* details their maltreatment, extreme privations, periodic slaughter, and discontent in what Eby views as an indispensible, iconoclastic corrective to the sentimentality of most histories: "To write within the boundaries prescribed by VALB [Veterans of the Abraham Lincoln Brigade] partisans is to enter a narrow space where mushy platitude and rusty propaganda have crowded out the air" (xiv).
26. Guttmann, 167–169.
27. In Nelson, *Wound*, 203.
28. Josephs, *Undiscovered*, 131.
29. Reynolds, *1930s*, 300.
30. "Indian Country and the White Army" (JFK: Item 496) and "The Monument" (JFK: Item 580a).
31. *FWTBT*, 334–335.
32. Wyden, 303.
33. Josephs, *Undiscovered*, 58.

34. *FWTBT*, 199–200.
35. *FWTBT*, 105–106.
36. *FWTBT*, 414.
37. *FWTBT*, 366.
38. *FWTBT*, 325–326.
39. *FWTBT*, 88.
40. *FWTBT*, 321, 327, 450.
41. *FWTBT*, 326.
42. "The Men That Are Falling," in Nelson, *Wound*, 66.
43. *FWTBT*, 164.
44. Josephs, *Undiscovered*, 133.
45. For example, characterizing Anselmo as a good man (*FWTBT*, 196); noting what Gomez doesn't know (417); and speculating on the result of Andrés's mission (423).
46. *FWTBT*, 285.
47. *FWTBT*, 112.
48. *FWTBT*, 99.
49. Beevor, 86.
50. *FWTBT*, 101.
51. Graham, 87.
52. *FWTBT*, 354.
53. Graham, 116.
54. *FWTBT*, 322.
55. Hemingway, "Preface," vii.
56. Norris, 62–63.
57. Hemingway, "Preface," x–xi.
58. In Josephs, *Undiscovered*, 13.
59. The Ambassador in France (Bullitt) to the Secretary of State, 30 April 1937, *FRUS* 1937 v.1, 292.
60. *FWTBT*, 333, 428, 432. Though as a holding attack it might have helped accomplish a great deal.
61. Beevor, 275–276.
62. Baker, *Story*, 310, 347. An offprint of the article ("'For Whom the Bell Tolls': The Origin of General Golz," by Jerzy R. Krzyżanowski, in *Polish Review* [1962]) is housed in Baker's papers (PU: Box 18, Folder 1, "1937"). A photo of Walter appears in *The Book of the XV Brigade* (205).

63. Baker, *Story*, 311.
64. Josephs, *Undiscovered*, 72; Meyers, *Life*, 49 (Hemingway to Wilson, 8 November 1952 [*SL* 794]).
65. Josephs, *Undiscovered*, 72 (Hemingway to Evan Shipman, 25 August 1942, [*SL* 538]).
66. Meyers, *Life*, 49; *Biography*, 605, n. 16.
67. Matthews, *Half*, 195.
68. Szurek, 183.
69. Szurek, 120. See also 98.
70. *FWTBT*, 8.
71. Szurek, 182–183.
72. Szurek, 143.
73. Szurek, 184–185.
74. Szurek, 171.
75. Szurek, 144–148. Szurek gets some things wrong: Hemingway did not, in July 1937, participate in "an International Anti-Fascist Congress in Valencia and later in Madrid" (143). He was back in the U.S. at that time.
76. Beevor, 196–197.
77. Beevor, 276.
78. Beevor, 277.
79. Beevor, 276.
80. *FWTBT*, 423.
81. *FWTBT*, 247.
82. Josephs, *Undiscovered*, 73.
83. Beevor, 276. Though I take exception to Beevor's charge of this battle causing "the first example of unrest." Unrest among the Internationals began at least as early as Jarama. Americans were deserting by March.
84. Capa, *Heart*, 36.
85. Schaber et al., plates 61–69.
86. "Hemingway: *Life* Documents His New Novel with War Shots," *Life* (6 January 1941), 52–57.
87. Schaber et al., plate 64; photo 13 in "Hemingway: *Life* Documents His New Novel with War Shots."
88. Schaber et al., plate 66.
89. See the *March of Time*, volume 3, episode 13, "Rehearsal for War"

(6 August 1937) at HBO Archives online (http://www.hboarchives.com/apps/searchlibrary/ctl/marchoftime).

90. In Capa, *Heart*, 36.
91. "Hemingway: *Life* Documents His New Novel with War Shots," 52, 56.
92. *FWTBT*, 2.
93. "Hemingway: *Life* Documents His New Novel with War Shots," 52.
94. Taro's include photo 13 in "Hemingway: *Life* Documents His New Novel with War Shots" (see Schaber et al., 23 and plate 64).
95. "Hemingway: *Life* Documents His New Novel with War Shots," 52.
96. For example, *Life*'s photo 3 is from the Bilbao front in early May (see Capa, *Heart*, 187), and photos 6, 7, 16, and 17 are from the Rio Serge, Aragon front (near Fraga) in November 1938 (see Capa, *Heart*, 193).
97. See Capa, *Heart*, 176.
98. See his map (*Undiscovered*, 2) as well as the narrative (*Undiscovered*, 52–53).
99. Josephs, *Undiscovered*, 60.
100. See Herbst, 155, and Hemingway's "Writer Says Rebels Seek to Force Foes to Attack" dispatch ("Dispatches," 37–39).
101. Josephs, *Undiscovered*, 53.
102. Hemingway, *Fifth Column*, 140.
103. Herbst, 161–162, 164.
104. Hemingway mentions the caves in his "Fall of Teruel" dispatch ("Dispatches," 67), and Quintanilla includes two sketches of civilians sleeping in caves in *All the Brave*.
105. "Dispatches," 53.
106. Carroll, 167–168. Exactly when Hemingway would have heard of this exploit is unclear. While he spent a little time with the field commanders during the attack, he also left before it was over to write and file his dispatches, and he left the country a few days later. See also Wolff's brief description of Goff and Aalto (in Nelson, *Remembering*, 13). See also Hodson on Goff, Aalto, and Kunslich in "Robert Jordan Revisited" (5), and Josephs's summary of Hodson's work (142).
107. "Dispatches," 61.
108. Matthews, *Education*, 99. Hemingway had already left the battlefield, on his way home, and missed the much larger traffic jam detailed by Matthews (*Education*, 109).

109. See Graham, 282–285.
110. Orwell, 180–181.
111. Meyers, *Life*, 38–39.
112. *FWTBT*, 163.
113. Koch, 236–237.
114. Koch, 240–241.
115. Hemingway, *Fifth Column*, 38, 80.
116. Hemingway, *Fifth Column*, 25. Dorothy Bridges has at least as much of the glamorous journalist Virginia Cowles in her as Martha Gellhorn. The two women would later collaborate on a play set during the Second World War, *Love Goes to Press*.
117. De Pereda also wrote a Spanish Civil War story called "The Denunciation" (HRC: Prudencio de Pereda Collection, Box 1, Folder 24).
118. Hemingway, *The First Forty-Nine Stories*, vi.
119. Koch, 256–257.
120. Koch, 257–258.
121. Koch, 276.
122. Donaldson, 441. Delmer witnessed the event that Hemingway turned into "The Butterfly and the Tank" (302). Did Hemingway not turn it into a dispatch because he agreed with the girl in the story, that to write it would tarnish the Republican effort? (Hemingway, *Fifth Column*, 106).
123. *FWTBT*, 228–239.
124. *FWTBT*, 136.
125. It may very well have begun that spring. But in his enthusiasm to tie everything to Soviet influence, Koch mistakenly dates Hemingway's dating of *FWTBT* from 18 to 21 May, the exact days of the "Soviet near-coup" of the Republican government (218). Those days do not correspond to the Guadarrama offensive and include no weekends. The novel's placing the second day on a Sunday (89) matches with Sunday, 30 May, the day before the offensive (though here Hemingway is a day off; the second day should have been Saturday, 29 May, in order for the battle to commence on 31 May, or the morning of *FWTBT*'s fourth day).
126. "The Aragon Front" dispatch of 13 September 1937 ("Dispatches," 48), though it should be noted that in the manuscript the last two sentences are in present tense, in accord with the rest of the passage.

127. Following Cecil Eby's 1966 article: Baker, *Story*, 348, 623; Martin, 59–61; and Wyden, 100n.
128. "Dispatches," 49.
129. "Dispatches," 48.
130. Matthews, *Half*, 208.
131. Josephs, *Undiscovered*, 82. Meyers continues the tradition of citing Merriman in his 1985 Hemingway biography (306–307), but by the fall of 1988 had changed his mind, when he presented his rejection of Merriman in a lecture at the University of Colorado (see Josephs, *Undiscovered*, 173). That lecture was first published in 1990 as "*For Whom the Bell Tolls* as Contemporary History" (see 102–104) and again in 2000 (in *Life into Art*; see 51–53).
132. Cecil D. Eby, *Comrades*, 83.
133. Cecil D. Eby, *Comrades*, 42.
134. Trogdon, *Racket*, 212.
135. "Docile" from Scribners letter to Harry Scherman of BOMC, 15 August 1940 (in Trogdon, *Racket*, 212). Hemingway also was apparently not particularly committed to Jordan's nationality, as he offered to change it from American to British.
136. *FWTBT*, 163, 305.
137. *FWTBT*, 425.
138. Josephs, *Undiscovered*, 82.
139. Merriman and Lerude, 24.
140. See Merriman and Lerude, 46–49.
141. Beevor, 205.
142. Wyden, 222n.
143. Josephs, *Undiscovered*, 118.
144. The 236th Brigade of the XIV Partisan Corps, with five hundred men (Szurek, 148).
145. Szurek, 144–145.
146. Szurek, 146.
147. Szurek, 147.
148. Szurek, 148. Watson's verification of Chrost's story is, as Josephs characterizes it, "a very strong circumstantial argument" that uses Hemingway's travel records and safe-conduct pass for that fall to make its claim. See Watson's three "Investigating Hemingway" articles from

the *North Dakota Quarterly* as well as Josephs's summary (*Undiscovered*, 143–147).

149. DePalma, 56. DePalma appears to have gotten his information from Moorehead's *Gellhorn*, though in this biography Moorehead simply states that Matthews was partially the model (along with Merriman) for Jordan (114). DePalma presumes, probably correctly, that Moorehead is giving us Gellhorn's stated belief.
150. Gellhorn, 486–487, 426. There was some speculation that Matthews was in love with Gellhorn, though she always denied it.
151. See unpublished interviews with Gellhorn (12 October 1981); Seldes (11 October 1981); and Ivens (4 June 1981), by Peter Davis.
152. George Seldes unpublished interview with Peter Davis, 11 October 1981.
153. Delmer, 328.
154. Meyers, *Biography*, 335–336.
155. In Nelson, *Remembering*, 13.
156. Cecil D. Eby, *Comrades*, 246–247. See also *The Book of the XV Brigade*, 237.
157. In McCormick, 34–35, 37.
158. McCormick, 162–163.
159. McCormick, 159–160.
160. Paul Patrick Rogers diary entry for 12 August, marked p130 (HRC: Paul Patrick Rogers Collection, Box 1, Folder 5, "Diary").
161. Paul Patrick Rogers diary entry for 13 August, marked p133 (HRC: Paul Patrick Rogers Collection, Box 1, Folder 5, "Diary").
162. "Gustav had a fever . . ." typescript (JFK: Item 442).
163. In Trogdon, *Reference*, 190.
164. Regler, *Owl*, 288.
165. See Regler's descriptions of his death in *Crusade* (444–448) and *Owl* (311–312). See also Regler's description of his appearance and background in *Crusade* (11–13). Regler's letter of 8 January 1939 asking Hemingway to write the preface for *Crusade* remarks that Luis Quintanilla has impregnated Heilbrun's widow, Almuth, though being in New York he has not learned this news (PU: Box 18, Folder 8, "1938").
166. Gertrude Licciardello (Mrs. "Trudy" Thomas) of Trumbull, Connecti-

cut, to Carlos Baker, 26 July [1964] (the letter has no year, but the postcard with it is postmarked 31 August 1964) (PU: Box 18, Folder 1, "1937").

167. The Pablo image can also be found in Capa, *Death in the Making*, in the lower right corner of the unpaginated "*The war of the man on the Street*" page, and in Capa, *Heart of Spain* (63), opposite another image of the same man operating a machine gun (62), both taken "Near Huesca, Aragon front, August 1936"—so indeed near the beginning of the war, as the *Life* caption says. The Maria head shot in the *Life* spread is of a young woman on a horse in *Death in the Making*, opposite the unpaginated "*Front in Andalusia*" section title page.

168. Cowles, 38–39. Baker buries a reference to this passage in an endnote (*Story*, 622).

6. PILAR AND MARIA

1. See Meyers, *Life*, 35; Waldmeir, 43–45. As Thomas E. Gould has demonstrated, the attraction between Pilar and Maria is far more blatant in the manuscript drafts than in the final novel. Hemingway's sensitivity to censorship as well as the American reading public's reaction led him to change the strong suggestions "that there once existed a sexual bond between the two women" to "one of platonic jealousy" (73–74).
2. Meyers, *Biography*, 337.
3. Stanton, 171–172; Josephs, *Undiscovered*, 76–78, 114.
4. In Josephs, *Undiscovered*, 75.
5. Rogers (HRC: Paul Patrick Rogers Collection, Box 1, Folder 5, "Diary," entry for 9 August 1937).
6. *FWTBT*, 32.
7. Guill, 90–93.
8. Thomas, 9, 235.
9. Josephs, *Undiscovered*, 68. See also Meyers, *Life*, 53.
10. Baker, *Artist*, 243.
11. *FWTBT*, 53.
12. Ibárruri, 162.
13. *FWTBT*, 63. For his acceptance of communist discipline, see 163.
14. *FWTBT*, 387. One is tempted to connect La Pasionaria's first husband

with Pilar's first lover, the bullfighter Finito, and La Pasionaria's wartime lover, a much younger man "of the new bureaucratic generation" who "never went to the front," with Pablo (Thomas, 754–755).

15. *FWTBT*, 95.
16. *FWTBT*, 284.
17. *FWTBT*, 54. See also 15.
18. *FWTBT*, 214, 90.
19. *FWTBT*, 55–57.
20. *FWTBT*, 15.
21. *FWTBT*, 163.
22. Baker, *Story*, 373.
23. Kazin, 109.
24. Though during the battle of Brunete, in July 1937, Bates was in Madrid at the writers conference.
25. Beevor, 107.
26. Beevor, 217.
27. Beevor, 218–219. See also 168.
28. Thomas, 690.
29. Orwell, 7. See also 13, 38, and 125.
30. In Nelson, *Wound*, 63.
31. See Mary Nash, *Defying Male Civilization: Women in the Spanish Civil War*, and Martha A. Ackelsberg, *Free Women of Spain: Anarchism and the Struggle for the Emancipation of Women.*
32. Lannon, 71; Thomas, 108.
33. Thomas, 499.
34. Preston, 207.
35. Beevor, 123.
36. Preston, *Spanish*, 206.
37. Barrington, 319. Graham confirms that the Nationalists "paid Moroccan troops in war booty that included access to 'red' women." Additionally, Nationalist officers debated whether such women were even Spanish (122).
38. *FWTBT*, 81.
39. Merriman and Lerude, 147–149. See Preston, *Spanish*, 245.
40. Wyden, 468. Though Baker names this Maria in his biography, Josephs finds this more detailed story in Wyden "a bit too perfect"

that nevertheless "probably represents a certain embellished truth" (*Undiscovered*, 79).

The Andalusian "Maria" woman in the *Life* spread and *Death in the Making* has fairly short hair. Gerda Taro wore her hair even shorter during the war, cropped much more like Maria's is described. Martha Gellhorn also wore her hair short; Hemingway sometimes called her rabbit (e.g., "We used to quarrell before attacks" manuscript fragment [JFK: Item 824]); and their intense romantic relationship during the war maps onto Jordan and Maria's.

Delmer writes about a Spanish woman named Maria who worked as the secretary of the Madrid Ministry of War, calling her "Red Spain's Joan of Arc." She was a "quiet little office spinster" who fell in love with a British deserter, Keith Scott-Watson. Three nights after their meeting, the secret police caught up with them and allowed Scott-Watson to leave Spain. But "Maria vanished, first victim among my personal acquaintances of the new pestilence that was for the next three years to ravage the Communist world" (303–307).

41. *FWTBT*, 352.
42. Such criticism is referred to in Stanton (173) and Josephs (*Undiscovered*, 92–93).
43. Guill finds some evidence of Maria as a "New Woman of Spain" (126–133).
44. Can we connect the novel's preference for conventional Maria over revolutionary Pilar with David Bourne's preference for conventional Marita over the transgressive Catherine in *The Garden of Eden*?
45. *Formación Politica: Lecciones para las Flechas*, translated by and quoted in Wright, 89.
46. "What is Fascism, 1932." Internet Modern History Sourcebook, http://www.fordham.edu/halsall/mod/mussolini-fascism.html.
47. Eisenman, 90–91.
48. *FWTBT*, 16.
49. *FWTBT*, 25, 137.
50. *FWTBT*, 32. I wonder too about a biographical reading of this. In an unpublished fragment, the correspondent-narrator doesn't let his lover "Rabbit" accompany him to a battle. ("We used to quarrell before attacks" [JFK: Item 824]). Did Hemingway experience some insecurity

due to Gellhorn's and the other women reporters' very presence? And Taro, who died getting as close to the fighting as Hemingway ever did? The first British fatality of the war was also a woman and an artist, the sculptor Felicia Browne (Lannon, 70).

51. *FWTBT*, 227.
52. *FWTBT*, 291, 344.
53. *FWTBT*, 164–165.
54. *FWTBT*, 203.
55. Hewson, 365, 368, 369.
56. *FWTBT*, 159, 379.
57. Strychacz, 108.
58. Beevor, 106.
59. Beals, 94. For other examples of Nationalist patria and fatherland language, see Thomas, 799; and Preston, *Spanish*, 32, 64, 201, 223.
60. Strychacz, 106–107, and quoting *FWTBT*, 370.
61. In Nelson, *Wound*, 77.
62. Jennifer Lester's 2007 article, while armed with such theoretical language, nevertheless replicates the mechanical warfare versus nature reading of the novel.
63. Guttmann, 170–175.
64. "Dispatches" 42, 78–79.
65. "[Spanish Civil War] Miscellaneous Fragments," (JFK: Item 716).
66. Guttmann, 173 (emphasis mine).
67. "Dispatches," 41.
68. Strychacz, 108.
69. *FWTBT*, 29, 63, 76, 79.
70. Romesburg, 149.
71. *FWTBT*, 161.
72. *FWTBT*, 321, 29.
73. *FWTBT*, 309.
74. *FWTBT*, 465, 469.
75. *FWTBT*, 21–22.
76. *FWTBT*, 170.
77. *FWTBT*, 263–274.
78. Gajdusek, 144.
79. Tyler, 126, 128.

80. Tyler, 127.
81. Tyler, 131.
82. Tyler, 132.
83. On the war poetry's following this tradition, see Nelson, *Wound*, 24.
84. Valis, 265.
85. Allen in Capa, *Death*, unpaginated fourth page. The woman, Juanita Rico, is not mentioned by Thomas, Beevor, or Preston (*Spanish*).
86. Link, 135.
87. *FWTBT*, 42.
88. Stanton, 175.
89. *FWTBT*, 137.
90. *FWTBT*, 23.
91. *FWTBT*, 264.
92. *FWTBT*, 341.
93. *FWTBT*, 312–313.
94. *FWTBT*, 348.
95. In Nelson, *Wound*, 193. See also Rolfe's poem "First Love" (in Nelson, *Wound*, 168).
96. Postwar cinematic reincarnations of Kiev appear in *Indochine* (1992) and *The Beautiful Country* (2004).
97. Wright, 4.
98. DeGuzmán, 190.
99. Murad, 90.
100. Valis, 264.
101. *TGE*, 52.
102. Wright, 4.
103. Allen in Capa, *Death*, unpaginated fourth page.
104. In Capa, *Death*, unpaginated first page.
105. *FWTBT*, 22, 158.
106. Ellis, 36.
107. *FWTBT*, 43.
108. Orwell, 101–102.
109. In Nelson, *Wound*, 164.
110. Josephs, *Undiscovered*, 78.
111. See *Life*, "Hemingway," 53; and Capa, *Death*, opposite the unpaginated "Front in Andalusia" section title page. Josephs is right in his rebuttal

of Arturo Barea's criticism of the novel's placement of characters based on Andalusian women in Castile (central Spain): "Hemingway was representing all of Spain in his mountain microcosm" (92). I have not read Barea's objection, but it appears to bespeak this internal Spanish racist regard for Andalusians.

112. Quotation and rumor from Szurek, 175–176.
113. Eisenman, 109.
114. Wright, 230.
115. Wright, 73.
116. Wright, 98–105.
117. Wright, 197.
118. Wright, 283. For a thorough analysis of *Pagan Spain* as an Anglo-American (and Southern) modernist response to Spain, see DeGuzmán (224–236). One way to account for a constructed difference between Spanish primitivism and African primitivism might be to return to Stein's words to Wright, promising in Spain not a trek to Africa but a return to the West's past: "You'll see what the Western world is made of" (in Wright, 4).
119. DeGuzmán, 187.
120. DeGuzmán, 218.
121. DeGuzmán, xii.
122. *FWTBT*, 43.
123. *FWTBT*, 175. In *The Fifth Column*, Rawlings's relationship with Anita, his "MOORISH TART," is infinitely less fanciful than Jordan's with Maria. The love triangle among Rawlings, Anita, and the materialistic Anglo-American Dorothy Bridges, deserves critical attention.
124. *FWTBT*, 93.
125. Stanton, 175. See also Josephs's support of Stanton, Teunissen, and others (*Undiscovered*, 80–81; 100–109; 136–138) for a view contrary to mine.
126. *FWTBT*, 270.
127. *FWTBT*, 70. See also 158.
128. *FWTBT*, 35.
129. Guttmann, 172; Stanton, 174.
130. Her possible impregnation receives comment (*FWTBT*, 79, 89). What Pilar teaches Maria might be about birth control (324), though Pilar

also tells her that she might be infertile (354)—symbolic of fascism's irreparable damage to Spain, or a trick to get Maria to sleep with Jordan to bring a new life to Spain?

131. *FWTBT*, 162.
132. *FWTBT*, 466.

7. FROM FREDERIC HENRY TO ROBERT JORDAN

1. Josephs, "Volatile Mixture," 183.
2. Josephs, *Undiscovered*, 11.
3. Excerpt of Hemingway letter to Duran "circa late August or early Sept. 1940" per Carlos Baker's notes (PU: Box 2, Folder 35, "Gustavo Duran").
4. Wagner-Martin, *Farewell*, 6.
5. *FTA*, 148.
6. *FWTBT*, 336.
7. *FWTBT*, 59.
8. "Dispatches" 62.
9. Reynolds, 271.
10. Nagel, 161.
11. Nagel, 172.
12. Nagel, 173. See Brenner's chapter "A Hospitalized World," 27–41.
13. Marcus, 208.
14. Fussell, 254.
15. *FTA*, 12, 59, 65, 144.
16. *FTA*, 108.
17. Ferguson shares the first name of Nick Adams's wife: Helen.
18. *FTA*, 115.
19. *FTA*, 322–323.
20. *FTA*, 332.
21. *FTA*, 28.
22. Donaldson, 348.
23. Norris, 73.
24. Norris, 71.
25. *FTA*, 84.
26. Strychacz, 95.

27. Quoted in Strychacz, 98.
28. Brenner, 28, 31–32.
29. See Norris, 58–77.
30. *FTA*, 149.
31. *FWTBT*, 336.
32. Vernon, *Soldiers*, 79.
33. Vernon, *Soldiers*, 81.
34. *IOT*, 19.
35. *IOT*, 71.
36. *FWTBT*, 386.
37. *FWTBT*, 336.
38. *FWTBT*, 386.
39. Wyden, 318n.
40. Watson, "Investigating Hemingway: The Novel," 13–15.
41. In Nelson, *Wound*, 64.
42. De Echeverria, 35.
43. *FWTBT*, 55.
44. Donaldson, 461.
45. Autobiographical sketch c. 1935 (HRC: Ernest Hemingway Collection, Box 3, Folder 1).
46. JFK: Item 717b. See Ivens's version in Bakker, 248.
47. 26 July 1939 (*SL* 493).
48. Young, 107–108.
49. Lynn, 488–491.
50. Koch, 218, 276.
51. *FWTBT*, 313–319.
52. *FWTBT*, 471.
53. *FWTBT*, 100.
54. *FWTBT*, 238.
55. *FWTBT*, 355.
56. *FWTBT*, 391.
57. *FWTBT*, 73.
58. *FWTBT*, 170.
59. *FWTBT*, 67.
60. *FWTBT*, 253.
61. *FWTBT*, 23.

62. *FWTBT,* 338.
63. *FWTBT,* 249–250, 371, 380, and others.
64. *FWTBT,* 148.
65. *FWTBT,* 20 (also 52).
66. *FWTBT,* 149.
67. *FWTBT,* 43.
68. *FWTBT,* 23–24, 45, 249.
69. *FWTBT,* 7–8.
70. *FWTBT,* 21.
71. *FWTBT,* 149.
72. *FWTBT,* 249.
73. *FWTBT,* 269.
74. Fleming, 127, 131. Yet Fleming then calls the novel Hemingway's "attempt to purge himself, through his art, of the debilitating psychological effects of his father's suicide," rendering the fact of Hemingway's eventual suicide "more provocative and more ironic" (132). If Fleming is correct that Hemingway used this book to purge himself of the suicide drive, its writing becomes a gesture like Jordan's throwing away his father's gun (an act Hemingway himself never undertook).
75. Donaldson, 461.
76. *FWTBT,* 470.
77. Lynn, 490.
78. *FWTBT,* 73.
79. *FWTBT,* 406, 410–411.
80. *FWTBT,* 447.
81. Eisenman, 52–53.
82. *FWTBT,* 160, 166.
83. *FWTBT,* 464.
84. *FWTBT,* 342.
85. Spilka, 215.
86. Eisenman, 65, 85.
87. William Aalto was "one of a half-dozen known homosexuals" (Carroll, 167).
88. Moddelmog, "Country," 19.
89. *FWTBT,* 17.

90. *FWTBT*, 338–339.
91. *FWTBT*, 134.
92. *FWTBT*, 248.
93. *FWTBT*, 210.
94. *FWTBT*, 437.
95. *FWTBT*, 206.
96. *FWTBT*, 213.
97. *FWTBT*, 404.
98. Richard Slotkin quoted in Carl Eby, *Comrades*, 219 ("androgynous" is Eby's word).
99. *FWTBT*, 337–338.
100. *FWTBT*, 339.
101. Spilka, 252.
102. Moddelmog, "Country," 11.
103. Moddelmog, "Country," 12–13.
104. Hewson, 369, 372.
105. *FWTBT*, 380.
106. Hewson, 369.
107. What are we to make of Maria's repeated rapings and torture given Graham's observation that that "which sparked the most vehement, pathological loathing and, in turn, some of the most extreme cases of ritual, violent humiliation was digression from rigid gender norms"? (Graham, 121).
108. Suzanne del Gizzo's study of Hemingway's transformation between the 1934–1935 and the 1953–1954 safaris might be a useful frame for this trajectory.
109. See Bleys, *The Geography of Perversion*; and Vernon, *On Tarzan*, 107–137.
110. Stanton, 168.
111. See Moddelmog, "Protecting," 101.
112. On homoeroticism, miscegenation, incest, cannibalism, and imagined primitive polysexuality, see Vernon, *On Tarzan*. The book's contention (chapters 6 and 7) that cannibalism potentially expresses the taboo subjects of homosexuality and incest in popular jungle narratives like Tarzan unfortunately neglects to emphasize miscegenation, probably

the most obvious taboo for which cannibalism stands in. *On Tarzan* also tentatively associates the modernist fetish for the primitive, the return to the garden, with a longing for death (160–161).

113. *FWTBT*, 436.

EPILOGUE

1. *FWTBT*, 188.
2. Preston, *Spanish*, 121. Allen reported 1,800 corpses; historians usually cite the 2,000 number.
3. Preston, *Spanish*, 104.
4. Thomas, 734. Though Thomas notes that "some corridas were held in the republic, mostly as benefits for hospitals or schools, despite the opposition of the anarchists" (734n2).
5. *FWTBT*, 184. The situation did not improve under Franco—see Wright, 124, 151.
6. See for example Edna St. Vincent Millay's "Say That We Saw Spain Die" (135) and Sol Funaroff's "The Bull in the Olive Field" (139).
7. *FWTBT*, 103.
8. *DIA*, 24.
9. *FWTBT*, 189.
10. *FWTBT*, 82.
11. Wright, 151.
12. James Meredith, "Hemingway's Spain in Flames, 1937," 12th International Ernest Hemingway Society Biennial Conference, Ronda, Spain, June 2006. Revised draft provided to the author in December 2009. Meredith's inclusion of *To Have and Have Not* follows from Reynolds's *Hemingway: The 1930s* (269–270).
13. See the material in Bruccoli, and Trogdon (*Reference*).
14. Wolff in Nelson, *Remembering*, 8.
15. See Jump.
16. Wolff in Nelson, *Remembering*, 10.
17. Two places to begin are Nelson (*Remembering*, 19–40) and Carroll (235–241, 315–319).

BIBLIOGRAPHY

Achtenberg, Ben. "Helen van Dongen: An Interview." *Film Quarterly* 30.2 (Winter 1976): 46–57.

Alexander, William. *Film on the Left: American Documentary Film from 1931 to 1942*. Princeton, NJ: Princeton University Press, 1981.

Alpert, Michael. *A New International History of the Spanish Civil War*. New York: Palgrave Macmillan, 2004.

Baker, Carlos. *Ernest Hemingway: A Life Story*. New York: Scribner, 1969.

———. *Hemingway: The Writer as Artist*. Princeton, NJ: Princeton University Press, 1980.

Baker, Carlos, ed. *Ernest Hemingway: Selected Letters, 1917–1961*. New York: Scribner, 1981.

Bakker, Kees, ed. *Joris Ivens and the Documentary Context*. Amsterdam: Amsterdam University Press, 1999.

Barrington, Ryerson. "A Foreign Volunteer in Spain." *New Republic* (21 April 1937): 317–319.

Beals, Carleton. "The Spanish War of Words." *New Republic* (2 June 1937): 94–96.

Beevor, Anthony. *The Battle for Spain: The Spanish Civil War 1936–1939*. New York: Penguin, 2006.

Bessie, Alvah. *Men in Battle*. Los Angeles: Pinnacle, 1977.

Bleys, Rudi C. *The Geography of Perversion: Male-to-Male Sexual Behavior Outside the West and the Ethnographic Imagination, 1750–1918*. New York: New York University Press, 1995.

The Book of the XV Brigade: Records of the American, Canadian and Irish Volunteers in the XV International Brigade in Spain 1936–1938. Pontypool, UK: Warren & Pell, 2003.

Brenner, Gerry. *Concealments in Hemingway's Works*. Columbus: Ohio State University Press, 1983.

Brogan, Jacqueline Vaught. "Parody or Parity: A Brief Note on Gertrude Stein and *For Whom the Bell Tolls*." *Hemingway Review* 15.2 (Spring 1996): 89–95.

Bruccoli, Matthew. *Hemingway and the Mechanism of Fame*. Columbia: University of South Carolina Press, 2006.

Capa, Robert. *Death in the Making*. Photographs by Robert Capa and Gerda Taro. Captions by Robert Capa. Translated by Jay Allen. Preface by Jay Allen. Arrangement by André Kertesz. New York: Covici-Friede, 1938.

———. *Heart of Spain: Robert Capa's Photographs of the Spanish Civil War*. New York: Aperture Foundation, 1999.

Carroll, Peter N. *The Odyssey of the Abraham Lincoln Brigade: Americans in the Spanish Civil War*. Stanford, CA: Stanford University Press, 1994.

Coleman, Arthur. "Hemingway's *The Spanish Earth*." *Hemingway Review* 2.1 (Fall 1982): 64–67.

Cowles, Virginia. *Looking for Trouble*. New York: Harper & Brothers, 1941.

Cowley, Malcolm. "To Madrid: II." *New Republic* (1 September 1937): 93–96.

———. "To Madrid III: Offensive on Two Fronts." *New Republic* (15 September 1937): 152–155.

———. "To Madrid IV: Three Spanish Kids." *New Republic* (22 September 1937): 179–182.

Davison, Richard Allen. "The Publication of Hemingway's *The Spanish Earth*: An Untold Story." *Hemingway Review* 7.2 (Spring 1988): 122–130.

DeGuzmán, María. *Spain's Long Shadow: The Black Legend, Off-Whiteness, and Anglo-American Empire*. Minneapolis: University of Minnesota Press, 2005.

Del Gizzo, Suzanne. "Going Home: Hemingway, Primitivism, and Identity." In *Hemingway: Eight Decades of Criticism*. Ed. Linda Wagner-Martin. East Lansing: Michigan State University Press, 2009. 479–512.

Delmar, Rosalind. *Joris Ivens: 50 Years of Film-Making*. London: British Film Institute, 1979.

Delmer, Sefton. *Trail Sinister: An Autobiography*. Vol. 1. London: Secker & Warburg, 1961.

Denning, Michael. *The Cultural Front: The Laboring of American Culture in the Twentieth Century*. London: Verso, 1997.

DePalma, Anthony. *The Man Who Invented Fidel: Castro, Cuba, and Herbert L. Matthews of the* New York Times. New York: Public Affairs, 2006.

Department of State, United States of America. *Foreign Relations of the United States*. 1937, vol. 1: General. Washington: Government Printing Office, 1954.

———. *Foreign Relations of the United States*. 1938, vol. 1: General. Washington: Government Printing Office, 1955.

Donaldson, Scott. *Fitzgerald & Hemingway: Works and Days*. New York: Columbia University Press, 2009.

Dos Passos, John. *The Theme Is Freedom*. New York: Dodd, Mead, 1956.

Eby, Carl P. *Hemingway's Fetishism: Psychoanalysis and the Mirror of Manhood*. Albany: State University of New York Press, 1999.

Eby, Cecil D. *Comrades and Commissars: The Lincoln Battalion in the Spanish Civil War*. University Park: Pennsylvania State University Press, 2007.

———. "The Real Robert Jordan." *American Literature* 38 (November 1966): 382–383.

Echeverria, Frederico de. *Spain in Flames*. Foreword by Robert I. Gannon. New York: Paulist Press, 1936.

Eisenman, Stephen F. *The Abu Ghraib Effect*. London: Reaktion Books, 2007.

Ellis, Havelock. *The Soul of Spain*. Boston: Houghton Mifflin, 1908.

Ferguson, Otis. "'And There Were Giants on the Earth.'" *New Republic* (1 September 1937): 103–104.

Fleming, Robert E. "Hemingway's Treatment of Suicide: 'Fathers and Sons' and *For Whom the Bell Tolls*." *Arizona Quarterly* 33 (1977): 121–132.

Franklin, Sidney. *Bullfighter from Brooklyn*. New York: Prentice-Hall, 1952.

Fussell, Paul. *The Boy Scout Handbook and Other Observations*. New York: Oxford University Press, 1982.

Gajdusek, Robert E. "Pilar's Tale: The Myth and the Message." In *Hemingway in His Own Country*. By Robert E. Gajdusek. Notre Dame: University of Notre Dame Press, 2002. 136–154. Originally published in *Hemingway Review* 10.1 (Fall 1990): 19–33.

Gellhorn, Martha. *Selected Letters of Martha Gellhorn*. Ed. Caroline Moorehead. New York: Henry Holt, 2006.

Gould, Thomas E. "'A Tiny Operation with Great Effect': Authorial Revision and Editorial Emasculation in the Manuscript of Hemingway's *For Whom the Bell Tolls*." In Sanderson, 67–81.

Graham, Helen. *The Spanish Republic at War 1936–1939*. Cambridge: Cambridge University Press, 2002.

Guill, Stacey L. *Hemingway and "The Spanish Earth": Art, Politics, and War*. Dissertation. Indiana University of Pennsylvania, 2006.

Guttmann, Allen. *The Wound in the Heart: America and the Spanish Civil War*. New York: Free Press of Glencoe, 1962.

Hanneman, Audre. *Ernest Hemingway: A Comprehensive Bibliography*. Princeton, NJ: Princeton University Press, 1967.

Hellman, Lillian. "Day in Spain." *New Republic* (13 April 1938): 297–298.

———. *An Unfinished Woman—A Memoir*. Boston: Little, Brown & Company, 1969.

Hemingway, Ernest. *By-Line Ernest Hemingway: Selected Articles and Dispatches of Four Decades*. Ed. William White. New York: Scribner, 1998.

———. *Death in the Afternoon*. New York: Simon & Schuster, 1995.

———. *Ernest Hemingway: Selected Letters, 1917–1961*. Ed. Carlos Baker. New York: Scribner, 1981.

———. *A Farewell to Arms*. New York: Scribner, 1995.

———. *The Fifth Column and Four Stories of the Spanish Civil War*. New York: Scribner, 2008.

———. *The First Forty-Nine Stories and the Play, the Fifth Column*. New York: Scribner, 1938.

———. *For Whom the Bell Tolls*. New York: Simon & Schuster, 1995.

———. *The Garden of Eden*. New York: Scribner, 1986.

———. "'Humanity Will Not Forgive This!': The *Pravda* Article." Intro. William Braasch Watson. *Hemingway Review* 72 (Spring 1988): 114–118.

———. *In Our Time*. New York: Scribner, 1930.

———, ed. *Men at War: The Best War Stories of All Time*. Introduction by Ernest Hemingway. Based on a plan by William Kozlenko. New York: Crown, 1942.

———. "Preface." In Regler, *The Great Crusade*, vii–xi. Reprinted in Trogdon, *Ernest Hemingway: A Literary Reference*, 218–219.

"Hemingway: *Life* Documents His New Novel with War Shots." *Life* (6 January 1941): 52–57.

Herbst, Josephine. *The Starched Blue Sky of Spain and Other Memoirs.* Introduction by Elizabeth Francis. Boston: Northeastern University Press, 1999.

Hewson, Marc. "A Matter of Love or Death: Hemingway's Developing Psychosexuality in *For Whom the Bell Tolls.*" In *Hemingway: Eight Decades of Criticism.* Ed. Linda Wagner-Martin. East Lansing: Michigan State University Press, 2009. 355–375.

Hodson, Joel. "Robert Jordan Revisited: Hemingway's Debt to T. E. Lawrence." *Hemingway Review* 10.2 (Spring 1991): 2–16.

Ibárruri, Dolores. *They Shall Not Pass: The Autobiography of La Pasionaria.* New York: International Publishers, 1966.

Ivens, Joris. *The Camera and I.* New York: International Publishers, 1969.

———. *Joris Ivens and China.* Film Archive of China and the Editorial Department of New World Press. Beijing: New World Press, 1983.

Josephs, Allen. "*For Whom the Bell Tolls*": *Ernest Hemingway's Undiscovered Country.* New York: Twayne, 1994.

———. "Hemingway and the Spanish Civil War or the Volatile Mixture of Politics and Art." In *Rewriting the Good Fight: Critical Essays on the Literature of the Spanish Civil War.* Ed. Frieda S. Brown, Malcolm Alan Compitello, Victor M. Howard, and Robert S. Martin. East Lansing: Michigan State University Press, 1989. 175–184.

Jump, Jim. "Milton Wolff." Obituary. *Guardian* (5 February 2008). http://www.guardian.co.uk/world/2008/feb/05/usa.obituaries.

Kazin, Alfred. *Starting Out in the Thirties.* Ithaca: Cornell University Press, 1989.

Keeley, Graham. "Revealed: Franco's Desperate Attempt to Hide the Truth about Guernica." *Times Online* (6 March 2009). http://www.timesonline.co.uk/tol/news/world/europe/article5852235.ece.

Kert, Bernice. *The Hemingway Women.* New York: Norton, 1983.

Knightley, Phillip. *The First Casualty: The War Correspondent as Hero and Myth-Maker from the Crimea to Iraq.* Baltimore: Johns Hopkins University Press, 2004.

Koch, Stephen. *The Breaking Point: Hemingway, Dos Passos, and the Murder of José Robles.* New York: Counterpoint, 2005.

Krzyźanowski, Jerzy R. "*For Whom the Bell Tolls*: The Origin of General Golz." *Polish Review* 7.4 (1962). One-off housed at PU: Box 18, Folder 1, "1937."

Lannon, Frances. *Essential Histories: The Spanish Civil War 1936–1939*. Oxford, UK: Osprey, 2002.

Lester, Jennifer. "Reading *For Whom the Bell Tolls* with Barthes, Bakhtin, and Shapiro." *Hemingway Review* 26.2 (Spring 2007): 114–124.

Link, Alex. "Rabbit at the Riverside: Names and Impossible Crossings in Hemingway's *For Whom the Bell Tolls*." *Hemingway Review* 29.1 (Fall 2009): 134–139.

Lynn, Kenneth S. *Hemingway*. New York: Simon and Schuster, 1987.

Marcus, Laura. *Auto/Biographical Discourses: Theory, Criticism, Practice*. Manchester, UK: Manchester University Press, 1994.

Marsh, W. Ward. "One Moment, Please." *Cleveland Plain Dealer* (24 July 1938), 9B. Reprinted in Davison, 122–124. Also as a standalone pamphlet by the J. B. Savage Company (1938), a copy of which is housed at the University of Delaware.

Marvin, Carolyn, and David W. Ingle. *Blood Sacrifice and the Nation: Totem Rituals and the American Flag*. Cambridge, UK: Cambridge University Press, 1999.

Matthews, Herbert L. *The Education of a Correspondent*. Westport, CT: Greenwood, 1946.

———. *Half of Spain Died: A Reappraisal of the Spanish Civil War*. New York: Scribner, 1973.

McCormick, Donald. *One Man's Wars, The Story of Charles Sweeny: Soldier of Fortune*. London: Arthur Baker Limited, 1972.

Mendelson, Jordana. *Documenting Spain: Artists, Exhibition Culture, and the Modern Nation, 1929–1939*. University Park: Pennsylvania University Press, 2005.

Meredith, James. "Hemingway's Spain in Flames, 1937." Conference paper delivered at the 12th International Hemingway Society Biennial Conference, Ronda, Spain, June 2006. Revised draft provided to the author in December 2009.

Merriman, Marion, and Warren Lerude. *American Commander in Spain: Robert Hale Merriman and the Abraham Lincoln Brigade*. Reno: University of Nevada Press, 1986.

Meyers, Jeffrey. "*For Whom the Bell Tolls* as Contemporary History." In *The Spanish Civil War in Literature*. Ed. Janet Pérez and Wendell Aycock. Lubbock: Texas Tech University Press, 1990. 85–108.

———. *Hemingway: A Biography*. New York: Perennial, 1985.

———. *Hemingway: Life into Art*. New York: Cooper Square Press, 2000.

Moddelmog, Debra A. "Protecting the Hemingway Myth: Casting Out Forbidden Desires from the Garden of Eden." In *Prospectus: An Annual of American Cultural Studies* 21. Ed. Jack Salzman. Cambridge: Cambridge University Press, 1996. 89–122.

———. "We Live in a Country Where Nothing Makes Any Difference: The Queer Sensibility of *A Farewell to Arms*." *Hemingway Review* 28.2 (Spring 2009): 7–24.

Moorehead, Caroline. *Gellhorn: A Twentieth-Century Life*. New York: Henry Holt, 2003.

Moreira, Peter. *Hemingway on the China Front: His WWII Spy Mission with Martha Gellhorn*. Washington, DC: Potomac Books, 2006.

Murad, David. "The Conflict of 'Being Gypsy' in *For Whom the Bell Tolls*." *Hemingway Review* 28.2 (Spring 2009): 87–104.

Nagel, James. "Catherine Barkley and Retrospective Narration." In *Critical Essays on Ernest Hemingway's "A Farewell to Arms."* Ed. George Monteiro. New York: G. K. Hall, 1994. 161–174.

Nelson, Cary, ed. *Remembering Spain: Hemingway's Civil War Eulogy and the Veterans of the Abraham Lincoln Brigade*. Urbana: University of Illinois Press, 1994.

———. *The Wound and the Dream: Sixty Years of American Poems about the Spanish Civil War*. Urbana: University of Illinois Press, 2002.

Norris, Margot. *Writing War in the Twentieth Century*. Charlottesville and London: University Press of Virginia, 2000.

Orwell, George. *Homage to Catalonia*. Introduction by Lionel Trilling. Orlando: Harcourt, 1980.

Quintanilla, Luis. *All the Brave: Drawings of the Spanish War*. Text by Elliot Paul and Jay Allen. Preface by Ernest Hemingway. New York: Modern Age Books, 1939.

Quintanilla, Paul. *Waiting at the Shore: Art, Revolution, War, and Exile in the Life of the Spanish Artist Luis Quintanilla*. Lulu Press, 2003.

Preston, Paul. *The Spanish Civil War: Reaction, Revolution, and Revenge.* Revised and expanded. New York: Norton, 2006.

———. *We Saw Spain Die: Foreign Correspondents in the Spanish Civil War.* New York: Skyhorse Publishing, 2009.

Regler, Gustav. *The Great Crusade.* Trans. Whittaker Chambers and Barrows Mussey. New York: Longsmans, Green, 1940.

———. *The Owl of Minerva.* Trans. Norman Denny. New York: Farrar, Straus and Cudahy, 1959.

Reynolds, Michael. *Hemingway: The 1930s.* New York: Norton, 1997.

———. *Hemingway: The Paris Years.* New York: Norton, 1989.

———. *Hemingway's First War: The Making of "A Farewell to Arms."* Princeton, NJ: Princeton University Press, 1976.

Romesburg, Rod. "Shifting Orders: Chaos and Order in *For Whom the Bell Tolls.*" In *Hemingway and the Natural World.* Ed. Robert F. Fleming. Moscow: University of Idaho Press, 1999. 139–152.

Sanderson, Rena, ed. *Blowing the Bridge: Essays on Hemingway and "For Whom the Bell Tolls."* New York: Greenwood, 1992.

Schaber, Irme, Richard Whelan, and Kristen Luben, eds. *Gerda Taro.* New York and Göttingen, Germany: International Center of Photography and Steidl Publishers, 2007.

Schoots, Hans. *Living Dangerously: A Biography of Joris Ivens.* Trans. David Colmer. Amsterdam: Amsterdam University Press, 2000.

Sontag, Susan. *Regarding the Pain of Others.* New York: Farrar, Straus, and Giroux, 2003.

Spilka, Mark. *Hemingway's Quarrel with Androgyny.* Lincoln: University of Nebraska Press, 1990.

Stanton, Edward F. *Hemingway and Spain: A Pursuit.* Photographs by Gonzalo de la Serna. Seattle: University of Washington Press, 1989.

Stott, William. *Documentary Expression and Thirties America.* Chicago: University of Chicago Press, 1986.

Strychacz, Thomas. *Hemingway's Theaters of Masculinity.* Baton Rouge: Louisiana State University Press, 2003.

Szúrek, Aleksander. *The Shattered Dream.* Trans. Jacques and Hilda Grunblatt. Boulder: East European Monographs, 1989.

Thomas, Hugh. *The Spanish Civil War.* Revised Edition. New York: Modern Library, 2001.

Trogdon, Robert W., ed. *Ernest Hemingway: A Literary Reference.* New York: Carroll & Graf, 2002.

———. *The Lousy Racket: Hemingway, Scribners, and the Business of Literature.* Kent, OH: Kent State University Press, 2007.

Tyler, Lisa. "Dead Rabbits, Bad Milk, and Lost Eggs: Women, Nature, and Myth in *For Whom the Bell Tolls.*" In *Hemingway and the Natural World.* Ed. Robert E. Fleming. Moscow: University of Idaho Press, 1999. 125–137.

Valis, Noël., ed. *Teaching Representations of the Spanish Civil War.* New York: Modern Language Association, 2007.

Vernon, Alex. *On Tarzan.* Athens: University of Georgia Press, 2008.

———. *Soldiers Once and Still: Ernest Hemingway, James Salter, and Tim O'Brien.* Iowa City: University of Iowa Press, 2004.

———. "War, Gender, and Ernest Hemingway." *Hemingway Review* 22.1 (Fall 2002): 34–55.

Viertel, Peter. *Dangerous Friends.* New York: Doubleday, 1992.

Wagner-Martin, Linda. *Ernest Hemingway's "A Farewell to Arms": A Reference Guide.* Westport, CT: Greenwood Press, 2003.

Wald, Alan M. *Trinity of Passion: The Literary Left & the Antifascist Crusade.* Chapel Hill: University of North Carolina Press, 2007.

Waldmeir, Joseph. "Chapter Number and Meaning in *For Whom the Bell Tolls.*" *Hemingway Review* 8.2 (Spring 1989): 43–45.

Watson, William Braasch. "Hemingway's Spanish Civil War Dispatches." *Hemingway Review* 7.2 (Spring 1988): 4–121.

———. "Investigating Hemingway: The Story." *North Dakota Quarterly* 59.1 (Winter 1991): 36–68.

———. "Investigating Hemingway: The Trip." *North Dakota Quarterly* 59.3 (Summer 1991): 79–95.

———. "Investigating Hemingway: The Novel." *North Dakota Quarterly* 60.1 (Winter 1992): 1–39.

———. "Joris Ivens and the Communists: Bringing Hemingway into the Spanish Civil War." In Sanderson, 37–57.

Waugh, Thomas. "'Men Cannot Act before the Camera in the Presence of Death': Joris Ivens' *The Spanish Earth.*" In *Documenting the Documentary: Close Readings of Documentary Film and Video.* Ed. Barry Keith Grant and Jeanette Sloniowski. Detroit: Wayne State University Press, 1998.

———. "Water, Blood, and War: Documentary Images of Spain from the North American Popular Front." In *The Spanish Civil War and the Visual Arts.* Ed. Kathleen M. Vernon. Ithaca: Cornell University Press, 1991. 14–24.

Weintraub, Stanley. *The Last Great Cause: The Intellectuals and the Spanish Civil War.* New York: Weybright and Talley, 1968.

Wolff, Milton. *Another Hill.* Introduction and afterword by Cary Nelson. Urbana: University of Illinois Press, 1994.

Wood, Jasper. "Introduction." In *The Spanish Earth.* By Ernest Hemingway. Cleveland: J. B. Savage Company, 1938. Reprinted in Davison, 124–127.

Wright, Richard. *Pagan Spain.* Introduction by Faith Berry. New York: Harper-Perennial, 1995.

Wyden, Peter. *The Passionate War.* New York: Simon and Schuster, 1983.

Yanagisawa, Hideo. "'International Eriend': Ernest Hemingway in the Classified Documents of China's Kuomintang." *Hemingway Review* 29.2 (Spring 2010): 133–147.

Young, Philip. *Ernest Hemingway: A Reconsideration.* University Park: Pennsylvania State University Press, 1966.

INDEX